YOUR GUIDE TO
RETIRING
TO MEXICO,
COSTA RICA
AND BEYOND

YOUR GUIDE TO RETIRING TO MEXICO, COSTA RICA AND BEYOND

SHELLEY EMLING

Avery Publishing Group
Garden City Park, New York

Interior Photographs: William P. McElligott, Ottawa, Canada
Interior Maps: John Wincek
Cover Photographs: William P. McElligott, Ottawa, Canada
Cover Design: William Gonzalez and Rudy Shur
Typesetter: Bonnie Freid
Printer: Paragon Press, Honesdale, PA

Library of Congress Cataloging-in-Publication Data

Emling, Shelley.
    Your guide to retiring to Mexico, Costa Rica, and beyond: finding
the good life on a fixed income / Shelley Emling.
        p.   cm.
    Includes index.
    ISBN 0-89529-719-1
    1. Retirement, Places of—Mexico.   2. Retirement, Places of—
Costa Rica.   3. Retirement, Places of—Guatemala.   4. Retirement,
Places of—Ecuador.   I. Title.
HQ1063.2.M6E56   1996
646.7'9—dc20   96-4180
                                                            CIP

Printed in the United States of America

10   9   8   7   6   5   4   3   2

Contents

To my two best friends –

my husband, Scott Norvell,
who is my partner in adventure,

and my mother, Lois Watton,
who has never let me down.

Introduction

So you're retired, or just about to be. The kids are grown and it's time for a change in routine—or perhaps just a change of scenery. As anyone who's done the math knows, living the good life—or even anything approaching it—on Social Security or a meager pension in the United States isn't easy these days. It can be done, however, in Latin America. Just ask any of the thousands of older expatriates who have chosen to spend their work-free years a little farther south than Florida or Texas or Arizona. They will tell you that pension dollars that barely bought the necessities in the United States will stretch luxuriantly in Latin America to cover everything from sirloin steaks to servants. They will rave about the eternally springlike weather, the relaxed pace, and the accommodating attitudes of the locals.

They may tell you about the live-in maid they hired in Mexico who did the cooking and cleaning for $20 a week, or about the gardener who came by twice a week for $5 a day. They will tell stories of elegant dinners with wine for less than $15 in Ecuador's capital, or about the 300-year-old Spanish colonial house they bought in Guatemala for less than $40,000.

For all these reasons and more, there are hundreds of thousands of older Americans who have put down roots in Latin America. My husband and I met scores of retired Americans during the two years we worked as journalists in Central America, traveling throughout the region and crisscrossing Mexico by car, bus, and plane more times than I can remember.

We played poker with snowbirds on Sunday nights past 1 a.m., and did aerobics with a group of older Americans year-round on the grassy lawn of a park dripping with bougainvillea and flowering orchids. For years I have wanted to capture what makes Latin America such a wonderful place to retire, and share it with people convinced they have few options—or who know about their options but need more information to take that first step.

There was a time when Mexico was the only country in Latin

America that came to mind when retirees started thinking about resettling in an exotic locale. Thankfully, that's no longer the case. While it's still a great place to retire, Mexico is not the bargain it was ten years ago. That's why you might consider looking farther south, and why I've included chapters in this book on Guatemala, Costa Rica, and Ecuador as well as Mexico. Services in all these countries are priced so that you can live like a king or queen. Maids and cooks can be hired for $5 a day. Dentists will clean your teeth for about $10. Attractive houses of the sort that could easily run $200,000 in a modest Los Angeles suburb can be purchased for $50,000.

But there are other reasons, besides price, to consider retiring in these countries. In Mexico, Guatemala, Costa Rica, and Ecuador, you can have it all—friendly neighborhoods, breathtaking landscapes, gourmet restaurants, cable TV, and enough money left over to fly back and forth to the States. And even if Latin America is more expensive than it used to be, it's still an easy place for Americans to live. English is widely spoken, crime is less of a concern than in many parts of the United States, and U.S. consumer products ranging from cereal to car parts are readily available (even more so now that the North American Free Trade Agreement is being implemented).

This book is intended as a down-to-earth, easy-to-read guide to retiring in these four countries. It's designed for people who haven't planned for retirement, as well as for those who have. People who've traveled extensively throughout the world will find in this book helpful tidbits of information available nowhere else, and those who've never left the part of the country they grew up in should gain encouragement from the anecdotes and advice given here.

This is not a travel guide; there are plenty of those to choose from. This book is written to help you make a decision about where to live during some or all of your retirement years. I've included the pitfalls of retirement in Latin America as well—and there are a few—so that you'll be able to make a well-informed decision about your retirement. For starters, I've included a broad introduction to the countries and what makes them tick, the people, the culture, and the politics. Every important detail about getting established and setting up a household is discussed—how to furnish your new home, how to import a car, how to find the foods you're familiar with, and so on. There are many organizations you might want to check with for more information before making a move, and I've included their names, addresses, and phone numbers for your convenience.

I've included items of interest to older Americans not found in other guidebooks. There's a section on finances that includes information about how to pay taxes and get Social Security checks, as well as one on staying healthy and dealing with Latin doctors and pharmacies. There's another on keeping busy and happy, with a list of expatriate and social organizations that can help lessen the initial shock of being separated from your own culture. New residents of San José, for example, can attend weekly seminars for new transplants from the United States and Canada, then join one of the dozens of bridge clubs, nature photography groups, golf clubs, or craft classes to meet new people and stay in touch with the huge North American population in that capital.

I focused on the parts of these four countries that are already home to lots of retired Americans. You're probably not going to want to live in Mexico City, for many reasons—namely, bad traffic, a high altitude, costly standard of living, and pollution problems—so only brief mention of this capital is warranted. As an alternative, I introduce you to the highland city of Guadalajara, Mexico's second metropolis. Located near Lake Chapala, Guadalajara is probably the most popular destination in Latin America for retirees because of its U.S.–like amenities and picturesque setting. It, and all other retirement havens, are thoroughly covered.

When applicable, I've included the dollar costs of expenditures like average rents, bus trips, dinner for two, household help, visits to the doctor, utility bills, and prescription medicines. Remember, though, that exchange rates can change, meaning costs can change. You'll notice also that this information varies by country. Prices in Ecuador and Guatemala are going to be less, for the most part, than in Costa Rica and Mexico. This book will try to convince you not to compare everything with the way it is back home. If everything were the same, there would be no reason to leave home in the first place. I remember so many good things about my time in Latin America, and returned to the United States only to start a family. I go back, though, frequently, and am already planning to return for good when my children are up and about.

Before you make a move to Latin America, you should by all means take an exploratory trip, stay a few months if possible, and decide if the environment is right for you. If you decide to take the plunge—and I sincerely hope you do—prepare a written checklist of everything you need to do before you go. Here's a quick "simplistic" sample:

❑ Decide whether to keep or sell your car.

❑ Determine whether to keep your bank accounts open and how you will arrange for bills to be paid.

❑ Check on your medical and auto coverage to be certain you will be covered abroad.

❑ Get a medical checkup and gather copies of all your medical records and prescriptions.

❑ Decide what to do with your house and furniture.

❑ Notify your utilities, the paper carrier, and other services of your departure date.

When moving overseas, you should have on hand certain documents. These include your birth certificate, or a certified copy; your marriage certificate; medical insurance cards and policy coverage information; copies of prescriptions, including one for eye glasses; your Social Security card; your driver's license; copies of important papers such as your will; credit cards and a record of the numbers; and extra passport photos.

Don't sweat the small stuff, and don't let a fear of the unknown stop you from experiencing a new adventure. I met many retirees in Latin America who had never even traveled to New York City, but were enjoying the high life in exotic locales. You can experience these feelings. So don't sit on the sidelines, and don't wonder what "might" have been. Your memories are waiting to be made.

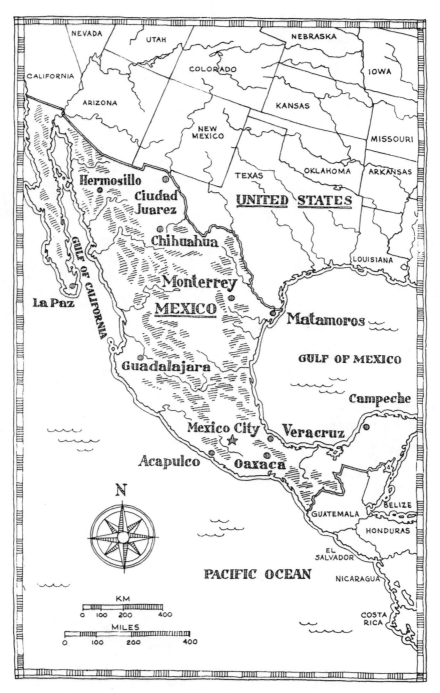

Mexico

Mexico

Ah, to retire to beautiful Mexico, where the pace is slower, the margaritas are tastier, and the pension dollars stretch further. Yes, it's true. Mexico is the dream retirement destination for tens of thousands of Americans.

Prices are not as good as they used to be, but the lifestyle sure is. Servants are still plentiful and inexpensive—indeed, you are almost expected to hire a maid and a gardener in Mexico. Baja California—which is actually part of Mexico—boasts some of the best fishing in the world. And an army of other equally adventurous retirees is ready to make your acquaintance; in fact, many communities offer a smorgasbord of social clubs and cultural events for retirees.

Mexico has become so popular that, today, it is home to more U.S. Social Security beneficiaries than any other foreign country. Every day, more and more people leave their cold climates, high utility bills, and humdrum lives to seek new challenges in Mexico. It most definitely is a foreign country, but it certainly is an easy one in which to retire. English is widely spoken, violent crime is not nearly the concern it is in the United States, and U.S. consumer products are readily available.

You won't have to give up cable television, *Newsweek* magazine, cocktail parties, or fine dining. But you will have to learn to like friendly neighbors, sunny weather, fresh fruits and vegetables, and lower prices.

Why Here and Not Florida?

Mexico is the third-largest country in Latin America and, with about 88 million people, it is the most populous Spanish-speaking country in the world. You'll come across all kinds of landscapes in Mexico—everything from swamp to desert, from tropical lowland jungle to high mountain vegetation, from dry soils to others so rich that they grow three crops each year. Mexico is about one-fourth the size of the United States, with which it shares a 1,700-mile border. On Mexico's southern frontier are Guatemala and Belize. Mexico has coastlines on the Gulf of Mexico, the Caribbean, the Pacific, and the Gulf of California.

The country's capital of Mexico City has ballooned in recent decades, and with more than 22 million residents, today it has the largest urban concentration anywhere in the world. This huge population is evident in the city's thick smog, heavy traffic, and high housing prices. Mexico City is the country's major industrial center, with 35,000 industrial plants. Most foreign banks and foreign companies have offices along the city's main street, the nine-mile Paseo de la Reforma. At the southern end of that street lies the Zona Rosa, an area characterized by fashionable, high-class shops, hotels, and cafés.

Guadalajara, a colonial town in central Mexico, is the second-largest city, with about 6 million people. Often compared to Washington, D.C., Guadalajara is known for its fine architecture, wide streets, and clean parks. In and around Guadalajara is where most American retirees choose to live.

Monterrey, the country's third-largest city, and other urban areas in the northern region of the country also have large populations of Americans, but do not have many retirees. There's little for the tourist in these cities, as they are largely business centers. Monterrey is the headquarters for Mexico's major banks and insurance companies, as well as most of the country's large corporations.

You'll find that many of Mexico's smaller cities and towns resemble those of Spain. The plaza or main square is planned in the same fashion, with a garden, a bandstand, and park benches; and is surrounded by a church, public buildings, and restaurants. The plaza is a convenient central place where people congregate on social and religious occasions. Traditionally, the Sunday *paseo*, or walk, around the plaza was a social event where the unmarried young people came to see and be seen. It's a tradition alive today in many towns.

When asked why they chose to retire in Mexico, most retirees top their list of reasons with the country's temperate year-round climate: the temperature in Mexico City rarely climbs higher than 70 or 75 degrees. Most homes, therefore, have no need for air conditioning or heating. The area in and around Guadalajara enjoys similar temperatures, although in Monterrey and Gulf Coast cities like Veracruz, the temperature can shoot up to 95 degrees in the summer. Close promixity to the United States is another reason retirees choose to live in Mexico. In case of an emergency, they can reach the Texas border in a day's drive or in a few hours by plane from such cities as Mexico City and Guadalajara.

The slower tempo is yet a third attraction, especially for those Americans who've spent years commuting in such frenetic cities as New York, Los Angeles, or Chicago. Mexicans don't place much emphasis on planning, taking each day as it comes at a pace all their own.

The low cost of living draws other retirees, even though prices have risen dramatically in recent years. It is still possible to hire servants for modest wages to do household chores, cooking, washing, ironing, and gardening. If you locate away from urban areas and shop in local markets, you can live fairly inexpensively. Many retired couples say they can live like kings and queens on $1,000 a month.

For example, a nice apartment rents for $200 to $300 a month. Bargains are to be had in the way of public transportation, utilities, prescription drugs, insurance, and medical care. Retirees aren't subject to Mexican state and national income taxes, although they still have to pay Uncle Sam, albeit after an $80,000 annual exemption.

Finally, many retirees winter in Mexico, choosing to enjoy part-time retirement in sunny weather during the coldest months back home and then return to their U.S. friends and families in the spring.

Don't move to Mexico if you want to live on $400 a month, or if you expect service always to be up to U.S. standards. You can no longer live that cheaply in Mexico, and you can't expect to change Mexican culture. But do move to Mexico if you want to live more cheaply than you would in the United States, if you want to make new friends, and if you want new challenges. Mexicans are loyal, generous people who treat foreigners with kindness and warmth. They will do everything they can to make you feel right at home.

FACTS AT A GLANCE

Population:	88 million
Ethnic groups:	Spanish-Indian mix 60 percent, Indians 25 percent, white 5 percent, other 10 percent
Religion:	90 percent Roman Catholic
Languages:	Spanish, several Indian dialects
Monetary unit:	Peso
Head of state:	President
Political system:	Federal republic of 31 states
Industries:	Mining and petroleum production
Literacy rate:	83 percent
Capital:	Mexico City
Crops:	Corn, wheat, coffee, and cotton
Average temperature:	70 to 75 degrees in Mexico City, in mountainous areas, and in Guadalajara; 85 to 95 degrees in northern Mexico and along the Gulf Coast
Square mileage:	761,604 square miles
Rainy season:	May through September
American population:	175,000

The People and the Culture

Mexico's population is growing in number, increasing by about 2.3 percent a year. It's also growing younger, more urban, and more middle class. About 31 percent of the population is now under the age of thirty. About 75 percent of the population lives in urban areas rather than rural ones. More than 25 percent of the population considers itself middle class. Yet a vast majority of Mexico's people still live in poverty—17 percent are illiterate—with a small percentage of the country considered the wealthy elite.

About 5 percent of Mexicans consider themselves white and

about 25 percent Indian; about 60 percent are *mestizos,* a mixture of Spanish and Indian; a small percentage are a mixture of black and white or black and Indian.

SOME BACKGROUND INFORMATION

Mexicans are a fiercely independent, passionate people who can be quite different from your neighbors in the United States. They love their families, enjoy making small talk, and won't hesitate to barrage you with questions. It's not that they are particularly nosy. It's just that they like getting to know people and making new friends. With those they like, they are incredibly loyal. Mexicans always like being with other people and pooh-pooh the notion of "doing your own thing." You're likely to find them warm-hearted, genuine, and intelligent.

While Mexicans will treat you with kindness and will be eager to get to know you, you might sometimes feel a little left out of their social scene because of the great importance they place on family life. Family-oriented activities take up a lot of the average Mexican's time, and outsiders usually aren't included. The elderly are highly respected in this country, and often you see whole families—aunts, uncles, grandparents, and cousins—spending weekends together picnicking in the park.

What do Mexicans like to do in their spare time? They love soccer, called *fútbol* in Spanish, and children are taught to play the game at an early age. They also like tennis, swimming, jai alai, and, in recent years, jogging. They enjoy watching soap operas, which are often discussed by friends and family members at great lengths, and reading, especially romance novels or short stories.

THE LOCAL CUSTOMS

You might find Mexicans annoying at times because of what appears to be their total disregard for promptness. Mexicans are not known for their ability to plan or to meet deadlines. They think nothing of arriving an hour or two late for appointments, or dropping in on friends and neighbors unannounced. But if you're not terribly impatient, don't mind a little procrastination, or rarely balk when someone shows up an hour late for an appointment, you'll do just fine in Mexico.

Everything moves a little slower in Mexico—everybody takes his or her time. What's the rush? Americans, Mexicans often complain, always seem to be in such a hurry. In Mexico, the seamstress who promised that your dress would be ready by Saturday might not have it ready for another two weeks. The neighbor who agreed to dinner at your house at 7 p.m. might not show up until 8 p.m. or later. The bank teller who should be waiting on you might first finish filing her nails. Dinner parties and doctor's appointments rarely start on time, but cultural and sports events usually do. If dinner is supposed to be at 8 p.m., you might not eat until 10 p.m.

The main meal for most Mexicans takes place between 1 p.m. and 3 p.m., and it may be followed by a siesta. Sometimes, a snack is eaten in the early evening before the late-evening dinner. Many businesses still close during lunchtime, although this practice is diminishing somewhat.

In general, Mexicans are emotional people. Sometimes they all talk at once, using their hands to illustrate what they're saying. They like small talk and they like to ask questions, wanting to know about everything, from your favorite television show to how much you spend on gasoline. They're not afraid to show their feelings with physical affection. Grown men are known to greet their fathers with a kiss. Women often say hello to each other with a peck on the cheek. Mexicans place little importance on the concept of privacy, and they don't like spending time alone.

Mexicans are also very polite. They usually greet everyone at a party before engaging in conversation with one particular person. They usually say goodbye to everyone upon leaving. I'm sure you've heard stories of tourists asking for directions in Mexico only to be given the wrong advice. These stories are true. Mexicans are so polite that they'd rather give you information that's wrong than have you be disappointed!

Mexicans consider titles very important. *Doctor* is often used, not just for a medical doctor but also for lawyers and professors. *Licenciado* is used a lot, too, for college graduates. Elderly people are often called *Don* or *Doña*, out of respect. As with titles, names take on a new meaning in Mexico. It is common in Mexico to take two surnames, the first from the father and the second from the mother. For example, someone with the name of Julia Hernandez Gonzalez is as follows: Julia is her first name, Hernandez is her father's last name and is the name used in everyday life, and Gonzalez is her mother's maiden surname and is used only on official documents. When a woman marries, she drops her mother's maiden surname and adds her husband's father's surname preceded by *de:* Julia Hernandez de Gomez.

A BRIEF HISTORY OF THE COUNTRY

A long string of advanced Indian civilizations has made Mexico their home, notably the Aztec, Maya, Toltec, Zapotec, and Olmec. The last great Indian civilization, the Aztec, was conquered by the Spanish in 1519. Exploiting the land and its people, the Spanish conquerors extended Spanish rule to all of Mexico and into the southwestern United States. Disease and subjugation caused a decline in the native population, from 28 million in 1520 to 1 million by the late eighteenth century.

A drive for independence began on September 16, 1810, led by Miguel Hidalgo, a Mexican priest, and was achieved eleven years later. Mexico was one of the first countries in South America to revolt and gain independence from Spain. But the territory of Texas seceded from Mexico in 1836 and joined the United States. With the end of the Mexican War in 1848, Mexico was forced to cede half its territory to the United States.

Porfirio Díaz, a reformist dictator, ruled Mexico from 1876 to the early twentieth century. The period was marked by stability and economic growth, but wealth was concentrated in the hands of a few leaders. Thus, the Mexican people's nationalism has its roots in the revolution of 1910, which started mostly because of the widening gap between the country's haves and have-nots. As the quarrel intensified, more and more groups were brought into the struggle for power, turning the political fight into a bloody battle to reform the country and divide up the landed estates among the landless peasantry. Emiliano Zapata and Francisco "Pancho" Villa are two figures who achieved fame during this time. During the revolution, which lasted until the 1930s, the political party called the Partido Revolucionario Institucional (PRI) was born, and it has governed Mexico ever since. Mexican affairs since the revolution have been mostly characterized by economic progress and political stability.

GOVERNMENT AND POLITICS

The PRI has held a virtual monopoly on all political activity since the 1940s. But this situation has started to change in recent years as dissatisfaction with the party has grown and charges of election fraud have been addressed. In 1989, a state governorship was conceded for the first time by the PRI to the right-wing party, Partido de Acción Nacional (PAN).

Carlos Salinas de Gortari ended six years of rule in late 1994. The one-time popular president who was largely responsible for the drafting of the North American Free Trade Agreement (NAFTA) saw his popularity plummet as a result of the country's economic crisis. That crisis began in December 1994, when his hand-picked successor, President Ernesto Zedillo, announced a devaluation of the peso and a decision to let it float against the dollar. The peso had been extremely overvalued, so as a result of this devaluation, the peso dropped in value against the dollar by more than 50 percent.

Historically, the country's most fundamental problem has been access to land, and it remains a big concern today. Life for the peasants is still hard. Their homes are often shacks with dirt floors and no windows, no water, and no sanitation. Many can barely afford a simple diet of beans, tortillas, and rice on their minimum-wage incomes. This lifestyle was behind the armed uprising by Indian peasants in the southern state of Chiapas in January 1994. The government is still negotiating with these peasants to address their concerns in order to quell the rebellion.

The most important thing for you to keep in mind about the country's history and politics is that Mexicans are extremely nationalistic. They hate the idea of the U.S. government's ordering them around or giving them handouts. This is why the United States' 1995 intervention in Mexico's economic problems has been so hard for Mexicans to swallow. The United States announced a $20 billion bailout plan for Mexico in February 1995, but the Mexican government had to use its precious oil revenues as collateral. So it's probably a good idea to avoid political and historical topics with Mexicans you don't know very well, especially topics such as recent economic problems or illegal immigrants.

Today, Mexican officials are bracing for more social tension and political struggle as people throughout the country react angrily to the severe economic austerity measures announced in March 1995. Businesses are expected to go bankrupt as the Mexican economy continues in recession. Interest rates of 90 percent and higher on mortgages, credit cards, and car loans have pushed many families into poverty. Gasoline prices have jumped a third and electricity costs have risen 20 percent. But real estate prices have remained stable. While all this sounds serious enough, and it is, it has little implication for the retiree moving to Mexico, except to make things cheaper for people paying with dollars.

A Look at Living Costs

There's been more discussion in books, magazines, and newsletters about the cost of living in Mexico than about anything else. Some experts claim that you can live in Mexico on $600 a month; others say the figure is more like $1,500. In surveys on the budgets of retirees, most respondents say that they live on anywhere from $500 to $2,100 a month. My research tells me that a couple can live quite comfortably on $1,000 a month, as long as they're not living in Mexico City.

Your budget will be determined by how "American" you want to live—whether you want to eat imported foods, shop at the branches of U.S. stores, and visit beach resorts so popular with U.S. tourists. With the devaluation of the peso in December 1994, prices have dropped considerably for everything but imported goods. But prices are ever changing, and they are likely to change again.

SOME SAMPLE PRICES

Gas (1 gallon)	$1.55
Auto insurance	$250.00 a year
Medical checkup	$50.00
Dental checkup and cleaning	$40.00
Cinema ticket	$3.00
Milk (two liters)	$1.08
Eggs (1 dozen)	$1.14
Nice dinner for two in Guadalajara, with wine	$20.00

Immigration Rules and Regulations

The Mexican government doesn't give any special tax breaks to American retirees, but it certainly welcomes them with open arms and makes it easy for them to live in or visit Mexico. And there are no indications, either economic or political, that it will become difficult to move to Mexico any time in the future.

Mexico gives all Americans a break by allowing them to enter the country on a tourist card good for six months. After six months, Americans can return to the border to get a new card. No problem. This way, they can explore the country and even live there for a few years without legal hassles and completing a lot of paperwork.

You can get a tourist card, called an FM-T, at any Mexican consulate, at border immigration offices, at travel agencies, or through airlines that fly to Mexico. Whatever you do, don't lose your tourist card because you cannot leave Mexico without it, and it takes about a week to get it replaced.

Most retirees in Mexico choose to reside in the country simply using their tourist card. There's no income requirement to get one and, as mentioned, the card can be renewed easily every six months by taking a trip outside Mexico. This isn't a problem for most people, since many retirees return to the United States at least once every six months to visit friends and relatives and to take care of personal and financial matters. The bad news is that tourist cards don't allow you to legally bring in household goods such as appliances.

The government does encourage Americans who decide to live permanently in Mexico to seek some sort of resident status. Obtaining the resident permits, called FM-2s and FM-3s, gives you some breaks, such as the ability to import household goods free of import duties. These permits, which grant permanent legal status, are renewable each year for five years and entitle the holder to reside full time in Mexico without having to leave the country every six months. After five years, the person is eligible for a permanent visa.

To get an FM-3 or FM-2, you must submit various paperwork and provide proof from a bank or other source showing that you receive $1,000 in income each month ($1,500 for couples). Check with a Mexican consulate for up-to-date information on income requirements, however, because they change often.

The Mexican Embassy stresses that every application for a resident permit is considered separately. There are many different categories—in addition to the FM-2 and FM-3—and different price ranges. Visas are required for those who will be working and receiving income in Mexico or for those who hold diplomatic, official, or special passports. Each permit has individual advantages, and you should inquire about these, if you so desire, after you've spent some time in Mexico as a tourist.

None of the various residency permits causes a loss of U.S. citizenship. After you hold a resident permit for five years, you are given the option of becoming an *inmigrado*. The same income requirements apply as for an FM-3 or FM-2. An *inmigrado* has all the rights of a Mexican citizen, including the right to work or operate a business. The only right refused an *inmigrado* is the right to vote. An FM-3 visa allows you to work, but is more difficult to get than an FM-2.

In summary, most of the retirees I have met say it's easiest to live in Mexico on a tourist card. About the only advantage to obtaining a resident permit is that it allows you to bring furniture and appliances with you into Mexico without a penalty.

Financial Matters

Mexico's unit of currency is the peso; it is written "P" outside the country, but within Mexico it is usually shown the same as the U.S. dollar—$1—although it is always written with just one vertical line through the "S." New peso bills (denoted N$) and coins were issued on January 1, 1993, equal to 1,000 old pesos. The old bills were no longer valid as of December 31, 1993.

On December 20, 1994, the Banco de México yielded to pressure from the government, devaluing the peso by 12 percent. The bank was then forced to let the peso fall freely until it found a stable international trading range. The peso fell by more than 50 percent against the dollar by March 1995.

Predicting what the peso will do is impossible at this point. It all depends on how well the country sticks to the economic austerity plan outlined by the president in March 1995. Because the peso is unstable, you should keep most of your savings and investments in the currency of your home country.

Personal checks are not widely used in Mexico and will not be accepted in most places. Even household helpers usually don't accept checks. ATMs at most Banco Nacional de México (BANAMEX) offices are on the Cirrus and Plus networks.

Major credit cards are widely accepted in Mexico, even in some supermarkets, although MasterCard and Visa are more useful than American Express. The Discover card is not widely accepted. Some banks will give cash advances in pesos to MasterCard and Visa cardholders. The American Express office in Mexico City is at Patriotismo No. 635, Piso 3, Colonia Nochebuena, Mexico, D.F. For information, phone 5-563-8689.

A retiree who lives outside the country can receive Social Security benefits at the U.S. Embassy. Social Security has a pamphlet called "Your Social Security Checks While You Are Outside the United States." For information call 800-772-1213.

CURRENCY EXCHANGE

You can freely change dollars into pesos at banks or exchange houses, called *casas de cambio*. These exchange houses will likely be quicker, and are apt to have longer hours than banks. There is an exchange house at the airport as you clear customs. The exchange rate at shops and restaurants is usually not as good as that offered at banks and exchange houses.

You should bring your money to Mexico in both cash and traveler's checks. Traveler's checks should be in dollars. There are no fees for converting traveler's checks to pesos.

Any purchases you charge on your credit card are recorded in pesos. You get the best exchange rate available on the day the credit card company records the transaction, which might be better or worse than the rate on the day of your purchase.

BANKING

Banking in Mexico is not unlike banking in the United States. You can open an account with a Mexican bank and you can get cash advances on your credit cards.

Mexican banks were privatized in the early 1990s, after having been nationalized in 1982 by then Mexican President José Lopez Portillo to prevent a run on the peso. Today, more than 102 foreign financial companies have filed a request to operate in Mexico. In late 1994, the Finance Secretariat awarded fifty-two licenses, eighteen of which were for banks. U.S. banks given the go-ahead included American Express, J.P. Morgan, Chemical Banking Corp., Republic New York, BankAmerica, NationsBank, Chase, Bank of Boston, and First Chicago. But although many foreign banks will be in operation in Mexico, only Citibank, which has operated a subsidiary in Mexico since 1929, offers retail banking services. Contact:

Citibank   Phone: 5-211-3030.
Paseo de la Reforma 390
Mexico, D.F

The California Commerce Bank of Los Angeles, California, a wholly owned subsidiary of Banco Nacional de México (BANAMEX), or the largest operating Mexican bank, offers a checking account designed specifically for North American retirees (fifty-five years and over) living in Mexico. The bank calls it the Friendship Senior Checking Program, or Programa Amistad. The main feature of this account is direct deposit of retirement checks, including direct deposit of Social Security checks. With a checking account at BANAMEX, you receive a free credit card and an ATM banking card. Checks are free and there is no service charge. For information, phone 213-624-5700.

TAXES: U.S. AND MEXICAN

U.S. retirees living in Mexico don't have to pay Mexican state or national taxes on earned income, nor do they have to pay any Mexican income tax on their U.S. income. Since U.S. retirees aren't usually employed in Mexico, the only taxable Mexican income they are likely to have is interest earned on deposits in Mexican banks, and that tax is withheld.

Americans in Mexico do, however, have to continue filing U.S. tax returns and paying U.S. income tax if they have income from the United States. However, the U.S. government allows Americans living overseas to earn up to $80,000 annually without being taxed.

If you need assistance with your U.S. taxes while living in Mexico, you can contact a special department at the U.S. Internal Revenue Service called IRS-International, designed to offer tax assistance to expatriates filing income tax returns. For information, contact the Internal Revenue Service at the address below. U.S. tax-payers living abroad should mail their completed returns to the Internal Revenue Service, Philadelphia, Pennsylvania 19255.

Internal Revenue Service   Phone: 202-874-1460.
Assistant Commissioner (International)
Attention: IN:C:TPS
950 L'Enfant Plaza South S.W.
Washington, D.C. 20024

In Mexico, you'll notice a 15 percent tax on many items that you purchase. This is a value-added tax, known as IVA (pronounced *ee-va*), that is assessed on goods and services. The tax does not apply to pharmaceutical items or basic foodstuffs. You'll also notice a 6 percent tax on the use of credit cards, and a $12 airport departure tax on international flights.

LOCAL INVESTMENT OPPORTUNITIES

You won't be able to work in Mexico unless you obtain an FM-3 permit, but Americans are allowed to invest and are encouraged to do so, especially since the North American Free Trade Agreement was implemented.

Most retirees do not get involved in heavy-duty investing. More than likely, if you do invest, it will be in real estate, the stock market, or via interest earned on bank deposits.

The stock market in Mexico is known as the Bolsa. While it is similar to stock markets in the United States, it is much smaller and fewer issues are traded. Although the Mexican stock market has taken a beating following devaluation of the peso in December 1994, there's probably some good money to be made in the future if Mexico sticks to its economic austerity plan and the economy begins to grow again.

Should you decide to learn more about business opportunities in Mexico, the following associations may prove helpful.

**American Chamber of
  Commerce of Mexico**
Lucerna 78, Colonia Centro
06600 Mexico, D.F.

Phone: 5-724-3800

**Comisión Nacional de
  Inversiones Extranjeras**
Blvd. Manuel Camacho 1
11560 Mexico, D.F.

Phone: 5-540-5659

**U.S.-Mexico Chamber
of Commerce (in U.S.)**
1211 Connecticut Avenue N.W.,
Suite 510
Washington, D.C. 20036

Phone: 202-296-5198

Also 730 Fifth Avenue, 9th Floor
New York, NY 10019

Phone: 212-333-8728

Also 5046 Biscayne Boulevard
Miami, FL 33137

Phone: 305-442-6236

**U.S.-Mexico Chamber
  of Commerce (in Mexico)**
Manuel Maria Contreras 133
Despachos 120 y 121,
Delegacion Cuauhtémoc
06470 Mexico, D.F.

Phone: 5-535-0613

TIPPING GUIDE

Tipping is very important in Mexico, where it often ensures you'll receive good service in the future. Therefore, it seems almost everybody is always giving tips to everyone, from postal workers to security guards to theater ushers.

At restaurants, tipping is more or less 10 to 15 percent of the price of the meal. Other tips include the following:

Mailmen	10 to 15 pesos on November 12 (Mailman's Day)
Gardeners	a week's salary at Christmastime
Security personnel	an extra 20 pesos each month
Reliable propane delivery people	3 to 5 pesos per trip
Parking lot attendants	1 to 2 pesos
Supermarket bag children	.5 to 1 peso
Gas station attendants	1 to 2 pesos
Garbage collectors	3 to 15 pesos per week

Taxi drivers don't have to be tipped, although a tip is appreciated if service is spectacular.

Rentals and Real Estate

In Mexico, you can have it all. Depending on your financial situation, you can choose among stately older homes along wide, tree-lined streets, apartments in high-rise buildings surrounded by security guards, plush condominiums with fine furniture in swanky American neighborhoods, or rooms in the colonial homes of accommodating Mexican families.

HOUSES, APARTMENTS, AND CONDOS

All types of housing are available, and they are available at varying prices. In years past, the growing army of retirees had nibbled at Mexico's affordable housing. While rental prices are still reasonable—lower than equivalent rentals in some parts of the United States—purchase prices had been increasing steadily over the last several years—until early 1995, that is. Though the peso has fallen, real estate values have remained stable, meaning that Mexican real estate is a good value.

For example, Century 21 recently advertised unfurnished condominiums priced from $19,000 to $60,000 in the area around Lake Chapala. A furnished two-bedroom, two-bathroom lakefront house with a phone, garage, terrace, and pool was selling for $139,000. A furnished one-bedroom condo was selling for $38,000. That's not bad. There are many bargains likely to be had, especially if you are willing to venture away from urban, highly populated areas.

Many long-time retirees suggest renting a furnished place on a month-to-month basis before signing a long-term lease or buying property. Many hotels rent apartments or suites by the week or month. These apartments come equipped with dishes, towels, and most everything else you need for day-to-day living, including daily maid service. You can't beat that.

After you secure a temporary place, then you can start looking at houses or apartments. Look for real estate clasified ads in newspapers like the English-language *Mexico City News.* Even local Spanish-language newspapers have some property advertisements in English. You can also check bulletin boards at grocery stores where people often post notices of properties for rent or sale. Also check with chapters of the American Society and with other American clubs to see what they recommend. Word-of-mouth is usually the best method for finding property.

Older houses often have lots of large rooms with high ceilings but no closets. You often have to purchase chests of drawers to store your clothing. The newer homes have smaller rooms with ceilings about the same height as their American counterparts. Older homes often have inner courtyards, arched verandas, and wrought-iron balconies. Homes will likely be adorned by both satellite dishes and brightly colored bougainvillea vines.

The kitchens in many Mexican homes won't be the same as kitchens in the United States. Instead of being roomy, pleasant places, Mexican kitchens are often small and drab, since Mexican families usually eat in the dining room and consider the kitchen the private domain of the cook. If you plan to employ a live-in maid, you must have an extra room and bath for her.

THE PLACES WHERE RETIREES LIVE

Many Americans claim to have discovered their own piece of paradise in Mexico. But one person's paradise can be another person's purgatory. Some retirees think the perfect spot is by the water. Others are accustomed to city life and claim they have to be surrounded by noise, cultural events, and a restaurant on every corner in order to be happy. Still others describe the perfect retirement haven as one with several golf courses and tennis courts. Everyone's different. That's why it's important for you to spend as much time as you can exploring the country and all it has to offer.

While I can't tell you where to live, I can tell you where other retirees have chosen to make their homes. Americans are clustered inland in cities such as Guadalajara, Oaxaca, Cuernavaca, and San Miguel de Allende. Many reside up and down the narrow finger of Baja California. Tens of thousands of Americans live in Mexico City and Monterrey, although most are employed by the U.S. government or are business people.

Guadalajara

Nowhere are there more American retirees than in Guadalajara and the nearby area around Lake Chapala. Guadalajara is the capital of the state of Jalisco, in central Mexico. The mile-high city and its neighboring counties—Tlaquepaque, Zapopan, Tonalá, and Chapala—have special appeal for foreigners because of their climate, which is springlike all year. Most are retirees, but many are students attending the well-known Universidad Autonoma de Guadalajara.

Many U.S. business people also live in Guadalajara, a major industrial center of 1.6 million people. Sometimes called the Mexican Silicon Valley, Jalisco exports more than $1 billion worth of electronic components each year and is home to branches of both Motorola and IBM. Guadalajara is often compared to Washington, D.C., with its wide, tree-lined avenues and multiple museums, plazas, and historic colonial buildings.

It's the little towns of Lake Chapala and Ajijic, near Guadalajara, that attract the most retirees. About 40,000 expatriates live in these towns, and several dozen social and civic clubs have sprung up as a result. Prices there are much lower than they are in urban areas, and pollution is not a problem. A huge airport in Guadalajara, just twenty minutes away, makes for easy access to the United States. Golf courses, museums, and the very active American Society of Jalisco provide retirees with plenty to do. (You can get low-cost medical insurance through the society.) The area is also close to Pacific beach resorts—about 150 miles. Around the lake, the warmest month, May, has an average high of 86 degrees and a low of 64 degrees. In January the high is 71 degrees and the low is 54 degrees. Ajijic has become a sort of Santa Fe (New Mexico), known as a community of artists. If you're not familiar with Mexico, I advise starting your search for a Mexican place to live in Guadalajara and its environs.

San Miguel de Allende

A colonial city that's less than a four-hour drive from Mexico City, San Miguel de Allende attracts thousands of American retirees and visitors each year with its reputation as a center for the arts. The city sits at 6,300 feet, so it's a little cooler than Guadalajara or Mexico City, but its fine colonial architecture, excellent art and Spanish schools, and recreational activities should not be ignored. With its narrow cobblestone streets, the city has been designated a national monument by the Mexican government.

In addition to San Miguel de Allende, you should check out the nearby towns of Guanajuato, Morelia, and Puebla. These are splendid cities where costs are extremely low, yet they are often overlooked by retirees.

Oaxaca

Oaxaca has no tall buildings, but it has a lively plaza ringed by sidewalk cafés. The city of about 350,000 is breathtaking, and for that reason it attracts a lot of tourists. From 500 to 750 Americans make Oaxaca their home; they generally are more interested in blending into the Mexican way of life than in becoming a part of a foreign enclave. You can find inexpensive housing in Oaxaca by renting a room or suite in one of the city's many affordable hotels.

Baja

One place that hasn't been overlooked by Americans in recent years is the Baja California peninsula, a strip of land stretching down from the California-Mexico border. It measures 800 miles long, and is about 140 miles at its widest point, 40 miles at its narrowest point.

Baja California is separated into two states: Baja California Norte, whose capital is the small town of Mexicali, and Baja California Sur, whose capital is La Paz. The area is noted for some of the best fishing in the world and some of the cleanest, most beautiful beaches.

South of Tijuana, the first place you might find North Americans is Rosarito Beach, which is within commuting distance of San Diego. There are bungalows, houses, mobile homes, and condominiums. Rosarito Beach is more like California than Mexico, but Americans who want to return to California in a hurry like it there.

Ensenada is farther south, the big urban area of west-coast Baja. Many retirees choose this spot because of the mild climate and beautiful ocean scenery. Fishing and tourism are the major industries in this city of more than 200,000 people.

Going south from Ensenada, you probably won't run across many North Americans until you get to La Paz. Here, the climate is almost perfect and there's hardly any rain. La Paz is home to 200,000 people and some clean trailer parks.

Other cities in Baja California worth checking out include Bahía de Palmas, about halfway between La Paz and Cabo San Lucas on the Sea of Cortes eastern side of the peninsula. Another is Todos Santos, noted for some of the prettiest beaches in Baja. Cabo San Lucas is popular for its incredible sailfish and marlin fishing.

Other Locations

All of Mexico's beach cities are popular with tourists, but not so popular with retirees because of their high costs. These include places such as Puerto Vallarta, Acapulco, and Cancún. It's better to make these spots your destinations for special weekends away than to choose them as a permanent residence. Mexico City is also popular with tourists but should probably be avoided by retirees because of its high costs, altitude, smog, and traffic.

That's not to say many retirees don't choose Mexico City as their home. Some people find the city's culture—especially concerts, opera, and dance performances—stimulating. Retirees with a lot of money and a penchant for Mexico City often rent homes or apartments in Cuernavaca, about an hour's drive away. The city sits in a lovely valley and is known for its high-priced mansions, well-manicured gardens, and ornate churches and palaces.

RENTING: WHAT IT WILL COST

Rentals in Mexico will likely be less than those along the west or east coast of the United States, but may be more than in some small towns of the Midwest. As in the United States, rentals are more expensive in or near large metropolitan areas than in small towns or rural areas.

Rents in Mexico City and in other large cities such as Monterrey are high. Accommodation at a reasonable rate can be found only far from the city center. Temporary furnished accommodation with cooking facilities, such as that in a hotel, is of limited availability and can cost $100 to $150 per day.

Monthly rents for a really nice furnished two-bedroom apartment in Mexico City with security can range from $1,000 to $3,000. Unfurnished apartments can go for $800 to $2,500. Obviously, you can find less expensive places the farther you venture from the city.

Now, before you close this book and decide you can't afford retiring in Mexico, consider the following: In Guadalajara and the Lake Chapala area, monthly rent on a nice furnished one-bedroom apartment ranges from $275 to $400. Monthly rent on a furnished two-bedroom apartment with several rooms ranges from $400 to $600. Monthly rent on a furnished two-bedroom condominium with a pool in one of the finest neighborhoods ranges from $600 to $750. Some retirees say you can find good housing for as little as $200 a month! Rentals in most parts of Mexico, outside Mexico City, are very affordable! You can find apartments and other rentals in Guadalajara in the *Colony Reporter* and *El Informador*, as well as on bulletin boards outside Sandi's Bookstore.

When you rent, you'll probably be asked to sign a six-month or one-year lease. Everything should be in writing, and you should read all fine print carefully before signing. Most of the terms will be in dollars, not in pesos. Be sure that all bills of previous tenants have been paid, and expect that rent will be due monthly, usually within the first five days of the month. Some landlords require two months' rent payable in advance with one month's rent required as a security deposit. Others require just a security deposit.

You should not have to wait more than ten days to move in after signing a lease if the property is unoccupied. It is customary for the renter to pay the equivalent of one month's rent to the buyer's agent, if one is used. Make certain you get receipts so that you'll have proof of your payments.

Before renting anything, here's a helpful checklist:

❑ Always check the plumbing and water pressure before signing a lease. Check the water pressure by turning on several faucets at once.

❑ Ask whether it's your responsibility to pay for utilities. It probably will be. Make sure that all utility bills are paid up to date.

❑ Realize that unfurnished houses rarely have a stove, refrigerator, screens, or other movable equipment such as lighting fixtures. Most new apartments will have such items, and will also have modern bathrooms and reliable hot water.

❑ Ask about repairs. The Mexican landlord often requires his tenants to pay for any repairs, maintenance, or improvements.

❑ Check for security (it is typically not included in the rent for homes, and must be contracted separately).

❑ Watch for signs of earthquake settling. Is the building secure?

❑ Locate the nearest grocery store, bus stop, and medical facility.

❑ Check for cleanliness. Are insects a problem?

❑ Look for electrical outlets. How dependable is electric service, and do the lights go out frequently?

❑ Pay attention to the surroundings. Is the house or apartment located on a busy street where noise might be a problem? What are the neighbors like?

❑ Ask about garbage collection. How frequent is it and how must it be handled?

Lastly, never ever *rent* a house or apartment that doesn't have a telephone. Always ask the owner, landlord, or real estate agent whether the property includes a working phone line. It can take weeks, even months, to get a new telephone line from Telmex.

If you have the misfortune of getting a home without a phone line, lines are for sale in the classified sections of most newspapers. A line bought on the thriving black market can cost upwards of $1,500. People without phones in their homes often rely on cellular phones. Always make certain to pay your phone bill on time. If you don't, and the phone company removes your line, it is extremely time-consuming and costly to obtain a new one.

Tax bills usually come to the place you are renting and should be given to the owner as soon as possible.

BUYING PROPERTY AND FINANCING THE DEAL

So you've heard that buying property in Mexico is a great investment. Or you're just looking forward to buying an old house and fixing it up with the help of cheap labor. It is indeed tempting to jump right into the real estate market if you've got some extra cash and a heavy dose of gumption, but a word of caution is in order.

The value of property in Mexico is often based on how much rent it will bring in. If inflation is high, tenants can't afford to pay high rents, meaning real estate isn't that great an investment. That's not to say good deals aren't to be had right now, especially now that the peso has been devalued.

Until December 1994, when that devaluation took place, real estate in Mexico was overvalued, like the currency. Costs had skyrocketed in recent years, closing the gap between what homes sell for in Mexico and similar properties in the United States. For example, along the coast of Baja California, furnished beachfront condominiums had been selling for hundreds of thousands of dollars. A beautiful colonial home in San Miguel de Allende had been going for a million dollars. But now that the peso has been devalued, everything is cheaper in Mexico, including property.

This means that you can probably snatch something up at a really good price, then turn around and sell it down the road and make a hefty profit. But how long the market stays this way remains to be seen.

Fortunately, it's not as difficult to purchase real estate in Mexico as it used to be. At one time, foreigners had to obtain a certain resident status to buy property, or they had to buy property through bank trusts, called *fidecomisos*, then lease the property back from the bank. But that's no longer the only way to purchase property. Today, anyone can buy property in Mexico—even tourists. Foreigners or anyone else can now hold fee-simple title deeds for property in their own names.

In general, it's about as easy to purchase property in Mexico as it is in the United States. Mexico has brokers who sell real estate throughout the country, but many Mexicans and retirees still sell their own homes, much as they do in the United States. Brokers are listed in the Yellow Pages under the headings "Inmobiliaria" or "Bienes y Raices." A few of the larger real estate companies from the United States and Canada have franchises in Mexico. Century 21 has offices in many parts of the country, and the bilingual staff has been recommended as being particularly helpful.

The Mexican government denies foreign ownership of land within sixty-two miles of any Mexican border or thirty-one miles of any beach, under a law known as La Zona de Restricciones, or the Restricted Zone. Despite the law, a Mexican bank may hold title to the property in a trust for up to fifty years at a time as a kind of silent partner, allowing a foreigner the full benefit of ownership of the land, even coastal land, including selling rights.

The Mexican government also has ruled that only it can own land within about sixty-five feet of a shoreline, under a law known as la Zona Federal, or the Federal Zone.

Before buying, most brokers suggest renting for several months so that you'll have time to get a feel for the country and where you want to buy. You should seek out reliable legal assistance from someone who fluently speaks both English and Spanish. Consult a reputable Mexican attorney to confirm that state codes do not conflict with federal provisions. Carry out a title search before investing. Don't be too trusting of real estate agents. The only requirement to sell real estate in Mexico is a business license issued by a local municipality. There's a new book that is apparently helpful to people wanting to buy property, called *How to Buy Real Estate in Mexico*, written by Dennis John Peyton and published by Law Mexico Publishing in 1994.

Homes in Mexico are often sold for cash and not with financing from a bank or mortgage company. Still, property owners, especially those of large developments, will sometimes finance.

UTILITIES: WHAT YOU'LL PAY

Utilities are not quite the bargain they are in other Latin countries such as Ecuador or Guatemala, but they will be inexpensive in the central plateau region of Mexico, where heating and air conditioning are not necessary. The prices below are for service in Mexico City. Outside Mexico City, prices tend to be lower, and you'll wind up paying less for utilities than you would in most parts of the United States, in most cases. Retirees report paying just $20 to $40 a month in utility bills for a typical home in the Lake Chapala area, for example.

Phone service costs $10 to $15 a month in Mexico City, with calls costing about 13 cents to 15 cents each after the first 100 calls per month. Telmex requires that all monthly bills be paid in full on the day before the due date—payments made on the due date are considered late. You must make your payment and work out your problems later if the telephone is out of order or if the company has mistakenly charged for calls not made. Because it has a long waiting list of customers seeking to obtain a phone line, Telmex doesn't hesitate to yank phone lines when bills are not paid promptly and to give them to someone else.

Electric bills vary, but will likely run $50 to $100 a month in Mexico City. Electric bills are usually in the owner's name or the previous tenant's name, but you'll likely be expected to pay them anyway. You can pay them at most banks, at Sears stores, or at the electric company's offices. The current in Mexico is 110 volts, the same as it is in the United States. Its strength can fluctuate, however, especially in rural areas. Three-pronged outlets are not common in Mexico.

Like electric bills, gas bills can vary widely, but are estimated to run $30 to $60 a month in Mexico City. Gas is delivered to individual homes by one of many gas companies and stored in tanks either on the roof or in an outdoor shed. You'll be responsible for contracting with one of the companies servicing your area for regular delivery if the property owner hasn't done so already. Always call early for a new supply, as delivery can take weeks, especially around the holidays. The gas must be paid for upon delivery, and the delivery men expect to be tipped at each visit.

Water is scarce in Mexico City, and some neighborhoods experience shortages, although a massive modernization program should improve the situation over the next decade or so. All tap water should be filtered, and ideally boiled before drinking. Homes in Mexico typically have water-holding tanks and cisterns near the street; you should have your water tank cleaned two to four times a year, maybe more. You'll receive a water bill about every two months for the water supplied by the water department. In addition to that bill, many people pay each month for purified bottled water to be delivered to their homes.

Setting Up, Settling In

Staying abreast of what's going on back home is often a concern when one moves overseas. But this need not be the case in Mexico. Not only will you be able to call and write your friends and relatives, but you'll be able to buy major U.S. newspapers and magazines in order to keep up with the news.

NEWSPAPERS, MAGAZINES, TELEVISION, MOVIES

You can purchase the *New York Times,* the *Wall Street Journal, USA Today,* the *Miami Herald,* and English-language magazines in locations around Mexico. *The News* in Mexico City is the local English-language newspaper and it's available all across the country. It offers world and local news. The *Daily Bulletin* is a free advertising publication aimed at tourists, covering world and Mexican news.

And you won't have to do without U.S. television. It seems almost every home in Mexico these days has satellite antennas allowing them to watch U.S. programming. People who don't have satellites pay for English-language cable service from one of the country's many cable companies. Those people with VCRs rent U.S. movies on videotape.

You can purchase U.S. publications and English-language books at many locations, including the Sanborn chain throughout Mexico City; the American Bookstore; the British Bookstore; Libros, Libros, Libros; and Casa Libros. Same-day delivery of the *Miami Herald* can be arranged from Promotora de Ediciones Internacionales, Narcisco Mendoaz 62, Col. Avila Camacho. For information, phone 5-589-0185, 5-581-0065.

MAIL SERVICE

Letters mailed from Mexico usually arrive at their U.S. destinations within a week or so. Mail service has improved, but I still wouldn't use it for anything of real importance; in other words, don't send checks through the mail or have them sent to you. Also, don't have packages sent to you unless it's absolutely necessary. Why? Because they will likely be held up in customs and probably come with a duty fee that is more than the value of the item mailed to you. Mail items at the post office rather than placing them in mailboxes along the streets since it may be some time before they are emptied.

To make certain you receive your mail, you might want to contract with a company such as Mailboxes, Etc., which sets you up with a U.S. address and a mailbox in Mexico City to which all your mail is couriered. The monthly fee is usually $20 or more. Mailboxes Etc. is located at Avenida Techmachalco 104, Col. San Miguel Techmachalco; phone 5-589-2477. You can also use courier services for your really important mail. DHL, Federal Express, and Airborne all have offices in Mexico City.

Instead of using the postal system, many people now use fax

machines to send important messages. Charges for sending or receiving a fax are usually based on the number of pages and are likely to be more expensive than in the United States. You can also use your computer and modem to send E-mail to the United States. For example, you can direct-dial the on-line service called CompuServe in Mexico. You just have to be a subscriber and have a U.S. credit card. To use the service from Mexico, though, will cost an additional $6 per hour. Furthermore, various companies have been established in Mexico that allow you to send faxes and E-mail by paying to use their fax machines and computer equipment.

TELEPHONE SERVICE

As in most Latin countries, phone service in Mexico isn't perfect. You can direct dial long-distance calls from Mexico, or you can use a credit card or call collect. In Spanish, a collect call is called a *llamada por cobrar*, and a credit-card call is called a *llamada con tarjeta de credito*. Long-distance calls are subject to a 39 percent tax, so calling collect is preferable. In general, calling from Mexico to the United States is more expensive than calling from the United States to Mexico.

To get an English-speaking operator in order to make an international call, dial 09; to call long distance within Mexico, dial 02. To call the United States from Mexico, dial 09-1-area code-local number. To call Mexico City from the United States, dial 52-5-number. To call Guadalajara from the United States, dial 52-36-number. To call Monterrey from the United States, dial 52-83-number. Remember that to dial any number in Mexico from the United States, you must first dial 011.

AT&T's USA Direct service is available from Mexico by dialing 95-800-462-4240. An AT&T operator will answer, then you can use this service to call collect or make calls billed to your AT&T Calling Card. (To me, this is the best way to make calls from Mexico.) You'll find coin-operated phones all over Mexico, although many public phones in Mexico City are free so you don't need coins. You can't call beyond the city limits with a coin-operated phone.

FURNISHING A HOME,
FROM SILVERWARE TO APPLIANCES

Moving across town can be a daunting experience even for the most organized of individuals. So what's moving to a far-away place going to be like? The transition won't be as hard as you think.

When moving to Mexico, one tough decision you'll have to make is what to take with you and what to leave behind. I think it's always preferable to travel as light as you possibly can, but it's up to you. You'll be able to import furniture and appliances free of duty fees only if you hold a resident permit. If you come into Mexico on a tourist card, you won't be able to do so and will wind up dealing with major hassles and charges involving Mexican customs.

But don't fret. You can buy most anything you need in Mexico, which is fortunate since many homes and apartments are rented unfurnished. You might even have to pay for the installation of electrical fixtures if you rent a house. Some apartments come with drapes and carpeting, but you'll have to buy things like linen, china, and kitchenware.

All U.S. appliances will function without conversion in Mexico and almost all brands and sizes are now available in Mexico at prices slightly higher than in the United States. If you prefer you might be able to squeeze some small appliances into your luggage. Portable gas or kerosene heaters are a good idea. Electric blankets are recommended, and you should bring your own since they're not widely available in Mexico. Because of frequent surges in the power supply, you should bring surge protectors with you to Mexico for all sensitive electronic equipment (microwaves, computers, stereos, etc.).

Last time I checked the rules, tourists could bring one radio and one TV set into Mexico as long as they registered them at the time of entry. (Check with a Mexican consulate on this before leaving because rules change often.) This might be something to consider, since a new color television in Mexico costs $600 to $1,000.

Some companies will supply you with all kinds of appliances for use in every country of the world at costs lower than what you'd pay in many foreign countries. Purchases in the United States are usually tax-free and the companies normally handle shipping. For more information contact:

Appliances Overseas
276 Fifth Avenue, Suite 407
New York, NY 10001-4509

Phone: 212-545-8001

L.A.W. International
13711 Westheimer, Suite L.
Houston, TX 77077

Phone: 713-558-5600

Fortunately, you'll be able to buy furniture fairly inexpensively in Mexico by watching the newspaper ads. While many Americans are moving to Mexico, some are returning to the United States and need to sell their stuff in a hurry. If you find an unfurnished place previously rented by Americans, you might be able to purchase the rugs, curtains, and so on. Try to avoid having custom furniture made, no matter how tempting the offer. It takes forever. Keep in mind also that the items you buy for your house may not be yours forever, don't spend a lot of money on unnecessary items, at least not at first. You may change your mind about living in Mexico some-day and return to the United States.

You'll be surprised at all the stores opening up to sell household goods. Pier 1 Imports plans to open branches in Sears stores throughout the country. Walmart, K-Mart, and other chains are also opening stores. In Mexico City, you can purchase household goods and appliances at Cyklos, Buenhogar, and Sears. Other major department stores include Liverpool and El Palacio de Hierro. You can also find bargains in used furniture stores.

CLOTHES YOU'LL WANT

Don't worry about bringing heavy winter clothing. Just a light jack-et and a few sweaters are necessary, plus a raincoat for the rainy sea-son. Spring clothes are usually acceptable year-round, but Americans who wear shorts are looked down upon in some areas (not in the resort areas, of course).

In general, North Americans living in Guadalajara and around Lake Chapala dress very casually. Lightweight pants or long shorts are appropriate. Men might not ever wear a tie. But Americans in Mexico City tend to dress more formally because Mexicans there dress more formally. Mexicans pride themselves on being very care-ful dressers, current on the latest fashions.

BRINGING BOWSER AND BUTTONS WITH YOU

Bringing your pets with you to Mexico is not difficult because, for one thing, there is no quarantine requirement. However, you will need to gather some documents.

❏ A health certificate issued by your veterinarian that's not more than 10 days old when your pet enters Mexico.

❑ Proof of vaccination for common dog and cat diseases—for example, rabies, viral hepatitis, leptospirosis, distemper, and parvovirus for dogs, rabies and feline panleucopenia for cats.

❑ An original rabies certificate issued by your veterinarian, showing proof of vaccination more than 30 days prior to the flight and not more than 180 days prior to flight. The original certificate must be signed in blue ink by your veterinarian.

You also may need an import permit, which you can probably obtain at the time of your pet's entry. Check with the nearest Mexican Embassy or consulate for the latest rules because they can change.

THE QUEST FOR PEANUT BUTTER AND OTHER NECESSITIES

Now that the Mexican economy has opened up, and the North American Free Trade Agreement is being implemented, you can find almost anything you could possibly want in Mexico. With trade barriers coming down, U.S. consumer goods from cereal to car parts are available. You'll even be able to continue shopping at large U.S. chains such as Walmart and K-Mart. Discount membership stores such as Sam's Club are currently in vogue.

Grocery stores in Mexico are very similar to those in the United States with only a few exceptions. Produce is usually weighed in the produce section rather than at the checkout counter. Food is usually sold by the kilo, not by the pound. Some items may be outdated, so check expiration dates closely. Alcohol can be sold at supermarkets in Mexico, and you'll notice different cuts of meat and new vegetables in the produce section. You're expected to tip bag boys and parking lot attendants.

One-stop shopping has become popular in Mexico, meaning you'll find supermarkets in some big department stores and a proliferation of large commercial centers housing all sorts of stores. But that doesn't mean that there's an absence of specialty stores. For example, one popular specialty store is the *panadería,* which is a bakery and a good place to buy *pan dulce,* or sweet rolls.

Unlike in the United States, where people often shop for a week's worth of groceries at one time, many Mexicans continue the habit of shopping daily at local market stalls. This is not a bad idea.

Fruits and vegetables are so fresh in Mexico that it's a shame to refrigerate them for a week.

You can find imported groceries at Mister Price, Super Duper, and Satelite and Super Importado. Grocery stores in American enclaves stock a wider variety of imported goods in response to requests from foreigners. Grocery stores around Lake Chapala, for example, started selling cheddar cheese recently after residents demanded it.

But if you choose to buy imported items instead of local brands, you'll end up paying 10 to 30 percent more in a trip to the supermarket than you would if you were still living in the United States. You should try local products and check out common grocery chains in Mexico, such as Gigante, Comercial Mexicana, Blanco and Aurrera, as well as open-air markets or streetside stands in towns across Mexico. They have an unbelievable smorgasbord of fruits and vegetables for the taking. Fruits such as pineapples, mangos, oranges, and avocados will have a wonderful new taste, since they are usually picked when ripe. Towns usually have weekly markets, at which people from miles around come to sell their wares, plus permanent but smaller markets that you can visit every day.

While many U.S. brands are available in Mexico without going to the import stores—things like Coke, Campbell's soup, Purina dog food—the Newcomers' Club in Mexico City recommends certain brands as being good substitutes for U.S. ones. Club members say that Anchor butter from New Zealand and Entremónt butter from France are both good. Chambourcy cheese is supposed to be tasty; the Herdez brand of canned produce is supposed to be reliable. *Crema de batir* is heavy cream in a carton used for whipping; *crema acida* is sour cream; *crema* is a thick cream used in Mexican cooking. Perigord is a recommended brand of *mermalada*, or jam. *Maizena* is cornstarch, and *descremada* is used to denote low-fat. Chambourcy yogurt is good, as is the Imperial brand of sugar. Mexico is known for its vast selection of herbal teas.

HOUSEHOLD HELP

It seems that almost everyone employs household help in Mexico. And maids serve many purposes. Not only do they clean but they often cook, do laundry, and are invaluable when you are away and don't want to leave your house unattended. While domestic service

METRIC MEASURES

Mexico operates on the metric system of weights and measurements. Here are some conversions to help you adjust.

1 gallon	equals	3.8 liters
1 quart	equals	.95 liter
1 pound	equals	.37 kilogram
1 ounce	equals	31.1 grams
1 mile	equals	1.61 kilometers
1 yard	equals	.91 meter
1 inch	equals	2.54 centimeters
1 kilogram	equals	2.2 pounds
1 liter	equals	1.06 quarts
1 gram	equals	.035 ounce
1 kilometer	equals	.62 mile
1 meter	equals	39.37 inches
1 centimeter	equals	.39 inch

is not always highly regarded in the United States, it is considered a noble profession in Mexico. Mexicans enjoy lots of perks working for Americans, who usually treat them as part of the family. Maids are efficient and energetic, and yours will likely become one of your most trusted allies and friends.

Wages for domestic help are generally quite low—about $15 a day for day help; $250 to $350 per month for live-in help; and $20 a day for gardeners. However, there are other costs to consider. Under the law, you must pay servants six days of paid vacation following one year of service. You must pay them an annual Christmas bonus, called an *aguinaldo*, of fifteen days' salary at the end of the year. You must pay for paid maternity leave of forty days both before and after birth. Servants are given one day off per week, usually Sunday, and receive eight paid holidays during the year.

It's always a good idea to have servants sign receipts for their wages and to have them sign written contracts in Spanish stating their wage, dates of pay days, duties, and a likely period of employment if it's known.

Maids usually prefer being paid on a weekly basis. Some will prefer wearing a uniform, while others will not. The best way to find a maid or other employee is through word of mouth. Check with new-comers' clubs and chapters of the American Society. Don't just hire someone off the street or from an agency that won't be able to take responsibility in case of a robbery. Be certain to spell out specifical-ly what your maid's responsibilities will be. Ask someone who can speak fluent Spanish for help with translating. If you want your maid to cook hamburgers for you, you'll have to tell her exactly how to do this, since she may not be familiar with such U.S. delicacies!

A gardener is called a *mozo* in Mexico, and is commonly a jack-of-all-trades. You can usually count on him to help with repair jobs and to assist the maid. Gardeners usually work for several families, serving each an hour or two a day.

Getting Around

One advantage to living in Mexico is that you'll have the whole country at your fingertips. You can explore seaside resorts, cos-mopolitan cities, and mountain villages and still stay within your budget by relying on Mexico's inexpensive network of public trans-portation. It's also possible to drive a private car in Mexico, with all the freedom that entails.

PUBLIC TRANSPORTATION

Unlike those of us in the United States who can't even imagine life without our cars, the vast majority of people in Mexico do just fine without them. Bus travel is the norm for most Mexicans, and it's cer-tainly the best way to absorb the local culture. Four bus stations oper-ate in Mexico City—located in the north, south, east, and west. Buses cover the entire capital and run along routes based upon their final destination. Buses serving the country as a whole are quite cheap but also quite slow. A faster alternative are the new more luxurious "executive" buses offering service between Mexico City and other cities, complete with clean restrooms and closed-circuit television. You can buy guaranteed seats on these from travel agents.

Other buses are lumped into three categories: first class, second class, and local. First-class buses assign you a seat although you may have to stand in line to get a ticket. Tickets for first-class buses are usually 10 percent higher than those for second-class buses. Second-class buses are usually older and quite crowded, and they tend to stop at every village or town along the road. You may have to stand some, but you'll definitely be living as a true local this way. Local buses are those that operate in strictly rural areas. Passengers are allowed to bring pigs and other animals on board, making these buses a true adventure.

While bus travel can be slow, train travel is probably even slower and not usually reliable. Rail service is designed for those of you who have a real spirit of adventure.

There is one popular journey from Chihuahua to the Pacific Coast that passes through the Copper Canyon and is highly recommended. There are also overnight Pullman trains traveling between Mexico City and Monterrey, Guadalajara, Veracruz, and Mérida. On all trains, air conditioning and reserved seats are available only in the first-class, or *especial,* cars. You should purchase tickets at the stations because travel agencies tend to charge a large commission.

For information about train travel, contact Ferrocarriles Nacionales de México, Avenida Jesus Garcia #140, Col. Buenavista, Mexico, D.F.; phone 5-547-4122/0402.

Mexico City is known around the world for its subway system, called the metro, which offers speedy travel in a clean, attractive setting. Designed by the French, the marble and onyx stations are usually quite clean and decorated with artistic designs. And the metro is safe. Eight lines covering most of the city are in service—more are under construction—and are identifiable by their colors and special symbols. Bus stations often connect with the subway. A ride costs just a few cents. Trains run until midnight during the week and later on weekends. But keep in mind that taking the subway during rush hour can be a nightmare because of the crowds.

Air travel within Mexico couldn't be easier. You can sometimes get discounts if you're a senior citizen. Terminal facilities in Guadalajara have been expanded as a result of NAFTA. And improvements are planned at five other airports in Mexico as part of a $40 million program. In Cancún, platforms are being extended and terminal buildings remodeled. Other projects are planned for airports in Veracruz and Zacatecas.

From the time you walk out of the airport in Mexico City, you'll have no trouble finding a taxi. There seems to be a countless number of taxis on the roads, and the cost is cheap. Most trips around town cost only a few dollars or less. You can hail them in the street or go to a taxi stand. Always check before taking off in a taxi to make certain it has a working meter. Then make sure that the taxi driver uses it. If he doesn't have a meter, negotiate a price for the trip before taking off.

Special taxis with English-speaking drivers especially for tourists are called *turismos.* The cheapest cabs are usually yellow and white, and green and white. Red and white cabs are usually more expensive because they're often associated with a particular location, such as a major hotel.

Don't assume that taxi drivers will be familiar with all addresses in urban areas. Mexico City, for example, is so large that drivers can't possibly be expected to know every area well.

DRIVING IN MEXICO

Passage of the North American Free Trade Agreement has done wonders for this country's infrastructure. There are all sorts of road improvements taking shape. A new multilane highway will soon cut the driving time from Guadalajara to Puerto Vallarta to less than four hours. The Reynosa-Monterrey toll road is now complete, as is the Monterrey-Saltillo toll road. Another new toll road linking Morelia and Guadalajara is under construction.

In general, Mexico's notoriously bad rural roads have been improved drastically in recent years with the privatization of the highway system (2,500 miles of four-lane road have been constructed since the late 1980s). Many are toll roads; however, that can take quite a chunk out of your wallet. Although things have improved, Mexico's reputation for potholes is still well deserved. Sometimes you come across a hole so big you feel like your car might fall in! (This is why it's important to carry a good spare tire with you at all times.)

So what about the country's traffic customs? Are they different from those in the United States? Most definitely yes! Any highway offense in Mexico is regarded as criminal rather than civil. Punitive action is immediate and severe, and Mexicans don't take the law lightly. Police officers with U.S. flags on their uniforms are supposed to speak English.

Some people may suggest that you pay a bribe to a police officer if stopped for an infraction. This is up to you. If you want to discourage this practice, which is looked down upon by most Americans, you may choose to take a ticket. Ask for the written ticket and request that the officer show you in the official rules of the road book which traffic infraction you are being charged with. This book will also tell you the amount due on the ticket.

If a police officer insists that you pay him a bribe, called a *mor-dida* in Mexico, don't argue the point. It will only make the situation worse. *Mordidas* are a way of life in many parts of Mexico and many police officers—all underpaid—don't consider bribes as dishonest. Some Americans think paying the bribe is a lot easier than getting a ticket, since taking care of a ticket usually involves a trip to the police station to pay the fine.

In addition to knowing how to deal with police, you should be aware of some other driving do's and don'ts. Driving in Mexico is on the right side of the road. Seat belts are required by law. The speed limit is usually 100 kilometers an hour, or about 60 miles an hour. Traffic lights in Mexico blink green, then flash yellow quickly before turning red. It is usually legal to turn right on a red light, but do so with caution. Curbs painted yellow mean no parking.

If a driver flashes his left-turn signal, it probably doesn't mean he's turning left. Rather, it means you are safe to pass him because no one is coming from the other direction. Everyone passes every-one in Mexico, so be careful when going around curves. Someone could be coming right at you, and in your own lane! Just drive slow-ly and you'll do fine. Never drive at night and be ready for anything, including livestock strolling in the middle of the road.

Driving has been restricted on occasion in Mexico City in order to reduce air pollution. The restriction is based on the last digit of the car's license plate. Each car must be kept off the road for one day a week, based on its license plate number. The ban includes rental cars driven by visitors.

You can get by in Mexico with a valid U.S. driver's license, but you should try to get a Mexican one if you plan to stay in Mexico for a long period of time. Legal residents with papers may get a Mexican driver's license at the Urban Auto Transport Booth locat-ed at the airport and at most police departments. A driving test is not required and the written test can usually be avoided, although some people are asked to take a quick eye exam. You will need copies of all your residency permits and your old driver's license, and will be asked your blood type.

Air-conditioned cars equipped with heavy-duty suspension and high-quality tires are the ones most often recommended for driving in Mexico. Internal combustion engines lose up to 25 percent of their power at Mexico City's altitude.

Gasoline is sold only by Pemex. The cost is the equivalent of 41 cents per liter ($1.55 per gallon). Service stations can be few and far between in rural areas, so tanks should be kept full; the gas station attendant will expect a small tip, as will the boys who wash your windshield. Unleaded gas is available and is called *magna-sin*. When filling up at a gas station, get out of the car to make certain the attendant gives you the amount of gas you ask for. Be sure to keep a lock on your car's gas cap. Sears auto-service centers are recommended by U.S. retirees.

One good thing about driving in Mexico is that almost everyone knows how to repair cars, even in the most remote areas. My husband and I have driven through Mexico umpteen times. On the one occasion our 1986 Pontiac konked out along a deserted highway in southern Mexico, we were immediately picked up by a friendly passer-by and transported to the nearest town, where we had no problem finding someone to fix our car. He wasn't a mechanic by trade and insisted we not pay him for his trouble. He managed to repair the car in about ten minutes and we were on our way!

Car Rentals

Car rental agencies are located in all major Mexican cities, particularly at the larger hotels and airports. The minimum age is twenty-one, the maximum seventy. Weekly rentals range from about $400 to $1,000 with unlimited mileage. Note any damage, however slight, to the car before leaving the agency so you won't be charged for it upon return.

The main offices include those operated by Avis, Budget, Dollar, Hertz, and National.

AUTOMOBILE CLUBS IN MEXICO

In addition to getting information regarding driving routes, you may also be able to get a Mexican driver's license through these clubs.

Asociación Mexicana
Automovilística
Orizaba 7, Colonia Roma,
Apto. 24-486
Mexico, D.F.

Phone: 5-511-1084

Asociación Nacional
Automovilística
Miguel E. Schultz 140/
Avenida Jalisco 27
06470, Mexico, D.F.

Phone: 5-546-9965

Importing Your Car

Cars may be imported on a tourist card, but make sure you get a permit for your car that matches the duration of your tourist card. After this initial permit expires, usually after six months, you'll have to renew the car permit every six months, just as you will your tourist card. And if you leave the country, you'll have to take the car with you. This rule was implemented to prevent Americans from bringing cars into Mexico and selling them for much more than they were valued in the United States. If you drive into Mexico, you can fly out of the country, but only if you complete a massive amount of paperwork and impound your car. You can't legally sell your car in Mexico. It's very expensive to purchase a car in Mexico and very difficult to get financing. For one thing, you have to have a cosigner who's a Mexican citizen. An annual car tax, known as a *tenencia,* must be paid on cars by February each year at banks or offices of the Treasury ministry. The rate will vary depending on the size and age of your car. Cars also require an emissions sticker, which requires an inspection.

If you do decide to bring your car into Mexico, there are some regulations to keep in mind. For example, entry and exit points must be from the same border crossing port of entry. The owner of the car should be present in the car at all times when it's in operation to avoid legal hassles with local authorities. You should contact the nearest Mexican consulate for the latest detailed information prior to departing the United States.

Car Insurance

All cars must be covered by liability insurance issued by a Mexican company. This is something you don't want to do without under any circumstance!

Liability covers you if you have an accident and harm someone or someone's property. It can also keep you from getting arrested in the event of an accident. Extra insurance such as fire, theft, or collision coverage issued by your home-country firm will probably be less expensive than from a Mexican one; carry insurance for property damage as well. Annual rates on the Mexican-issued insurance run anywhere from a few hundred dollars to more than $800.

It is important to insure heavily. Insurance agents in Mexico are like trustworthy friends. In an accident, they sometimes find you a place to stay and make sure you're treated fairly by the judicial system.

Remember, you can be arrested if you do not have Mexican insurance.

Mexican insurance may be purchased at the border and within border states in the United States. Sanborn's Insurance Service, with offices in almost all border towns, is a good place to get insurance. It will cost about $3 to $6 per day, but remember that it is essential. Long-term insurance is cheaper than short-term insurance.

To get really good rates, you might consider joining a travel club, which offers its members group rates on auto insurance. (See page 45.)

SECURITY CONCERNS

If you live in the United States, you know that you can't turn on the TV news without seeing reports of murders, kidnappings, and other violent crimes. It's inescapable in any urban area, and the problem appears to be growing worse.

Obviously, Mexico has crime, but I'd still bet that most parts of Mexico are safer than the streets of most U.S. cities. In fact, I feel safer traveling through Mexico than I do traveling through Atlanta, where I currently reside. I'm not saying that street crime is not a problem in Mexico—because it is—but violent crime in Mexico isn't nearly as common as it is in the United States.

Just as crime is less prevalent in small U.S. towns, so is it less prevalent in small Mexican towns. In places where retirees reside, violent crime is almost nonexistent. Juvenile delinquency is not the menace it has become in the United States, and drug use is considered a gravely serious offense.

One reason for this may be that such a great emphasis is placed on family in Mexico, and no one, not even a troublesome teenager, wants to suffer the wrath of his or her grandparents, aunts, uncles, and older siblings. Families tend to socialize together on the weekends and during the evenings, meaning there's less time for kids to get into trouble.

All of this is not to say you don't have to take precautions when in Mexico. But if you follow these common sense rules of thumb, you should not encounter any problems with criminals.

Mexico West Travel Club Inc.
P.O. Box 1646
Bonita, CA 91908

Phone: 619-585-3033

Vagabundos del Mar
P.O. Box 824
Isleton, CA 95641

Phone: 707-327-5511

Remember, drivers, especially foreigners, who are involved in accidents are sometimes subject to arrest and detention, particularly if they don't have insurance. This applies even if you aren't at fault. Bail bonds and lawyer's fees are not included in Mexican insurance. The judicial process is long and costly, so one must take special precautions.

❑ Do be careful when driving at night because robbers have been known to target drivers along isolated roads.

❑ Don't wear expensive jewelry or carry valuables on you when walking the streets of urban areas such as Mexico City.

❑ Wear a money pouch around your neck or around your waist, and clutch your purse tightly if you must carry one at all. Pickpocketing is a growing concern in Mexico.

❑ Keep valuables in your hotel's safe, since maids have been known to burglarize the rooms of foreigners.

❑ If you have to leave your home in Mexico for an extended trip, ask your maid or someone else you trust to look after it while you're gone. The windows and doors of many homes in Mexico are protected by steel bars.

Unfortunately, carjackings are on the rise in Mexico. Police say thieves target imported models such as Cadillacs and convertibles. Apparently, carjackers have a favored method of stealing. They like to lightly bump the rear of the victim's car at an intersection or traffic signal. When the victim gets out to look at the damage, the carjacker jumps into the victim's car and takes off. If someone bumps your car, you might consider sounding your horn if people are nearby, or pretending that you're making a call if you own a cellular phone.

If you're concerned about your security, you can get the latest U.S. State Department travel advisory on Mexico by calling 202-647-5225.

Because of this, most people don't even call the police when they are involved in an accident. They just work issues out among themselves, with the help of their insurance agents. Mexican police do not have the power to assign fault in an accident; it's for a judge to decide. You should report accidents as soon as possible. You may lose your claim with the insurance company if you wait too long.

Staying Healthy

For years, Americans have been bombarded with horror stories of tourists becoming sick in Mexico from drinking contaminated water or eating contaminated food. Who *hasn't* heard of Montezuma's revenge? While alarming on the surface, these stories should not keep you from considering Mexico as a retirement destination.

DON'T DRINK THE WATER AND OTHER SAFEGUARDS

While I'm sure many tourists have become ill from eating or drinking something they shouldn't have, the vast majority of Americans, especially those living in Mexico, don't suffer any problems. You just don't hear their stories the way you do the horror stories. If you drink bottled water, wash vegetables and fruits in purified water, and take other simple precautions, you're not likely to get sick. In fact, you'll probably feel better than you've felt in years!

Just because you can't drink tap water doesn't mean you can't drink mineral, bottled, or filtered water, which makes the water issue a really trivial one compared with all the health benefits of living in Mexico. For one thing, the climate in many parts of Mexico probably beats what you'd be leaving behind.

Mexico boasts a dryer climate and moderate year-round temperatures, meaning you're likely to spend more time outdoors. Because of the climate, most homes need no air conditioners or heaters, so you won't be breathing in stale, recycled air all the time. The country is also likely to be better for your emotional health, meaning you'll feel physically better and more energetic as a result. Many retirees say that living in Mexico offers them new challenges, new friends, and a new lease on life that's invigorating. And a slower pace of living means less stress, while more to do means less lethargy, boredom, and fatigue.

Let me say one more thing about the water issue. While it's true that you sometimes can't drink the water in Mexico, many hotels and other establishments now use filters so that even the tap water is safe. Under the law, ice at restaurants must be made from *agua purificada,* or purified water. But if you're still nervous, bottled water is available everywhere.

Most residents of Mexico buy purified water in ten-gallon bottles for their homes. Tehuacan mineral water is sold all over Mexico. Water-sterilizing tablets and water-purification solution, Microdyn, can be purchased at most pharmacies. Maids are well educated in how to maintain a safe water supply and prepare safe-to-eat fruits and vegetables.

If you do get a gastroenterological infection (a big term that simply means stomach problems caused by bacteria transmitted through contaminated food and water), you'll likely suffer from one or more of the following symptoms within seventy-two hours of infection: cramps, fever, nausea, diarrhea, and vomiting. To avoid getting sick, simply wash all produce well in purified water. Peel all fresh produce. Don't drink or cook with the first water out of the tap each day, since you don't know how long it has been sitting in the pipes. Avoid food and beverages sold by street vendors. Avoid uncooked seafood and cold seafood salads. Purify water by boiling it (you just need to bring it to a boil, not boil it for 30 minutes).

So, really, as you can see, there's nothing to worry about regarding water or food. What you will have to worry about, unfortunately, are things such as air pollution if you choose to reside in a highly congested, highly populated area. I've heard lots of troubling stories about residents of Mexico City being asked to stay home on occasion because of heavy pollution on a particular day. Most diplomats appointed to Mexico are warned to leave behind their very small children because of the pollution.

Why is it so bad? Mexico City is located in a valley, which creates a thermal inversion, trapping warm pollution under cold mountain air. Because of this, ozone levels have exceeded approved international standards for more than 80 percent of days for the last few years. The air pollution, coupled with Mexico City's high altitude—7,000 feet—can cause problems for the elderly and persons with high blood pressure, anemia, and respiratory or cardiac problems.

To deal with pollution, you should try to find a home as far from downtown Mexico City as possible, if you have to live near the capital at all. If you do decide to live in or around Mexico City, listen to the news. Warnings about especially high pollution levels will be broadcast. Avoid strenuous exercise outdoors. Use air filters, which are available in Mexico City from NSA Environmental Systems, phone 5-515-9645. They are also available from Enviracare, phone 5-557-9777.

Another thing to worry about is altitude. Many of the places frequented by retirees outside Mexico City are more than 5,000 feet in altitude, which can have a negative effect on people with heart trouble or respiratory ailments. You should probably consult your doctor before moving permanently to a high-altitude locale. In general, most people who take it easy and avoid alcohol for a day or two eventually adjust to high altitudes.

If you still have health concerns, the Centers for Disease Control and Prevention can help. By making one phone call, you can obtain CDC documents via fax. A good first step is to request a copy of the system's international travel directory, which will list documents available—everything from vaccination recommendations to malarial medication. The phone is 404-332-4565.

DOCTORS AND HOSPITALS: WHAT IF YOU GET SICK?

You will have no problem finding well-qualified, English-speaking doctors throughout much of Mexico, especially in urban areas. In fact, many doctors in the United States received their education in Mexico after being turned away by U.S. medical schools that had exceeded their capacity.

Many hospitals in Mexico offer quality care, similar to what you'd receive in the United States and at much lower prices. In fact, low-cost health care is what attracts many retirees to Mexico in the first place. Some hospitals even give discounts to members of Mexico's various American Society chapters.

Centros de salud (health centers) and *hospitales cívicas* (civic hospitals) are open to everyone and are quite cheap. I've heard, though, that the quality of care can be lacking and that the social-security hospitals are apparently of higher quality and more up-to-date. Many foreigners use private clinics, which are more expensive but top-notch, for their health-care needs. Health facilities in Mexico City and Guadalajara and other places frequented by Americans are especially good. Furthermore, the Mexican government plans to open twelve bilingual medical centers in major tourist areas that will operate twenty-four hours a day and will work in conjunction with several U.S. medical centers.

Here are a few hospitals in Mexico City that are frequently used by foreigners:

American British Cowdray Hospital
Observatorio and Calle Sur 136

Phone: 5-277-5000;
emergency 5-515-8359

Clínica Germán
Calle Eucker 16-601

Phone: 5-545-9434

Hospital de los Angeles
Camino a Santa Teresa

Phone: 5-652-2011

Other than Mexico City, Guadalajara has the finest medical facilities in Mexico. There are two large medical schools, public and private facilities, well-trained specialists in every field, five hospitals with intensive care units, and many doctors and dentists who have had some training in the United States and speak English very well. Mercy Hospital of San Diego is constructing the new Guadalajara Mercy Hospital, which will be affiliated with the eighteen Mercy Hospitals across the United States. Almost all U.S. medical insurance will be honored at this facility.

Monterrey also has fine medical facilities; medical care at Hospital Muguerza and Hospital San José is recommended.

When dealing with Mexican doctors, you should be aware that many will try to do several things at once during an office visit. They may take a personal call while you're sitting in the office. This is not considered rude in Mexico; it's just the way things are done. On the plus side, retirees tell me that patients in Mexico are given the chance to make more decisions pertaining to their treatment than they would be in the United States. For example, prescriptions are usually returned to you when they are filled, except in the case of narcotics. Furthermore, you can usually get a blood test at a laboratory without a doctor's referral. Often, you can keep X-rays after having them taken.

There are many English-speaking doctors working in Mexico who have been trained in the United States or Europe. You can get a list of English-speaking doctors from the U.S. Embassy in Mexico City. You can also get a list of well-regarded doctors and hospitals abroad from Intercontinental Medical. The company's source is a database of 5,500 doctors and hospitals, compiled from medical directories, U.S. consular lists, and hospital associations. The company will customize a list specifically pertaining to Mexico. For more information call the company at 800-426-8828.

Here are a few doctors in Mexico City you should know:

Ernesto Fernandez Reyes   Phone: 5-272-0200
Sur 136, Suite 407

Jorge Goldberg   Phone: 5-540-7300
Palmas 745

Jamie Feldman   Phone: 5-294-7166
Pte. Piramides 1, 2nd floor
Tecamachalco

DEALING WITH EMERGENCIES

It's a good idea to know exactly what you'd do in the event of an emergency when you're at home, and even more so when you're in the unfamiliar surroundings of a foreign country. By preparing yourself, you'll have a peace of mind that will allow you to do what you came to Mexico to do: enjoy yourself.

Ambulance service in Mexico has a reputation for being slow and not very reliable, which is why you should take the time to familiarize yourself with the route to the nearest hospital and keep on hand the phone numbers of reliable taxi services.

Also, know how to ask for help in Spanish. Make a list of all emergency numbers for your area and place them near your phone. Emergency numbers for fire, police, and ambulance services should be printed in the front of the phone book.

Know how to say your address in Spanish, and learn other key phrases. Be certain your maid knows what to do in case of an emergency.

In Mexico, one emergency to be prepared for—although it's a highly unlikely one—is an earthquake. In 1985, Mexico City experienced a catastrophic earthquake that measured 8.2 on the Richter scale and killed or injured tens of thousands of people. Although much of the pressure along the fault line was released by this earthquake, the possibility always exists that another quake may occur. To prepare yourself, put together an earthquake kit that includes candles, a flashlight, extra batteries, a transistor radio, a first aid kit, bottled water, and dry and canned food. If an earthquake does occur, get under a strong structural door support and do not take an elevator. Turn off your gas and all electricity, and report your status to the Embassy.

In the unfortunate event of a death of a U.S. citizen in Mexico, the following steps should be taken: Contact Consular Services at the

U.S. Embassy immediately. Call the deceased's doctor for a death certificate. Contact a funeral home—the Embassy can recommend one—because embalmment must be done before the deceased will be allowed to leave the country. The Embassy will issue a "Report of Death of an American Citizen Abroad," which is legal proof of death.

Before going to Mexico, you might want to contact one or all of the following services that cater to travelers faced with an emergency situation:

Centers for Disease Control and Prevention

Phone: 404-332-4555

The CDC provides updated information regarding diseases and vaccinations.

International SOS Assistance
P.O. Box 11568
Philadelphia, PA 19116

Phone: 215-244-1500

This service provides subscribers with professional help worldwide in any medical or personal emergency. Services range from telephone advice to medical evacuations.

Medex Assistance Corporation
P.O. Box 10623
Baltimore, MD 21285-0623

Phone: 410-296- 2530

This service provides assistance similar to that of International SOS Assistance. Multilingual specialists answer calls twenty-four hours a day.

INSURANCE FOR OVERSEAS HEALTH CARE

Each year about 23,000 Americans are hospitalized overseas. Many suffer financially because their health insurance policies do not cover care outside the United States. Elderly travelers, in particular, are at risk, since Medicare usually does not cover medical assistance in foreign countries.

Since rules vary company by company, you should check with your insurer before going anywhere to determine exactly what care is covered and what care is not. Some U.S. insurers will reimburse you for medical expenses in Mexico. Some insurers refuse to cover emergency medical evacuations, a concern since the cost of these ranges from $5,000 to $20,000. Blue Cross will usually cover hospital stays in Mexico.

Many affluent Americans who live in Mexico decide against purchasing health insurance and instead choose to pay cash for their medical expenses, citing the low cost. Because of Mexico's close proximity to the United States, other Americans maintain their insurance policies with U.S. companies and simply travel to the United States when they need medical care. Other retirees often choose to get treated in the United States so that Medicare will cover the costs.

Meanwhile, more cautious Americans buy a medical assistance insurance policy before they'll even travel outside the country for a short period of time. This kind of policy generally covers medical expenses and evacuation in case of sudden illnesses or accidents. Travelers can buy this insurance by itself or as part of a package that includes baggage insurance. Travel insurance companies and travel agents usually sell this type of insurance.

Instead of dealing with U.S. insurers at all, many retirees instead choose to participate in the group insurance plan offered through the American Society in Mexico, which has chapters in most major cities. Still other retirees join the Mexican social security system, which covers almost all medical expenses. One retired couple told me they pay $240 a year for complete coverage under this system. The plan apparently covers drugs, dental and eye care, and medical and hospital costs. You can apply for coverage in January, February, July, or August. Ask other retirees about these plans upon your arrival.

If your insurance policy won't cover you in Mexico, you can get more information about insurance by contacting the following:

Amex Travel Protection Plan
P.O. Box 919010
San Diego, CA 92191-9970

Phone: 800-234-0375

Travel Assistance International
1133 15th Street N.W.,
Suite 400
Washington, DC 20006-2710

Phone: 800-821-2828

Travel Assure, Teletrip Company Inc.
3201 Farnarm Street
Omaha, NE 68131

Phone: 800-228-9792

Travel Insurance Services
2930 Camino Diablo,
Suite 200, Box 200
Walnut Creek, CA 94596

Phone: 800-937-1387

Travel Insured International
P.O. Box 280568
East Hartford, CT 06128

Phone: 800-243-3174

MEDICINES, PHARMACIES, AND PRESCRIPTIONS

Many medicines that would require a prescription in the United States can be bought over-the-counter in Mexico. If you have your prescription bottle and drug name, it's likely that you'll be able to find it in Mexico. Most pharmacists keep a book to look up the corresponding drug name and drug company in Mexico. Still, it's probably a good idea to bring a hefty supply of your prescription drugs from home just to be on the safe side until you're sure you can get them in Mexico. You might find yourself unfamiliar with some drugs in Mexico because they are sold under a different name.

Almost all drugs will be less expensive in Mexico than they are in the United States—most cost less than 20 percent of what they would in the United States. Some U.S. insurers will reimburse the cost of medicine with a receipt, so check with your insurance company before leaving.

Some pharmacies in Mexico City stay open twenty-four hours a day, including the Farmacia Arrocha off the Periférico next to the Hospital de Seguro Social. Long-time residents claim that the Sanborn's chain and El Fénix discount pharmacies have the most complete selections.

DENTAL CARE

There are many English-speaking dentists working in Mexico and many have been trained in the United States or in Europe. Fees can vary widely, but dental care in general costs about one-third what it does in the United States.

Many retirees consider low-cost dental care one of the biggest perks to living in Mexico. You should be able to get your teeth cleaned and X-rayed for about $40, and a tooth filled for about $40. You can obtain a list of reputable dentists from the U.S. Embassy. The following are just a few English-speaking dentists in Mexico City:

Nathan Aron
Campos Eliseos 325

Phone: 5-520-9208

Antonio Bello
Palmas 745-1001,
Lomas de Chapultepec

Phone: 5-202-9812

Jaime Cohen
Plaza Polanco, Torre C / 7th flr

Phone: 5-358-8855

Paul Goldberg
Avenida Las Fuentes 141A-303,
Tecamachalco

Phone: 5-294-0859

Nathan Stein
Homero 1804-501, Polanco

Phone: 5-580-3354

Staying Busy and Happy

Once you're in Mexico, what will you do with your spare time? This is a good question since many of you who choose to live permanently in Mexico will consequently choose to employ maids and other household help and will have lots of spare time.

LEISURE ACTIVITIES

Believe me, filling time will never be a problem. Many retirees in Mexico claim to be busier now than they were before they retired. Large American communities in sites across Mexico, with their wide range of social clubs, outdoor events, and cultural activities, make the transition to Mexico easy. Bridge clubs, lending libraries, and dance classes abound. What's more, a battalion of enterprising and friendly retirees already living in Mexico is on hand to draw out even the most reserved of newcomers.

To get an idea of what there is to do, you should purchase English-language publications that will certainly have long listings of all entertainment and sporting activities, social clubs, churches, and the like. For example, you can consult *Tiempo Libre* magazine and the *Mexico City News* for such information.

To give you an idea of how much there is to do in Mexico, let me share something I saw recently in a weekly English-language newspaper called the *Guadalajara Reporter*. The newspaper lists activities scheduled each day in the area around Lake Chapala. According to the newspaper, here's what was happening on one particular Wednesday:

❑ Meeting of a tennis club

❑ Meeting of Alcoholics Anonymous

❑ Free dance class

❑ Meeting of an aviation club

❑ Seminar called "Harmonizing Mind, Body and Spirit Through Exercise"

❑ Services at the New Apostolic Church

❑ Meeting of the bridge club

❑ A party hosted by the American Legion

And that was just one day's worth of activities!

If a daily schedule like that won't keep you busy enough, you can always skip over to a resort area such as Puerto Angel or Acapulco for a short, action-packed getaway. (I don't recommend these places for retirement because of their high prices.) Puerto Vallarta, for example, has everything: scuba diving, sports fishing, kayaking, boating, rafting, and so on. On land, you can play eighteen holes of golf, practice your tennis, go horseback riding, or try duck and dove hunting.

In resort areas, as well as in all major urban areas, and especially in Mexico City, the nightlife is always hopping. Some popular nightclubs in Mexico City include La Fonda de Recuerdo, Las Glorias del Barco, and Caballo Negro. Popular bars include the Muralta Bar (great view), the Lobby Bar (good place to talk), and La Cantina (good Mexican music).

If you like sports but want to sit on the sidelines, go see a baseball game. The Mexican National League includes some U.S. players who come to Mexico during their off-season to keep in shape. Look in the newspapers for game times and places. You can also have fun attending Mexican rodeos, which are steeped in tradition and folklore. Rodeos are usually held on Sunday afternoons. Soccer is probably the most popular sport among spectators, although people also enjoy watching horseracing, jai alai, and polo. The bullfighting season in Mexico City is November through April. When buying a ticket, you may choose between *sol* (sun) and *sombra* (shade), *sombra* seats being the more expensive ones because they are cooler and closer to the action.

If you don't want to sit on the sidelines, you can enjoy horseback riding at various clubs, mountain biking and hiking, running, sailing, squash, swimming, and tennis. Guadalajara alone has five golf courses! In Monterrey, cycling, bowling, tennis, golf, swimming, and sports clubs are popular. Day trips could include mountain climbing at Chipinque or water sports at Presa de la Boca.

Mexico is full of cultural events, and you won't have to forgo your weekly dose of theater or opera just because you live in a foreign country. For concerts, Mexico even has its own Ticketmaster network with outlets in various locations. Tickets can be purchased to events such as the ballet and orchestra concerts. The main spots for cultural events include the Palacio de las Bellas Artes, home to the National Symphony and Ballet Folklórico; the Teatro de la Ciudad, where all kinds of plays and concerts are held; and the National Auditorium, site of various music and dance performances. Guadalajara has its own symphony orchestra, plus a steady stream of music and dance performances, art exhibits, and theatrical events.

Good museums in Mexico City include the National Museum of Anthropology, the Museum of Modern Art, the Frida Kahlo Museum, and the San Carlos Museum. In Guadalajara, you'll find the Museo Regional de Guadalajara. Many museums are closed on Mondays. All the major cities have movie theaters, which show first-run U.S. films about six months after their U.S. release, usually subtitled in Spanish.

HOW TO MAKE FRIENDS

You'll have no problem meeting people and making friends in Mexico. I've found that foreigners living overseas tend to come together much more quickly than they do in Smalltown, U.S.A. Since Americans in Mexico usually don't work, neighbors are home during the day and they get to know each other, unlike many neighbors in the United States.

In addition to meeting other foreigners, I hope you'll take the time to meet some locals. This is something that might take some effort, particularly if you're living in an American enclave like Lake Chapala. Mexicans are well-known for being friendly, open, and loyal.

Upon arrival in Mexico, and if you're a woman spending any amount of time at all in Mexico City, you should definitely contact the Newcomers' Club. The Newcomers' Club invites all English-speaking women to participate in its classes, tours, and seminars, designed to make adjustment to Mexico easier and happier. The club holds monthly meetings as well as sponsors all types of events—everything from book clubs to monthly dinners to movie nights. From what I've heard, this is a great way to meet other women and to acclimate yourself to your new surroundings. There are also Newcomers' Club chapters in Monterrey and Guadalajara.

There are plenty of other special interest groups to join in Mexico City. The American Society of Mexico (phone: 5-202-4600) is a big one, and it holds all sorts of social events while serving as a referral service for other groups in Mexico. Other groups include the Daughters of the American Revolution, the Mexico City Quilt Guild, Republicans Abroad, Democrats Abroad, and various alumni associations. Self-help and support groups include Weight Watchers, Narcotics Anonymous, Alcoholics Anonymous, and Adult Children of Alcoholics and/or Dysfunctional Families.

There are groups to join in other sites popular with American retirees as well. In Monterrey, you'll find English clubs such as the International Quilters, the Cosmopolitan Club, the Newcomers' Club, the American Society of Monterrey, the Garden Club, and the Women's Guild of Union Church. Around Lake Chapala, Americans belong to golf, sewing, bridge, and square dancing clubs, among others, and attend classes in painting, gourmet cooking, and music appreciation. Although San Miguel de Allende is a tiny city, you'll find classes in yoga and dance as well as golf, riding, amateur string quartets, an American Legion post, a bridge club, a garden club, and lots of concerts, theater performances, and dance recitals.

Always a good source for meeting people are the English-language churches found in most urban areas. In Mexico City, these include the following:

Capital City Baptist Church
Calle Sur 138,
Colonia Tucubaya

Phone: 5-516-1862

Christ Episcopal Church
Monte Escandinovos 405
Lomas de Chapultepec

Phone: 5-520-3763

St. Patrick's Catholic Church
Bondojito 248,
Colonia Tucubaya

Phone: 5-515-1993

Union Evangelical Church
Reforma 1870,
Lomas de Chapultepec

Phone: 5-520-0436

English-speaking churches in Monterrey include:

Holy Family Church   **Union Church**
Rio Jordan,   Oscar F. Castillon and
Sombrerete and Teotihuacan Streets   Larralde Streets
Colonia Mitras Centro   Colonia Chepevera

Immaculate Catholic Church
Rio Eufrates and
Rio Ganges Streets
Colonia del Valle

LANGUAGE SCHOOLS: HOW MUCH SHOULD YOU KNOW?

Your experience in Mexico will be so much more rewarding and enjoyable if you learn at least some Spanish before traveling. And the Mexican people you speak with will be so appreciative if you at least try to speak their language. Just think how impressed you'd be if a foreigner traveling in the United States spoke to you in English.

Granted, if you move to Lake Chapala or some other American stronghold, you're not likely to have to speak much Spanish. Still, it will be better for you if you know how to negotiate with taxi drivers, speak with secretaries, question bus drivers, and chat with servants in their own language.

It won't be as hard as it looks. More than 3,000 words in the Spanish language are very similar to their English counterparts. First try to learn common verbs, such as *ask, say, bring,* and the names of household objects. Also learn how to ask questions. Memorize numbers.

One of the first things you should do upon moving to Mexico is to sign up at a Spanish-language school, even if you already know some Spanish. The schools are well regarded, plus they're a wonderful way to meet other people, take field trips, and explore new parts of Mexico with teachers who really know the country.

Try to find a school that emphasizes conversation. Learning to speak Spanish is much more important than learning how to write a gramatically correct sentence in Spanish. Many schools offer the option of living with a Mexican family. This is a good idea because it allows you to practice your Spanish and save money, since room and board are usually minimal. Other good ways to learn Spanish in

Mexico include practicing with your maid and/or gardener and watching Mexican television. Many people recommend watching the *telenovelas*, or soap operas, that are so popular throughout Latin America. It's easy to tell what is happening, so it's easy to pick up the language. Listening to television newscasts and the radio will help as well.

Before leaving the United States, you can get a running start on your education by taking a Spanish class that emphasizes conversation. Check with your local colleges. You also might buy cassette tapes to listen to at home or in your car. Listening carefully and really trying to understand what the person is saying is so important. Many Americans get to Mexico able to speak some Spanish, but have no idea of what is being said when someone speaks back to them in Spanish.

You'll find Spanish schools everywhere in Mexico. Just check in the local newspapers and English-language publications for listings. San Miguel de Allende is a beautiful colonial city and a popular place to study. Schools there include the Instituto Allende, the Academia Hispano Americana, and Inter/Idiomas. Programs at all schools range from a few hours a day to eight hours a day. Studying eight hours a day can be tiresome and can cause you to burn out pretty quickly. Taking a few hours and practicing with the locals in your off time might be a better way to learn the language without tiring yourself out. After all, you are supposed to be in Mexico to enjoy yourself!

The National Registration Center for Study Abroad will advise on tuition within a worldwide network of language schools. It will also make all arrangements for study in Mexico. The center has affiliated schools in several locations including Mexico City, Guadalajara, San Miguel de Allende, and Oaxaca. For more information write 823 North Second Street, P.O. Box 1393, Milwaukee, WI 53201; phone 414-278-0631.

Here are some other Spanish schools you can check out upon arrival in Mexico. I haven't attended any of these schools, so it might be a good idea to talk to other students before signing up for a long-term study program.

Cemanahuac
San Juan #4, Las Palmas
62051 Cuernavaca, Morelos

Phone: 73-12-1367, 73-12-6419

Center for Bilingual Multicultural Studies
San Jeronimo #304,
Colonia San Jeronimo
62170 Cuernavaca, Morelos

Phone: 73-17-1087, 73-17-0694

Centro de Idiomas Dinámicos
Luz Savinon #13, Oficina 902,
Colonia del Valle
Mexico, D.F.

Phone: 5-543-7066

**Instituto Cultural
Mexicano Norteamericano**
de Jalisco, A.C.
Enrique Diaz de León
(Tolsa) 300
44170 Guadalajara, Jalisco

Phone: 36-25-4101

**Instituto Mexicano
Norteamericano de
Relaciones Culturales**
Hamburgo 115,
Colonia Zona Rosa
Mexico, D.F.

Phone: 5-525-3357,
5-511-4720

Universal
J.H. Preciado #332,
Colonia San Anton
62000 Cuernavaca, Morelos

Phone: 73-18-2904,
73-12-4902

**Universidad Internacional de
México, A.C.**
La Otra Banda #40,
Colonia Tizapan San Angel
Mexico, D.F.

Phone: 5-548-7646,
5-550-4073

EXPATRIATE ORGANIZATIONS: A USER'S GUIDE

In Mexico, you'll find a range of expatriate organizations—organizations designed to assist U.S. citizens living or traveling in Mexico. These groups will help smooth the adjustment to your new home.

BUSINESS SOURCES

**American Chamber of
Commerce of Guadalajara**
Avenida 16 de Septiembre
730-1209
Guadalajara, Jalisco

Phone: 31-614-6300

**American Chamber of
Commerce of Mexico**
Lucerna 78, Colonia Centro
06600 Mexico, D.F.

Phone: 5-724-3800

American Chamber of Commerce of Monterrey
Picachos 760, Despachos 4 y 6
Colonia Obispado
64060 Monterrey,
Nuevo León

Phone: 83-48-7141

Asociación Nacional de Importadores y Exportadores (ANIERM)
Monterrey 130, Piso 2
Colonia Roma
06700 Mexico, D.F.

Phone: 5-564-8618

Cámara Nacional de Comercio de la Ciudad de México
Paseo de la Reforma 42,
Apto. 32005
Mexico, D.F.

Phone: 5-592-2677

Confederación de Cámaras Industriales
Blvd. Manuel Contreras 133
Del. Cuauhtemoc
06597 Mexico, D.F.

Phone: 5-546-9053

Mexican Association of Industrial Parks
Genova 33-902, Colonia Juárez
06600 Mexico, D.F.

Phone: 5-208-4770

U.S.-Mexico Chamber of Commerce (in Mexico)
Manuel Maria Contreras 133
Despachos 120 y 121,
Delegacion Cuauhtemoc
06470 Mexico, D.F.

Phone: 5-535-0613

U.S.-Mexico Chamber of Commerce (in U.S.)
1211 Connecticut Avenue
N.W., Suite 510
Washington, DC 20036

Phone: 202-296-5198

Also 730 Fifth Avenue,
9th Floor
New York, NY 10019

Phone: 212-333-8728

And 5046 Biscayne Boulevard
Miami, FL 33137

Phone: 305-442-6236

CLUBS AND ORGANIZATIONS

American Benevolent Society
Copenhague 21-PH,
Colonia Juárez 06000
Mexico, D.F.

Phone: 5-514-5465
or 5-207-2961

American Legion Post Home
Celaya 25,
Colonia Hipódromo
06100 Mexico, D.F.

Phone: 5-574-4053;
in Guadalajara, 36-31-1208

**American Society
of Jalisco (AMSOC)**
San Francisco 3332
Colonia Chapalita

Phone: 5-621-2395
or 5-621-0887

Also Apartado Postal 5-510
Guadalajara, Jalisco

Phone: 36-21-2395
or 36-21-0887

American Society of Mexico
Monte Escandinavos 405
Lomas de Chapultepec
11000 Mexico, D.F.

Phone: 5-202-4600

Mexican Golf Association
Cincinaty 40-104
Napolese, Mexico, D.F.

Phone: 5-553-9194

EMBASSIES

**Embassy of Mexico
in the U.S.**
1911 Pennsylvania Ave. N.W.
Washington, DC 20006

Phone: 202-728-1600

*Consular offices are found in New
York, Chicago, Dallas, Austin,
Denver, El Paso, Los Angeles,*

*Phoenix, Houston, Miami,
Seattle, and San Francisco.*

U.S. Embassy in Mexico
Paseo de la Reforma 305
Colonia Cuauhtemoc
06500 Mexico, D.F.

Phone: 5-211-0042

*Consular offices are found in
Ciudad Juarez, Guadalajara,
Hermosillo, Tijuana,
Matamoros, Monterrey, Nuevo
Laredo, Merida, and Mazatlán.*

TOURIST OFFICES

**Mexican Government
Department of Tourism**
Marieno Ascobierdo 726
11560 Mexico, D.F.

Phone: 5-211-0099

**Mexican National Tourist
Office**
405 Park Avenue, Suite 1401
New York, NY 10022

Phone: 212-755-7261

Secretaría de Turismo
Avenida Presidente Mazaryk 172
11560 Mexico, D.F.

Phone: 5-250-8555

VOLUNTEER OPPORTUNITIES

Mexico has more opportunities for would-be volunteers than probably any other country mentioned in this book. The country shares

a long history with the United States and, as a result, U.S. citizens have resided in Mexico for decades, carving out all sorts of volunteer opportunities for themselves.

Giving to charities in Mexico can be more rewarding than giving to charities in the United States because, often, you can personally witness the effects of your efforts, since charities in Mexico often benefit local projects such as orphanages. Many Americans living in Mexico choose "charity work" that benefits their servants and their servants' family members. Many help their servants financially or in other ways such as by tutoring them.

Here are just a few places to contact for more information on volunteer organizations and charities:

American Benevolent Society

Phone: 5-525-5991, 5-525-2943, or 5-207-2961

Provides support for U.S. citizens in Mexico who need medical, social, or economic assistance.

Fondo Unido I.A.P.

Phone: 5-535-4541
or 5-566-3957

Collects money for charity groups in Mexico and is affiliated with United Way.

Humane Society

Phone: 5-570-3433

Rescues injured and abandoned animals and assists at shelters.

International Executive Service Corps

P.O. Box 10005
Stamford, CT 06904-2005

Phone: 800-243-4372.

Places skilled Americans—everyone from judges to carpenters—in positions around the world. Some expenses are paid for volunteers, including airfare, and usually a per diem to cover housing, meals, and other expenses.

Salvation Army

Phone: 5-789-1511, 5-575-1041, or 5-559-5244

Works with the homeless, alcoholics, drug addicts, refugees, mentally ill, battered women, and children in several orphanages.

Shriners Hospital for Crippled Children

Phone: 5-524-8818

Provides medical care for children up to age 18.

Veterans of Foreign Wars

Phone: 5-553-4383

Assists U.S. veterans living in Mexico.

Your Exploratory Trip

Certainly, you don't have to decide right now if retirement in Mexico is right for you. I strongly urge you to spend a few months in the country before coming to any decision. For example, you may decide you don't want to stay in Mexico year-round.

ADVANCE PREPARATION

Whether you go to Mexico for a few days or for a few years, you will need a passport. In Mexico, passports are not required of U.S. citizens for stays of up to 180 days, but proof of citizenship is. Proof of citizenship includes a passport, birth certificate, voter registration card, and the like. It's a good idea to carry a passport because photo-bearing identification, such as a passport or driver's license, is often requested when cashing traveler's checks and exchanging currency.

To get a passport, you must present, in person, a completed passport application at a U.S. passport agency, or at almost any post office or federal and state courthouse. Along with your application, bring proof of U.S. citizenship, such as a certified copy of your birth certificate, an ID that includes your signature and photo, and two identical 2-inch photos. The fee is $65, and a new passport is valid for ten years.

Before you go to Mexico, it's a good idea to read all you can get your hands on about your destination. Consider subscribing to a new quarterly journal called *Retire in Mexico*. To do so, write Retire in Mexico, 40 Fourth Street, Suite 203, Petaluma, California 94952; phone 707-765-4573.

There's another quarterly magazine on retirement published by Mexico Retirement & Travel Assistance. You might want to check it out by writing to M.R.T.A., P.O. Box 2190-23, Pahrump, Nevada 89041-2190.

You also might consider contacting a so-called settling-in service, or a firm that is designed to provide you with information in areas such as housing, medical care, shopping, social clubs, and the hiring of household help. These services include the following:

Contacto En Monterrey, S.C.   Phone: 8-388-6390
Monte Palantino 290,
Col. Fuentes del Valle, Garza
Garcia, N.L.
66220 Monterrey

International Relocation   Phone: 5-570-7592
Service
Privada Rosaleda 11,
Col. Lomas Altas
11950 Mexico D.F.

You'll have to decide whether to drive or to fly. If you're going just for a short visit to check things out, you'll probably want to fly and then rent a car or take public transportation. Driving across the country, whether in your own car or in a rented car, is really the best way to see Mexico. You can control your itinerary, stop where you want when you want, and get a feel for how hard it is to find your way around, should you choose to make a permanent move.

FLYING TO MEXICO

If you fly into Mexico City, you'll be arriving at the Benito Juárez International Airport, which is about eight miles from the city center. United Airlines, Aeromexico, Mexicana, and some other airlines fly from New York, Miami, and Los Angeles to Mexico City. Other U.S. airlines, including Delta, American, and Continental, also fly from various cities such as New York, Miami, Houston, and Dallas. It takes about four hours to fly from New York to Mexico City, three hours from Chicago to Mexico City, and two hours from Dallas to Mexico City.

Guadalajara is home to the country's second-largest airport, with 300 flights each day, 68 to and from the United States on five different U.S. carriers and several Mexican carriers.

You might want to rent a car to see the country. There are rental car agencies at the airport. (See the section earlier on "Driving in Mexico.") Of course, until you familiarize yourself with the Mexican way of life, you might want to take taxis, which are cheap, or some other form of public transportation. In Mexico City, you'll have no problem getting around; the subway system in Mexico City is one of the best in Latin America.

DRIVING TO MEXICO

Two years ago, the Mexican government enacted strict rules for bringing a car into Mexico that substantially increased the paperwork. However, travelers driving into Mexico can now avoid long delays at the border by preparing most of the paperwork beforehand.

In December 1994, Mexico's tourism ministry authorized Sanborn's Insurance Service, with offices in many border towns, to issue tourist cards and to prepare the documents needed to drive a car beyond Mexico's border area. Some American Automobile Association offices near the Mexican border can also provide these forms for their members. According to the Mexican government, only Sanborn's and the AAA are authorized to provide the documents. (Anyone driving into Mexico is advised to stop at a Sanborn's to get a copy of their mile-by-mile Mexico travelog, which is invaluable.)

Sanborn's service costs $10 for those who buy insurance from Sanborn's (see "Car Insurance" section earlier in this chapter) and $25 for others. Drivers have to have a tourist card, a valid driver's license, their original vehicle registration and title, and evidence of citizenship, such as a passport, voter registration card, or birth certificate. The title of the vehicle must be in the driver's name.

When all the paperwork is complete, drivers get a permit good for six months, during which time they are allowed to cross into the United States and back as many times as they want.

A free booklet "Traveling to Mexico by Car" explains the requirements, and can be obtained at Mexican government tourism offices and consulates. Sanborn's Insurance Service can be reached at 210-686-3601 or P.O. Box 310, McAllen, Texas 78505. American Automobile Association members should contact their local chapter. You should also stock up on roadmaps for Mexico, available from both Sanborn's and AAA.

There are lots of border crossings along the 1,700-mile U.S.-Mexico frontier, from Tijuana on the Pacific to Brownsville on the Gulf. I haven't had the opportunity to cross at every one, but many Americans report that the crossing at McAllen, Texas, is easiest. With all your paperwork in hand, crossing anywhere shouldn't be a problem and should take no longer than twenty to thirty minutes.

In the 1980s, Mexico launched an ambitious road-building project, and lots of fine new highways have been built. But there's a price to be paid. Heavy tolls are charged on many highways—not 50-cent tolls, but tolls totaling several dollars each. And despite these wonderful new highways, Americans driving into Mexico still need to be on the lookout for potholes, since often these new highways haven't been maintained very well. This is one reason not to ever drive at night. Other reasons include livestock that roam freely, including onto the road. Another is that highway workers tend to leave rocks and other debris in the middle of the road when they have finished working for the day. Four-lane highways are rare, as are roadway shoulders.

The quickest route from the Texas border to Mexico City is through the border town of Brownsville. Go along the Gulf Coast to Tampico, then on to Tuxpan, and then cut across to Mexico City. (It's quicker because the terrain is flat.) The more scenic but slower route is through the border town of Laredo. Head toward Monterrey, then follow the road to San Luis Potosí, Querétaro, and Mexico City.

Will You Be Retiring in Mexico?

As I noted at the beginning of this chapter, the prices in Mexico are not as good as they used to be, but the lifestyle is still relaxed and easy-going. You can live well in Mexico, enjoy its pleasant year-round climate, and have the company of thousands of other Americans who have chosen this country as their second home. Mexico, particularly, has the advantage of close proximity to the United States, so you're never really that far from relatives and friends. I've outlined the reasons why many other retirees have chosen Mexico—maybe you will choose it, too.

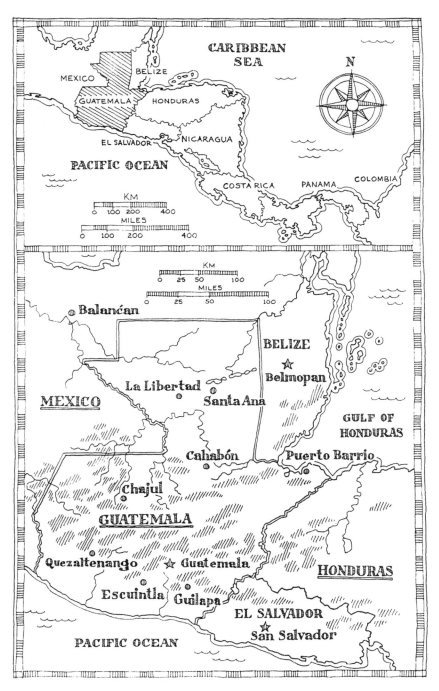

Guatemala

Guatemala

Along a cobblestone street in the colonial town of Antigua, just outside Guatemala City, stands a popular store called Jades, which sells everything from fine jewelry to bagged coffee. When I visited the store recently, English-speaking employees were passing around a flier that advertised the following:

For Rent
Charming colonial cottage
with a small patio, 24-hour
guard service, maid service,
and gardener. With antiques,
living room, bedroom
with fireplace,
modern kitchen
with microwave, stove,
refrigerator, phone and cable TV.
$275 a month.

What a reason to think about retiring to Guatemala!

Why Here and Not New Mexico?

Roughly the size of Ohio, this Central American country is too small to be intimidating, even to those who've never traveled outside their home state before.

With just 10 million people, Guatemala is bordered by Mexico to the north and west, and Belize, Honduras, and El Salvador to the east and south. The distance from the Mexican border to the

Salvadorean border is no more than 200 miles. From the Atlantic to the Pacific coasts, there are just over 300 miles. And in either direction, you might see pine forests, active volcanoes, mineral hot springs, and rugged mountain chains.

You can easily divide Guatemala by its geography. The west is characterized by a slender Pacific plain that flows into the western highlands, an area noted for its large Indian population. There, a line of volcanoes towers over a fertile landscape of corn and bean fields worked today by descendants of the ancient Maya. Most of the rest of Guatemala's population lives in the valleys surrounding the more than thirty volcanic peaks in the southern highlands.

Guatemala City is located in one such valley, as are Antigua and Lakes Atitlán and Amatitlán. Meanwhile, the coastal lowlands hug the Pacific coast. The coast is a hot, humid, sparsely populated area where bananas, sugar, and tropical fruits grow like wildflowers. It is also the site of Puerto Barrios, Guatemala's principal port.

There's also the northern panhandle, called the Petén, which covers one-third of the country and is the least populated area of Guatemala. This flat, forest-covered region was home to the famous civilization, the Maya, that built the giant pyramids of Tikal.

There are thousands of Americans now living in Guatemala. Ask any of them why he or she lives there, and climate, proximity to the United States, the excitement of completely new surroundings, the slow pace, and the cheap cost of living top the list. It is still possible to hire servants for a few dollars a day to do cooking, cleaning, washing, ironing, and gardening. Yet it's easy to hop on a plane and be in Miami in two and a half hours. It's also conceivable to spend days doing absolutely nothing, or to fill them with activities as varied as scuba diving and volunteer work.

Guatemala City is the capital, though few retirees choose to make it their home. Much of the city is filled with bus fumes, the roar of mufflerless vehicles, and pickpockets, although you can avoid most of these by staying out of the downtown area and in the fashionable Zones 9 and 10, where streets are canopied with crimson bougainvillea. Although most retirees don't choose to live in Guatemala City, many go there for shopping or entertainment. U.S. consumer products fill the shelves of grocery stores. Dunkin' Donuts, Ace hardware store, and Circle K are there. Even the golden arches ascend into the city's skies, as they do in the United States.

So where do the retirees live? Most choose to reside about a forty-minute drive west of Guatemala City, in the colonial town of Antigua. This city of 40,000 served as Guatemala's capital for more than 200 years, until it was nearly destroyed by an earthquake in 1773. Today, Antigua looks as if it has stood still in time; the government has declared the city a national monument. Antigua is also known for its Spanish-language schools—there are more than thirty—and its lively, active foreign community. Retirees lounge in the sun around the flowing fountains of Antigua's central plaza. They play poker on Sunday nights. They enjoy yoga, bridge games, and cocktail parties.

Panajachel is another popular spot with retirees. It is a village that lies along the shores of spectacular Lake Atitlán, where rough dirt roads wind past crumbling adobe houses and colonial churches, and where Indian women dry their wash on flat rocks. This is a slow-paced haven with a free-and-easy ambiance reminiscent of the 1960s. Along the shore, a boardwalk teems with an array of people from around the world, from bikini-clad blondes playing volleyball to Indian women in ankle-length skirts and high-piled black hair.

In general, Guatemala's attractions are strong—a warm, sunny climate, a slower tempo, a completely new culture and environment, a reasonable cost of living. It's much more affordable than, say, Miami, and it is close to the United States. Retirees say that the clear, sunny days and exhilarating air (I'm referring to the air *outside* smog-filled Guatemala City) do wonders for their health, even when compared with Florida. The temperature is consistently moderate, never rising much above 80 degrees. During the rainy season, which lasts from May through November, the late-afternoon showers are of short duration, and morning invariably brings a return of the sun.

Guatemala's government encourages Americans to spend their retirement years in its country, and officials there are willing to help with the transition. Guatemalans themselves are a friendly, warmhearted people. They genuinely like North Americans, unlike some residents of Nicaragua, El Salvador, and Panama. They are curious about, and fascinated by, the U.S. way of life.

One final word. For years most of us have read about the raging civil war in Guatemala and the violence of military regimes. Don't worry. U.S. tourists and residents marvel that they have absolutely no fear of trouble. All in all, Guatemala is a great place to consider making your new home, or even choosing it as a winter home, for you and your family during what are likely to be the best years of your lives.

FACTS AT A GLANCE

Population:	10 million
Ethnic groups:	Mix of Indian and European ancestry 50 percent; Indian 50 percent
Religion:	Roman Catholic
Languages:	Spanish and 22 Indian languages
Monetary unit:	Quetzal
Head of state:	President
Political system:	Constitutional republic
Industries:	Pharmaceuticals, textiles, tourism
Literacy rate:	55 percent
Capital:	Guatemala City
Provinces:	22 departments
Crops:	Coffee, cotton, sugar, and bananas
Average temperature:	70 to 75 degrees
Square mileage:	42,042 square miles
Rainy season:	May to October or November
American population:	13,000

The People and the Culture

About 50 percent of the total population of Guatemala, which is about 10 million people, are classed as Indian, while the rest are called Ladino. The indigenous people of Guatemala—who truly make this the most interesting country in Central America—are mainly of Maya descent. They speak twenty-two recognized languages and a hundred or more dialects. Accordingly, their culture is a varied and colorful one.

SOME BACKGROUND INFORMATION

Many of the Indians you encounter on back roads outside of the cities don't speak any Spanish, let alone any English. Among these

Indian groups are the Mam, Cakchiquel, Kekchi, Quiché, Chuj, and Ixil. They live life much the way it was lived 500 years ago. They plant and harvest corn, and they worship ancient gods. Their history is full of mystery and wisdom.

Experts still can't explain the sudden deterioration of the Maya civilization, which spanned 2,000 years and left behind awesome ruined cities, now overgrown by jungle. Shortly after the Spaniards arrived from Mexico City in 1523 to subdue the Maya, the brash young Spanish officer Pedro de Alvarado was able to take control of almost all of Guatemala, helped by a smallpox epidemic that wiped out thousands of Indians.

But despite their so-called success, the Spanish failed to find the precious metals they were looking for and many Spaniards abandoned the mission. Some stayed behind, however, settling in the southern highlands around Guatemala City and Antigua, and intermarrying with native subsistence farmers. This is the basis of the present mestizo population living in the cities and towns, as well as those in all parts of the southern highlands and in the flatlands along the Pacific coast. The indigenous population is still at its most dense in the western highlands and the Alta Verapaz.

Because of this history, two distinct cultures have formed in Guatemala: the almost self-supporting indigenous system in the highlands, and the Ladino commercial economy in the lowlands. At first sight the two seem to have much in common, for the Indian economy is also monetary, but a gulf exists between the two cultures. To an Indian, trade is seen as a social act, not done out of need, and not from any impulse to grow rich. This is certainly in sharp contrast to traditional Western commerce.

The Indian regions west of the capital have superb scenery and are full of color. In the towns and villages are colonial churches, some half ruined by earthquakes but often with lavish interiors. The Spaniards transformed the outer lives of the native people. Today, the Indians sing old Spanish songs, and their religion is a blend of image-worshipping rites and outward forms of Catholicism. But the inner nature of these Indians remains the same as it has always been.

The markets and fiestas—there seems to be one every day somewhere—are of outstanding interest and should not be missed. The often crowded markets are quiet and restrained: no voice raised, no gesture made, no anxiety to buy or to sell. But the fiestas are a rush of noise, a flow of processions, usually carrying saints—all of it marked by grand fireworks displays and masked dancers. The chief fiesta is always named for a town's patron saint, but all the main Catholic festivals and Christmas are celebrated to some extent everywhere.

Indian dress is unique and attractive, little changed from the time of the Spaniards: colorful headdresses, *huipiles* (tunics), and skirts for the women; often richly patterned sashes and kerchiefs, hatbands, and tassels for the men. You can tell which village an Indian is from by the manner of dress. While men are starting to adopt modern dress in many villages, women still hold tight to their traditional dress, especially older women.

The word *Ladino*, used most commonly in Guatemala, applies to any person with a Latin culture, speaking Spanish and wearing Western clothes, even though he or she may be pure Indian by descent. (Be aware that in other areas, *Ladino* has a different meaning.) Someone whose dress, language, and culture is Indian would be referred to as an *Indígena*.

The Indians you encounter hours away from the capital city are still not accustomed to Americans. They may come out and touch your automobile, especially if it is a shiny, bright color. Don't be put off if they follow you through town, wanting to touch your blonde hair, for example. They are just being curious and friendly.

Guatemalans are a very religious people. The Guatemalan man may be out cheating on his wife on Saturday night, but he'll be in church with his family on Sunday morning. There is no official religion, but about 70 percent consider themselves Roman Catholic. The other 30 percent are Protestant, mostly affiliated with Evangelical churches.

With much of its population not participating in official society, Guatemala's literacy rate of 55 percent is the lowest in the hemisphere, and its 51 percent rate of primary-school-age children enrolled in school is also the lowest.

THE LOCAL CUSTOMS

Guatemala, and Guatemalans themselves, can test your patience. So if you choose to retire there, you must tell yourself that you can't become impatient at delays, procrastination, and the seeming irresponsibility of service people.

The electrician may not come when he's supposed to, or he may not come at all. The upholsterer may not have even started work on your chair on the day it was supposed to be ready. I had a friend in Guatemala City who had to travel to Antigua to see if the pair of end tables she was having built were ready. Every day she would make the forty-minute trip to Antigua because the worker didn't have a phone and always promised they would be ready. They were ready, finally, several weeks later.

Guatemalans are extremely family oriented, much more so than Americans, and they revere their older relatives. Maids and servants may want to bring their children or other family members with them when they work. So you may have a small adopted family on your hands when you hire help. Enjoy getting to know them.

Guatemalans always kiss each other when they greet one another. They will kiss you on both cheeks at first meeting. Even the most macho man shows no embarrassment at being warmly embraced by a friend.

If you decide to do business in Guatemala, keep in mind that personal relationships will be your key to success.

Being able to say that so-and-so referred you will be much better than starting out cold. Titles are very important, and almost everyone carries a business card. *Licenciado* applies to anyone with a university degree. *Doctor* is for a medical doctor, *profesor* is for a professor, *ingeniero* is for an engineer.

When speaking, try to use a soft voice rather than a loud overpowering one, which is considered rude. Avoid criticizing the country, and discuss, instead, topics like travel, children, and hobbies. Don't bring up the violence of recent years, as many Guatemalans resent foreigners who complain about human rights violations.

A BRIEF HISTORY OF THE COUNTRY

Guatemala's history has been marked by oppression, often brutal. The target of much of this brutality has been the Maya, the most enduring culture, which began around 1000 B.C., and whose people made great strides in the fields of astronomy and mathematics.

The Maya civiliation flourished until the early sixteenth century, when Spanish conquerors came in search of precious metals. Spain subsequently ruled Guatemala, along with most of Central America, for 300 years. It wasn't until 1821 that political leaders proclaimed independence from Spain, as part of a federation of Central American states. But by 1847, the federation had collapsed and conservative Guatemalan leader Rafael Carresa declared the country an independent and sovereign nation.

Guatemala's modern period began with the administration of

Justo Rufino Barrios (1871-1885), a reformer who founded a national bank, supervised road building, started construction of a railroad, and set up a national school system. Thereafter followed a period of both economic improvement and political repression. Indeed, during much of the twentieth century, Guatemala has remained a political hotbed. The army has been the ruling party for a good part of the time, choosing each new president from among its ranks.

In the late 1970s and early 1980s, tens of thousands of Indian peasants were reported murdered as a result of the government's antiterrorist campaign. Hundreds of thousands fled to Mexico. International pressure partly helped bring democracy to this country in 1985, with the election of Vinicio Cerezo Arevalo. Subsequently, tourism increased, with hundreds of thousands of people visiting the country each year since that time.

A civil war has brewed in Guatemala since the early 1960s. But the end of the civil war in neighboring El Salvador has put new pressure on the Guatemalan government to resolve the conflict at home. Former President Jorge Serrano pushed hard for a settlement, beginning a series of peace talks in April 1991. But it became obvious after months of meetings that neither side was willing to make the necessary concessions. The military refused to recognize the guerrillas as anything more than terrorists; the guerrillas refused to even consider putting down their weapons.

Throughout the peace process, political violence—ranging from assassinations to minor bombings in some cities to full-scale combat in northern rural areas—has continued, although at levels nowhere near those of the early 1980s. Foreigners are almost never affected, and are usually unaware that there is even a civil war going on.

POLITICS AND ECONOMICS

First, disregard just about every newspaper article you've read about the horrors of Guatemala. Not because they're untrue, necessarily, but because they will only scare you unnecessarily. Indeed, Guatemala is a country with a powerful military, an institution that was responsible for unthinkable atrocities in the early 1980s. Today the country is marked by democracy—although that's not to say the military isn't influential.

Guatemala is a republic with a single legislative house with 116 seats. The head of state and of government is the president. The country is administratively divided into twenty-two departments.

The governor of each is appointed by the president, whose term is five years in length. The latest constitution was dated May 1985.

The election of President Jorge Serrano in 1990 marked the first time in history that one democratically elected civilian had succeeded another.

However, when Serrano projected his autocratic personality into politics, dissolving the congress and declaring martial law, the people and business community protested to such an extent that the military ran him out of the country. This just proved the extent to which the private sector now influences the military. Congress selected a new president, Ramiro De León Carpio, who was formerly the country's human rights ombudsman, and the democratic process resumed.

Guatemalan politics will likely never affect you, but they're fun to observe because they are never boring. With stability in the country's political situation has come stability in the economy. Guatemala's private sector accounts for some 88 percent of the gross domestic product, one of the highest ratios in the world. The Guatemalan constitution guarantees the right of private property, and government development programs seek to promote private enterprise. No distinction is drawn between domestic and foreign capital.

Agriculture remains the heart of the economy, contributing more than a quarter of the gross domestic product, employing half the workforce, and shipping three-quarters of the country's exports. Principal exports are coffee, cotton, sugar, meat, cardamom seed, and bananas. As recently as 1986, coffee accounted for 48 percent of Guatemala's exports, but shipments of nontraditional products, principally textiles and apparel, fruits, winter vegetables, and flowers, have expanded significantly and now account for one-quarter of all exports.

Taken as a whole, the country remains on a strong footing. Inflows of foreign capital, rising tourism revenues, and increasing diversification of exports are likely to continue. As a result of strong economic policies, the currency is likely to remain stable as well.

A Look at Living Costs

The cost of living in Guatemala is lower than it is in Mexico or Costa Rica, but is slightly higher than it is in Ecuador. In any event, your dollar certainly goes further here than it would in Florida, Arizona, or Southern California.

SOME SAMPLE PRICES

Telephone rates	$0.75 for residential use for 200 local calls per month
Water service	Usually not more than $2 a month
Laundry services	About $1.75 a load
Cornflakes (1 box)	$2.80
Lettuce (1 head)	$0.55
Onions (1 pound)	$0.16
Potatoes (1 pound)	$0.15
U.S. Lean Cuisine	$4.00
Heinz ketchup (28 ounces)	$3.90
Local brand ketchup	$1.60
Rice (1 pound)	$0.40
Ground beef (1 pound)	$1.50
Wheat bread (1 loaf)	$0.55
Pepto-Bismol (1 large bottle)	$3.00
Palmolive soap (1 bar)	$0.30
Premium unleaded gas (1 gallon)	$1.75
Oil change	$15.00
Weekly U.S. newsmagazine	$2.00
Dinner for two at a nice restaurant in Guatemala City, with wine	$20.00
Cinema ticket	$1.25

One-bedroom apartments can be found for as little as $100 a month, on up to nearly $1,000, depending on where you live and the style of the building. Houses rent for as low as $200 a month on up to more than $1,000. Houses sell for $30,000 on up to more than $1 million. Location is the key. Apartments and houses in Panajachel and Quetzaltenango are cheaper than those in Antigua and Guatemala City, for example. Regarding location and cost, you have to weigh the advantages against the disadvantages. It's nice to live in Antigua because there are so many retirees there, the surroundings couldn't be more beautiful, and there are plenty of activities, but rental and purchase prices are higher than in the countryside.

A city like Quetzaltenango, which is a three-and-a-half-hour drive from Guatemala City, offers inexpensive properties, but you won't find much English spoken there or many retirees as neighbors.

An American couple can probably live very well on less than $1,000 a month. However, that couple can live on much less than that if they choose to live in Panajachel or a town outside Antigua and shop in local Indian markets, for example. (Many people do.) They could also live on a lot more if they dine out in fancy restaurants every night and rent a colonial house just off Antigua's central square. Thus, how much you spend is up to you, but you can live inexpensively if you choose. Utilities, domestic help, medical care, and entertainment such as movies are all bargains in Guatemala.

TIPPING GUIDE

Granted, the service is usually not up to par with that in the United States, but you're still expected to tip.

At restaurants, 10 percent is recommended. If your party is a large one, you might find that gratuities have been included in the bill.

You might give a taxi driver a quetzal for his trouble, although taxis are so expensive that most people don't tip the driver.

Give airport porters a quetzal for carrying a piece of luggage. Some Americans give their maids a few extra quetzales each week, more if they really like them.

Immigration Rules and Regulations

You will be given a tourist card good for a ninety-day visit when you enter Guatemala. Even though you could obtain a five-year multiple-entry visa from a Guatemalan consulate, it is still good for only ninety days at a time. What's funny, or maybe not so funny, is that even though you obtain permission for a ninety-day stay, your car permit—which is issued by another government agency—is legal for only thirty days. While *migración* (immigration) hands out tourist cards, *aduana* (customs) hands out car permits.

But don't fret. At the end of the thirty-day period (you should apply before the thirty days is up) you can ask for an extension at what is called the Finanzas office in Guatemala City, located on the 12th floor of the Centro Civico at 8th Avenue and 21st Street in Zona 1. Finanzas will give you a car permit that totals the time on your new visa. At the end of ninety days, you can apply for another visa good for another ninety days, at which time you can get a car permit for the same amount of time. If you don't want to deal with all this paperwork, hire a *tramitador*—or a Guatemalan who knows his way around governmental red tape—to help you. We always hired a *tramitador*—who can be found by word-of-mouth. The fee charged, usually $20 to $50, is well worth it.

After the second car permit expires, you will be required to take your car out of the country for a few days before bringing it back. This is not hard to do, since you can simply drive to Mexico for a few nights, or you can cross into Honduras and spend a few days at one of the beach resorts on the Caribbean coast, popular with North Americans with the same problem.

With all the hassles, it's sometimes hard to believe that the government of Guatemala is actually delighted to have you apply for resident or retirement papers. You have to remember that excessive paperwork is a staple of life in almost all Latin American countries. Government officials do encourage retirees to settle in their country, knowledgeable of the fact that they'll be contributing to the economy with their pension money and that they're likely to be respectable, law-abiding citizens.

If you've spent time in the country, and now have decided that you'd like to become a resident, the first thing to do is to visit a Guatemalan consular office in the United States for information and to authenticate all necessary documents. When you arrive in Guatemala City, go to the Foreign Relations office (9th Street 14-69,

Zona 1) to legalize those documents signed by the consular officer and translate any English documents into Spanish.

It's important to visit, and familiarize yourself with, the tourist office known as Inguat, located at 7th Avenue 1-4, Zona 4, in the Civic Center, because it is responsible for considering residency applications. From there, you'll probably be sent to the Immigration Office for registration and authorizing visas.

It may take a year for all the paperwork to be completed. However, once you submit an application, you won't have to leave the country every ninety days as if you were a tourist; you will be given papers that are valid until you get your resident permit. According to Elizabeth Lopez at Inguat, it takes only two to six months for some people to get residency. "Most retirees live here most of the year, although they may travel two to three months or go back to the United States in April to pay taxes," she said.

There are two categories of residents under Guatemalan law: Resident Retired Citizens—those who receive pension money from their government or a private company; and Resident Renters—those fifty years of age or older, who are not retired yet receive steady, long-term income from outside Guatemala. To fit into one of these categories, you must provide written proof showing you have at least $300 a month in income that can be used for living expenses while in Guatemala.

You must deposit a minimum of this amount each month into a Guatemalan bank account as proof that you have enough money to live on. If you return to the United States for a long period of time, you have to offer proof that you've deposited enough money to cover six months of deposits in advance of your trip. In order to keep your residency papers current, you can't remain out of the country for more than a year.

Although rules change, you will likely have to include the following with your application for residency in addition to proof of a monthly income: a photocopy of your passport, a certificate issued by your police department concerning your and your spouse's police records, a list of articles to be imported and their values, your birth certificate, your marriage certificate if applicable, a medical report, and two photographs of yourself. All documents coming from abroad must be certified by the Guatemalan consulate officers in your home country.

Because retirees make such a positive contribution to the economy and development of the country, the Guatemalan government, back in 1973, decided to codify the rules and regulations so that those considering retirement would understand the procedure. These rules are presented in a booklet titled "Law for Resident Retired Citizens and Renters," which you can obtain by writing to or visiting the following offices. This booklet explains in detail what needs to be done to become a resident or a retiree.

Guatemala Tourist Commission,
299 Alhambra Circle, Suite 510,
Coral Gables, Florida 33134

Phone: 305-442-0651 or
442-0412.

Instituto Guatemalteco de Turismo
Centro Civico, Cuidad de Guatemala,
Central America

Phone: 2-23-13-33

At one time, residency provided substantial tax benefits. Household effects and automobiles could be imported duty-free. But, like Costa Rica, the Guatemalan government rescinded these laws in November of 1992.

Financial Matters

The Guatemalan currency is the quetzal, and one quetzal is made up of 100 centavos. Notes come in denominations of 100, 50, 20, 10, 5, 1, and .50. Try not to accept damaged notes because sometimes businesses won't accept them, leaving you in a predicament.

The best currency to have is U.S. dollars, in either cash or traveler's checks. You should probably carry most of your money in traveler's checks and a little in cash. Credit cards, such as American Express, Visa, and Mastercard, are generally accepted at stores, hotels, car-rental companies, and restaurants in major cities. And no, you can't use your U.S. money machine card in Guatemala.

You will be able to easily receive Social Security benefits outside the country as long as you are eligible. You should call the Social Security Administration in Washington, D.C. (phone 800-772-1213) for information, and request a pamphlet entitled "Social Security Checks While You Are Outside the United States." The U.S. Embassy—which you will find to be an amazing resource—distributes Social Security checks by courier, cost-free. It also distributes veterans' civil service checks and IRS refund checks. To get this service, you must sign up with the Social Security Administration in the United States before going to Guatemala, and then sign up with the

U.S. Embassy upon arrival. By the way, you can also have money wired to you through the U.S. Embassy. It will even loan you money if you're in a desperate situation.

One advantage for retirees living overseas is that not only can they receive distributions from a 401(k) plan, they might be able to begin distributions earlier than they could if they were residents of the United States. Distributions normally begin when someone reaches 59 years 6 months, becomes disabled, leaves the company that established the plan, or dies. But distribution may begin earlier in cases of a hardship. According to one accountant, "Living abroad isn't considered a hardship, but the move might cause you to have an immediate and heavy financial need without any other reasonably available resources. In this case, the plan could make a 'hardship distribution.'"

CURRENCY EXCHANGE

Exchange rates used to be fairly volatile in this region of wild inflation, but not anymore. The exchange rate has been about the same—5.70 quetzales or so to a dollar—for the last few years. You'll get a slightly better rate on the black market, though you must be careful never to hand over your cash first, and make sure you're given the correct amount of quetzales before walking away.

Exclusive hotels and some shops change money, as does a daily exchange service at the airport. However, it's a good idea to have exchanged a little money into quetzales before arriving in Guatemala because this exchange service keeps odd hours. If you fly into the country, keep in mind that a taxi charges $6 or more to take you to most hotels, even if the hotel is only a mile or two away. Taxi drivers will take dollars.

Banks are the safest bet when changing money, and there is one in every town. Some of the more established banks are Lloyds Bank, Banco Industrial, Banco de Guatemala, Banco del Ejercito, and Banco del Agro. The daily exchange rate floats, and is always displayed. Banking hours are normally Monday through Friday from 9:00 a.m. to 3:00 p.m., although a new emphasis on service has resulted in some banks staying open later and on Saturdays.

American Express cardholders can easily get cash at the American Express office located in the basement of the Banco del Café, Avenida La Reforma in Zona 9. They can also replace lost traveler's checks and request a block on the account of a stolen or lost card at this office.

Quetzales can be bought with Visa or Mastercard at Crediomatic in the basement of 7 Avenue, 6-22, Zona 9. This is how we survived for two years in Guatemala. When we needed cash, my husband or I took our American Express cards to this office and wrote a personal check from an account in the United States. The office would issue us a traveler's check, which we would change in the bank. It was very easy, and the office allowed us to write up to $1,000 in checks every three weeks.

BANKING

One of the most worrisome aspects of a move abroad is personal finances: paying bills at home and transferring funds from one country to another. Things can go wrong even within the most sophisticated banking systems, but I hope you won't have to spend undue time trying to locate funds lost in transit and bills lost in the mail.

How you handle your finances will depend on your personal situation. If you plan to visit Guatemala for only a few months, perhaps you can pay your bills ahead of time or ask a relative to handle them for you while you're gone. If you plan to live in Guatemala but return to the United States fairly frequently, perhaps you can take care of finances on your return trips. For those headed to Guatemala for good, or for at least a year or more, you can now open savings and checking accounts in Guatemala, but only in quetzales.

You might be able to cash your Social Security checks at the U.S. Embassy. If not, you'll have to deposit them into your account in a Guatemalan bank.

The following U.S. and British banks have opened branches in Guatemala City. Many Guatemalan banks have reciprocal wire services with foreign banks:

Citibank
3 Calle 7-14, Zona 9

Phone: 2-31-76-06
on the Avenida Reforma
between Calles 15 and 16,
Zona 10.

Lloyd's Bank International
8a. Avenida, 10-67, Zona 1,

The bank also has offices at:
Plazuela 11 de Marzo,
7a. Avenida 4-87, Zona 4;
Autovía Mixco 4-39, Zona 11;
Calle Marti 14-57, Zona 6.

TAXES: U.S. AND GUATEMALAN

Retirees are not taxed on their Social Security or retirement income in Guatemala. Likewise, they do not have to pay income tax in Guatemala on any income generated outside the country. Resident retirees do not have to pay duties on the visas required for entry into Guatemala, neither are they charged what's known as the annual alien head tax. However, laws in Guatemala change all the time, and this is something you should check before making a move.

Living overseas, you also won't have to pay any taxes to the U.S. government on annual income totaling $80,000 or less.

You will, of course, still have to file a yearly U.S. income tax return. U.S. taxpayers living abroad should mail their completed returns to the Internal Revenue Service, Philadelphia, Pennsylvania 19255. The U.S. Internal Revenue Service has a special department, IRS-International, for expatriates filing income tax returns. The department offers tax assistance over the phone and in person, distributes tax guides, sponsors workshops, and conducts a variety of other outreach programs. For further information, contact the Internal Revenue Service, Assistant Commissioner (International), Attention: IN:C:TPS, 950 L'Enfant Plaza South S.W., Washington, D.C. 20024. For information, phone 202-874-1460.

The U.S. Embassy in Guatemala does not have a tax advisor on staff. However, once a year, usually in March, an advisor from Mexico City visits the Embassy to conduct tax seminars for U.S. citizens. Tax forms are available year-round at Citizens Services at the Embassy.

There are businesses in Guatemala that will complete individual and business tax returns for a fee; they advertise in the *Classifieds Revue* and other English-language publications.

At one time, residency in Guatemala brought substantial local tax benefits. Under a 1973 law, *pensionados* did not have to pay import taxes on cars and furniture, but as of 1992, that's no longer the case. There are no more special benefits. However, the financial scenario is not all bleak.

You can import household effects to the tune of $8,000 once, without customs duties or import taxes. When you become a resident in Guatemala, you may also import one car for personal or family use, free from import duties and sales duties. Thereafter, you can import another car with these same benefits every three years. But check this before you go, because laws can change.

LOCAL INVESTMENT OPPORTUNITIES

Foreign residents in Guatemala are not entitled to work at a job without government permission. But excluded from this prohibition are those who, in the opinion of the Ministry of Economy, invest in activities that are beneficial to the country. That means that if you invest in a business that helps tourism and provides jobs, you can work in that business. I know several foreigners who say they've had no problems doing business in Guatemala.

Guatemalans are eager for foreign investment, and they are open to all kinds of business ideas. You can start a business with virtually no capital investment of your own if you have contacts, possess or have access to the necessary technology, and have expertise in a certain area. Among Guatemalans, you'll find many with both the money and the inclination to back foreigners interested in starting businesses here. In 1993, Guatemala shipped $1.3 billion worth of merchandise worldwide. U.S. citizens are exporting Guatemalan handicrafts, furniture, flowers, and all sorts of nontraditional exports.

To attract and help foreign investment, the government has developed free trade zones and drawback laws. These include fiscal incentives, such as tax holidays and duty-free imports and exports for businesses operating under free trade zone status. And you can qualify for such status without having to locate within an industrial park. The country passed a law in 1989 that allows a single business, anywhere in the country, to qualify as a stand-alone free trade zone.

Taxes on business income are exempt for ten to fifteen years, and there are no duties on the import or export of raw materials, equipment, or finished products between an approved free trade zone and any non-Central American country. Best of all, the country's laws give equal treatment to local and foreign investments and permit 100 percent foreign ownership of any business.

Another incentive for investors has been the introduction of "one-stop windows" for the quick processing of export permits and for the registration of any new business. At the one-stop window, permits are supposed to be ready within forty-eight hours; at the one-stop investment window, documents for a new company are supposed to be processed in approximately two weeks.

If you are interested in doing business in Guatemala, you should contact the following offices:

Guatemalan Business Office
299 Alhambra Avenue,
Suite 510
Coral Gables, FL 33134

Phone: 305-444-0600

This office is funded by FUNDESA and provides foreign investors with advice on investment opportunities, as well as help in establishing a business relationship in Guatemala.

Guatemalan Development Foundation (FUNDESA)
Edificio Camara de Industria, Ruta 6, 9-21, Zona 14, 01004, Guatemala City, Guatemala

Phone: 2-34-68-72

This agency is sponsored by the private sector and would be delighted to offer assistance. Everyone associated with this organization is friendly, knowledgeable, and dynamic.

Rentals and Real Estate

You'll have nothing if not plenty of choice. In Antigua, you can choose from Spanish colonials with stucco roofs, well-maintained courtyards with extensive gardens, and lots of windows for as little as $50,000 or as much as $1 million. In Guatemala City's posh Zona 15, the newest of the upper-class residential areas, you can select from dozens of high-rise apartment buildings.

In another part of the capital city, called Las Conchas, a twenty-four-hour guard watches over spacious homes with patios and gardens and all the modern conveniences. In Panajachel, you can choose from beachfront property that sells for $120,000 or houses a short walk from the beach that sell for $50,000. Apartments can be had for as little as $100 a month.

HOUSES, APARTMENTS, AND CONDOS

A typical home has high ceilings and tiled floors. Do not expect dishwashers or garbage disposals. But neither will you have heating or air-conditioning bills. Walls are about two feet thick and retain heat and cool air. Most homes are sold with a one-car garage. They usually don't have carpets, so you might want to purchase some area rugs.

Like houses, apartments are usually spacious, with no carpeting or dishwashers. Many are furnished, and most lack the closet space you're used to in the United States.

About half of the Americans who choose to retire in Guatemala buy property, while the other half rent. To do either, they walk the streets, checking out the signs in windows and the bulletin boards of popular restaurants in search of the best deals. In Antigua, the flier-plastered bulletin board at Doña Luisa's restaurant is the best place to look for houses, apartments, condominiums, and rooms in houses. In Panajachel, the bulletin board at the Al Chisme restaurant is building a strong reputation.

Property is also found by word-of-mouth and usually not through a real estate agent, as is typical in the United States. In Guatemala, prospective buyers or renters rely on people-in-the-know, or those who have lived there a long time and who have a good relationship with foreigners. For example, in Panajachel, you can check with Ivan García or his British wife, Sandra, at Panajachel Tourist Services if you're interested in buying property. They've lived there for years and can point you in the right direction.

The good news about buying or renting right now is that the price of both rentals and purchases has dropped over the last year, thanks to a series of travel advisories issued by the U.S. government against Guatemala since the uprising of peasants in Chiapas, Mexico, in January 1994. These warnings have caused the number of gringo visitors to drop considerably, which in turn has caused prices to go down.

If your goal is to purchase property, I suggest renting an apartment or condominium for a few months first, both to make certain you can adapt to your new environment and to give you ample time to scope out various neighborhoods.

THE PLACES WHERE RETIREES LIVE

When you step off the plane at the La Aurora Airport in Guatemala City, or make your first venture through Zona 1 by car, you'll wonder why anyone would want to live in this capital city. And you're right. Only those who absolutely can't live without the hustle and bustle of a metropolitan area will make their home here. Most retirees make immediate tracks away from the city in search of a place to settle, ultimately deciding on Antigua or Panajachel. But before I take you to these two attractive locations, allow me to first discuss Guatemala City, home to about 6,000 Americans. Parts of the city have a special ambiance of elegance, sophistication, and convenience, albeit on a much smaller scale than you'd find in

Mexico City, Buenos Aires, or Bogota. Its 2 million residents are spread thinly throughout the seemingly endless grid of avenidas (avenues) and calles (streets).

Guatemala City

Since it was leveled in 1917 by earthquakes, Guatemala City has few points of historic interest. But there is lots of activity here: crowded streets, deluxe hotels and gourmet restaurants, active nightlife, and many shops and boutiques.

Guatemala City is home to most of the country's government agencies, leading banks, newspapers, valued schools, and major businesses. Older buildings remain in the center of the city, but sparkling new ones have cropped up in Zonas 9, 10, and 13, and 14. You'll find KFC, Hickory Farms, Kids R Us, and a host of other recognizable names here.

Guatemala City is divided into nineteen zones. You'll want to stay as far from Zona 1—full of beggars, traffic, and pollution—as you possibly can. Addresses at first may seem confusing, but are easy once you get used to them. They are purely numerical. For example, 19 C, 4-83 is on 19 Calle between 4 and 5 Avenidas.

A good rule of thumb is that the higher the zone number, the better the lifestyle is likely to be. In other words, Zonas 9 and 10 are particularly quiet when compared with Zonas 1 and 2. The relative peace is due to the fact that homes here are hidden behind high walls and barbed wire. Guards stand outside the entrances of what are some of the finest residences I've ever seen, sealed off from the rest of the world. Vista Hermosa in Zona 15 is an exceptionally beautiful neighborhood on the western edge of the city, where the streets begin winding up toward the mountains. Here there are luxury condominiums where the residents' parking lot is on an upper floor for added security.

Homes can be found in Zonas 11 and 12 for $70,000 on up. Keep in mind that the parts of Guatemala City most crowded with Americans are going to be the most expensive. The Guatemalan daily newspaper *Prensa Libre* once published an article that compared property values in Guatemala with those in Paris, concluding that those in Paris were cheaper. The article, though, was considering the prices of homes in Guatemala's most upscale neighborhoods, where the high cost of property has been brought on by corrupt government officials, who put their ill-gotten gains into property, and drug traffickers, who buy property with cash as a means of money laundering. And, as I mentioned earlier, the prices have dropped a lot over the last year.

Despite its less appealing features, many retirees live in Guatemala City, or "Guate," as it is sometimes called. We lived in the city for more than a year, renting a secure, furnished apartment in Zona 13 for $300 a month. For us, the attraction was its proximity to political and business contacts, since we were both freelancing for U.S. publications at the time. But for retirees, the attraction is more likely to be the city's sophistication, ambiance, and wealth of activities. Yes, parts of the city are tinged by beggars, pollution, and traffic jams. But if it's excitement you're looking for, or a closeness to fine shops, all-night nightlife, and good restaurants, Guatemala City might be just for you. (Many people who live in Antigua and Panajachel drive to Guatemala City to do their shopping.)

Antigua

From 1543 to 1773, the capital city of the Kingdom of Guatemala—which comprised part of Mexico as well as Guatemala, Belize, El Salvador, Honduras, Nicaragua, and Costa Rica—was what is today known as Antigua, the place retirees love most. In 1773, it contained 60,000 people, 32 churches, 18 convents and monasteries, 15 hermitages, 10 chapels, 1 university and 7 colleges, the most beautiful cathedral in Central America, 5 hospitals, an orphanage, spectacular fountains set in carefully tended parks and gardens, elegant private mansions, and some of the most exquisite buildings ever built in the New World. Unfortunately, much of the city was destroyed in an earthquake in 1773, and the capital was moved to present-day Guatemala City. But its wealth, splendor, size, and sophistication had been rivaled only by Mexico City and Lima.

Today, Antigua has a population of more than 40,000, and many of its cobblestone streets have changed little since 1773. There are no signs jutting out across the streets, few buildings are more than one story high, and the center of town is full of colonial-style homes with metal grilles; ornate, metal-studded doorways; whitewashed walls; and tile roofs. And everywhere still stand the churches and palaces, mansions, fountains, convents, and other monuments— some in ruins after the earthquake of 1976—reminders of Antigua's glorious past.

The abandonment of Antigua following the earthquake in 1773 is largely responsible for the impression that Antigua is suspended in time. People were very slow in returning. Sprawling ruins of churches, convents, and government buildings remained undisturbed through the centuries. It wasn't until World War II that tourists started to discover Antigua. Those tourists included a few retirees from the United States and Canada, captivated by the city's charms as early as the 1940s.

To accommodate this new influx, hotels and businesses were built. Realizing what a gem it had in this city, the government intelligently decided in 1944 to prohibit modern high-rise construction and flashy signs. So today, colonial buildings must be restored to their original condition under the law, or if that isn't possible, they must be left exactly as they fell during earthquakes or other calamities. It's because of this preservation effort that Antigua today is more like an original Spanish colonial town than any other place in Latin America.

Americans looking to Guatemala as a retirement destination should definitely consider this town, which is the most popular of all retirement destinations in Guatemala. Culture shock is less severe here for Americans who are not used to living in a Third World country.

Antigua is easy to reach, located about thirty miles west of Guatemala City. Sometimes there seem to be more Americans living here than Guatemalans, since many gringos pass through on business or to attend one of the town's Spanish schools. Prices for property near the center of town are going to be higher than those for property farther away. To meet demand, there's lots of construction going on along the road leading out of Antigua, just beyond the Ramada Inn. The best deals to be found if you want to live close to Antigua, but are trying to save on money, are just outside Antigua. You can find nice homes for sale in Jocotenango for $50,000 or $60,000, and in San Pedro el Alto for $33,500.

Panajachel

Another ideal spot for long-term living or retirement is Lake Atitlán, principally around the town of Panajachel. The accent falls on the last syllable: *Pan-a-ha-CHEL.* It's sometimes called simply Pana. Novelist Aldous Huxley described Atitlán as the most beautiful lake in the world, and most people still do. Encircled by mountains with three sharp volcanic peaks presiding over all, the crystal-clear waters of the lake are truly a spellbinding sight.

Lake Atitlán itself measures 11 by 8 miles and is more than 1,000 feet deep. Surrounded by exotic flowers, fruits, birds, and animals, the lake has various patches of color that appear to change with the hour. It's sometimes deep green, sometimes blue, sometimes purple.

Panajachel is a tropical resort on the shores of Lake Atitlán, some seventy miles from Guatemala City. Lodging and housing here range from luxury hotels to the most basic accommodations. The food is very good and hundreds of Americans call this place home. There is no central square in Panajachel. Rather, people wander up and down the main street, or stroll the boardwalk along the shore of the lake, or congregate at one of the many cafés.

To get to Panajachel from Guatemala City by car, take Calzada Roosevelt northwest out of Guatemala City, passing through Chimaltenango to Los Encuentros. At Los Encuentros, there is a gas station and a small restaurant, and a road leading north to Chichicastenango. Two miles after Los Encuentros, turn left to Sololá and Panajachel, eleven miles from the junction, descending the narrow, winding mountain road to the lake. It takes about two and a half hours to make the drive.

In Panajachel, a furnished three-bedroom house on the beach costs $120,000, while something away from the beach might go for $50,000. Of course, usually the properties on the beach are the most plush. One house on 1,000 square meters of beachfront, with four bedrooms, two baths, and phone, as well as two sailboats, a power launch, and a golf cart, was recently listed for $180,000. There are also lots of homes and condominiums going up among the breathtaking views of coffee *fincas* (plantations) and volcanoes.

Quetzaltenango and Other Options

If you really want to live on the cheap, take a peek at property in Quetzaltenango, a city located about a three-and-a-half-hour's drive west of Guatemala City. The owner of one colonial house there advertised a room in his house, which included complete access to television, phone, kitchen, and laundry room, for $7 a night, with special weekly and monthly rates available.

In general, better bargains all across Guatemala might be houses still in need of repair as a result of the 1976 earthquake. Labor is cheap; the best way to find a handyman or a plumber, for example, is word-of-mouth. Construction-supply stores are popping up all over the place, many with English-speaking employees and free delivery. One woman told me she had bought an attractive adobe one-bedroom house, built around a large courtyard but in need of some repairs, in Antigua for $10,000.

RENTING: WHAT IT WILL COST

Once again, let me emphasize the benefits of checking the bulletin boards at Dona Luisa's and Al Chisme, as well as other restaurants and bookstores, for rentals. Here's a sampling of the postings I saw on a recent visit to Antigua:

❏ Furnished two bedroom, one bath apartment for rent. With stove, refrigerator and phone. Just $330 a month.

❏ House for rent fifteen minutes from Antigua in San Bartolo. Lovely, unfurnished, two bedrooms, yard, garage, appliances, hot water. $250 a month.

❏ Furnished rental house fifteen minutes away on a small coffee finca. Garden, kitchen, bedroom, living room, study, bath, shower, open patio, parking space, secure. $275 a month.

Obviously, the farther you go from the center of Antigua, the less expensive the rentals will be. Of course, you'll also be farther from stores, English-speaking residents, and all the pleasures Antigua has to offer. But staying ten to fifteen minutes away is not a problem if you have a car, or if you don't mind riding the bus or walking. Still, most Americans prefer staying as close to the center square as possible, at least when they first arrive, because everything is then within walking distance.

In Antigua, more than any other location in Guatemala, you have the opportunity of renting not only a house or an apartment but a room in a private home. A large number of older single men and women, as well as retired married couples, take advantage of this inexpensive way of living. And there is lots of turnover, meaning it's usually easy to find something, since Spanish students often rent rooms during their one- to two-month stints in Antigua.

We rented a room in a house for six months in Antigua and it was the best deal we've ever found. We had a huge bedroom with private bath, use of the kitchen, and almost complete run of the house. It came with a maid, a fax machine, a phone, cable television, and a beautiful courtyard where we spent evenings sipping wine and watching the sun set. Our American landlady had been married to a Guatemalan, was widowed, and liked to spend the weeks in Guatemala City with her daughter. She spent only Saturdays and Sundays at the house. The cost? Just $200 a month, and it was located a few blocks from the central square in Antigua.

If you choose to rent an apartment or house in Guatemala City, you'll likely choose from new, high-rise buildings or houses sealed off from the street with gates or concrete walls. Typically, apartments are two- to three-bedroom, many with balconies. Most apartments have guard services, and furnished units are available. One-story homes, or split-levels, are most common. Furnished housing in new sections of town can be difficult to find, and is far more expensive than unfurnished homes. This is the one time I'd suggest looking in the classified sections of the local newspapers for rentals, rather than relying solely on word-of-mouth or bulletin boards.

You'll find rentals in Panajachel to be cheaper than those in Guatemala City or Antigua, running from $100 on up. Outside Panajachel, they will be even more inexpensive. In the lakeside village of Santa Catarina, the rental of a two-bedroom house with two fireplaces, an equipped kitchen, TV, VCR, washing machine, and gardener was advertised for $400.

Retiree Wally Johnson rents a one-bedroom studio in Panajachel for $100 a month. "It has a kitchen, furniture, and beautiful garden with peacocks too!" he said. "It doesn't have a phone, but I didn't want one."

All landlords require leases, which normally run for six months to one year with renewal rights. The tenant is usually expected to pay any legal fees associated with drawing up a rental contract, and these cost about $50. Many landlords of the better addresses will require that renters have a *fiador*, or a co-signer of sorts, sign the lease. *Fiadors* are generally well-established residents who can be responsible for any unpaid rent or expenses if the lease is broken.

Rents are almost always paid monthly, and on the first day of the month. Almost all landlords will require that the rent be paid in U.S. dollars or the equivalent in quetzales.

BUYING PROPERTY AND FINANCING THE DEAL

North Americans looking to purchase property in Guatemala will find not only an affordable retirement haven but also a good long-term investment. Real estate prices, which have dipped in recent years, are expected to increase as more and more North Americans and Europeans discover this little Central American treasure.

Property owners are looking for North American buyers with cash. Guatemalans are always in desperate need of dollars. A show of cash will get you a lower price—and it will save you the hassle of dealing with a bank.

Property in Guatemala is sold by word-of-mouth or through classifieds in the local daily newspapers, including *La Prensa* and *Siglo Ventiuno*. You usually do not use a real estate agent; instead, your lawyer acts as an intermediary between you and the seller.

The U.S. Embassy can recommend reputable, English-speaking attorneys. You can also contact lawyers who advertise in English-language publications, such as the *Classifieds Revue*, although I'd double-check their reputation with the Embassy.

Foreigners have the same rights as Guatemalan citizens when purchasing land. You cannot purchase property within sixteen kilometers (ten miles) of the country's borders, lakes, rivers, or other waterways. The one problem you may encounter, although it's not likely, is local prejudice. A few Guatemalans feel that Guatemalan properties should remain in Guatemalan hands, and will not sell their homes to North Americans for any amount of cash. It is possible for North Americans to arrange a mortgage in Guatemala. But you should think long and hard before you do so. Interest rates can run more than 20 percent. And Guatemalan banks usually offer mortgages for no more than five years. They require at least 20 percent down and usually a letter from a bank in the United States guaranteeing your financial stability.

UTILITIES: WHAT YOU'LL PAY

The low cost of utilities is one of the benefits of living in Guatemala. Water bills, for example, average only a few dollars every two months. Electricity is between $5 and $10 a month, and twice-weekly garbage pickup costs about $2 a month. The telephone rate for residential use is 75 cents for 200 local calls a month. Of course, if you rent a room in a home, you'll not likely be burdened with utility bills, except phone.

Because of the weather, central heat and air conditioning are almost nonexistent, which really does save on electricity. Fireplaces and electric blankets provide all the warmth you might need, even on the coldest nights.

Guatemala's electricity is 120 volts 60 cycles, alternating current (the same as in North America), so appliances may be brought from home without fear of their burning out. Power outages and brownouts are common, and usually short lived, but not always. Just a couple of years ago, the government rationed electricity for several months following a severe drought, meaning that residents, depending on what zone they lived in, had use of electricity for a certain number of hours each day. Like the electricity, the system was very erratic, meaning that your electricity didn't always come on at 6:00 p.m. even though it was supposed to.

Like electricity, the country's water supply can be sporadic. During the dry season, I've heard that water pressure occasionally drops so low that there is little or no water in some homes, although I've never known anyone to have such problems. The water supply is, in general, more reliable in apartment buildings that have installed auxiliary tanks.

Utility bills are delivered monthly to the home and they usually arrive on time. If they don't, however, it's your responsibility to follow up on them. You might have to stand in line at the utility office and get a copy. Never pay your bills through the mail. Rather, pay them in person at either the utility company or at some banks—or you can send someone, like the maid, which is what most people do.

Setting Up, Settling In

Finding an apartment or house is only the first step in establishing a retirement residence. You'll want to know how to stay informed of world events, receive mail, and telephone home, as well as furnish your home and obtain household help. These matters are all easily arranged in Guatemala.

NEWSPAPERS, MAGAZINES, TELEVISION, MOVIES

You won't have any problem keeping up with what the U.S. government is doing, or the latest on peace in the Middle East. In Guatemala, you can buy all kinds of English-language publications—everything from *The New York Times* to *Time* magazine. Many people rely on the international edition of the *Miami Herald* for their news. Other sources of information are two locally published English-language news weeklies, *Central American Report* and *This Week*. If you understand Spanish, a weekly news magazine, published locally, called *Crónica* has a fine reputation.

Guatemala has a modern television system, with three or four local channels. The local news is not very good. However, soap operas beamed from Mexico are amusing and a great way to learn Spanish.

Many foreigners sign up for cable, which costs about $12 a month for twenty channels, including CNN and the three basic U.S. networks. However, the number of channels constantly fluctuates. For a while, Guatemala was pirating cable to the point that customers received dozens and dozens of channels, including all so-called premium channels. But the U.S. government has worked out an agreement with the Guatemalan government to protect intellectual property rights, which simply means that the Guatemalans don't steal as many channels as they used to.

Video stores are starting to grow in popularity, and you can find U.S. movies. Movie theaters show recent English-speaking films at about one-fourth what you pay in the States. Spanish subtitles are printed over the lower part of the screen, which gives you another opportunity to learn Spanish by reading Spanish and listening to English at the same time.

MAIL SERVICE

Domestic and international mail service is reasonably efficient by Latin American standards, but slow by North American and European standards. Letters to the United States can take a week or longer; to Europe, about ten days. Registered mail to the United States may be sent through the Guatemalan postal service and return receipts obtained. Guatemala offers "express" mail, which costs about double the normal mail rate. This is not overnight delivery, but does assure a reasonable delivery time. The most reliable of the express-mail services, with offices around the country, is King Express.

The best bet for long-term residents is to rent a post office box from one of the various companies that provide daily courier service to and from Miami. Subscribers are provided with a post office box number in Miami to which all their mail is delivered, after which it is flown to Guatemala. Fixed monthly rental rates on these boxes allow you to receive up to about five pounds of mail a month.

Rates usually run $25 a month or more, depending on the company. After you meet the limit, charges are incurred on a per-ounce basis. Outgoing mail is also allowed for a fee of about $1 a letter.

In Panajachel, the Panajachel Tourist Services operates a post office box service. Owner Ivan Garcia says mail is brought down three times a week from Miami. The service costs $10 a month. You get mail in five to seven days. You can send a letter back for $1.25 a letter. It's couriered to Miami and dropped in regular mail. You can also send and receive faxes through this service.

Never place letters in mailboxes situated along the streets, because the mail is hardly ever picked up. It's far better to take your mail to the post office. The main post office in Guatemala City is located at 7 Avenida and 12 Calle, Zona 1.

When writing to someone within Guatemala, such as an attorney, here's the address format you should use on your envelope:

> Gabriel Orellana Rojas
> 6 Calle 5-47, 5o. Nivel, Zona 9
> Guatemala City, Guatemala

To avoid the postal service altogether, many people communicate by computer. Services in Guatemala and Antigua allow you to send and receive E-mail messages for about $5 for every 2,500 characters. Telegrams at these same services cost $10.

Throughout Guatemala, you'll find shipping services that will pack and ship supplies; provide custom packaging; offer next-day and second-day air services, ground delivery, and parcel post; and offer international air and ocean freight and import and export services. Check in the phone book or scan the ads in local papers.

TELEPHONE SERVICE

Never rent a house or apartment that does not come with a telephone—if you want a telephone. The demand for new phone lines in Guatemala City is such that requests for service, if they can be met at all, may involve delays of several years. Sometimes, homeowners must wait four years or even longer for a telephone line, which is not necessarily purchased with a home.

So when you're looking at houses, be sure the owner is not intending to sell the telephone line to someone else—or to take it with him when he moves. In the daily newspapers, you'll notice telephone lines on sale for as much as $1,000.

Phone bills are considered late after sixty days and service will be cut off without notice. It is very difficult and time-consuming, if not impossible, to have your telephone service reconnected once it's turned off, as they may sell your line to another customer. If weeks have passed and you haven't received a phone bill, it's your job to check with the phone company on the whereabouts of the bill. In other words, even if the bill was lost in the mail, it's still your responsibility to pay it.

Indeed, the one area of communication in which you can expect major headaches is from the phone system in Guatemala, which can be both unreliable and exasperating. Guatel, the state-owned and operated telecommunications company, provides domestic and international telephone service. Direct dialing is available twenty-four hours a day, although service is unreliable.

While living in Guatemala, our phone once stopped working for three days because of heavy rains. When service went out, it was impossible to discover if it would remain out for three days or three months. Guatel employees are not known for their prompt attention to service problems.

Calls to the United States and Europe are often easier to place than calls across town. Guatemala also has some public pay phones from which you can place calls, but few actually work. Some pharmacies have them, and many hotels have pay phones in their lobbies. Public phones take 5, 10, and 25 centavo coins.

The area code for Guatemala is 502. You must always dial 011 before calling any number in Guatemala from the United States. If you are dialing a number inside Guatemala City and you are within Guatemala, but outside Guatemala City, the number should be preceded by dialing 02.

International calls can be placed on public phones, but a better alternative is to call from your hotel or home. In general, the best way to make a call is to obtain an AT&T calling card before leaving the States. Then all you have to do is call 190 when you get to Guatemala from any private phone. A pleasant-sounding operator will answer in English, and place the call in a matter of seconds once you give the telephone number you are calling and your calling card number. You can also make collect calls this way.

If you don't want to deal with Guatel, private phone services like Intertel in Antigua offer calls to the United States for about $1.50 a minute. You can receive international calls at these services for 25 cents a minute, or send a one-page fax for $3.

Many publications in Guatemala have started advertising cellular phone rentals as the answer to communication problems. According to the ads, you can rent a personal, transportable phone, but it's not likely to be cheap.

FURNISHING A HOME, FROM SILVERWARE TO APPLIANCES

As of 1992, foreigners can no longer import furniture cost-free. That's why most retirees either find furnished houses or apartments or buy what they need in Guatemala. However, many people do bring appliances with them, especially if they plan to live for several months in Guatemala, because the cost of appliances in this country can be fairly steep. I'd advise against bringing in large appliances, however, because they may not fit into Guatemalan houses, and shipping and customs duties make it expensive to bring them into the country.

Air conditioners are generally not necessary, but fans can be useful, not only for keeping cool but to drive away mosquitoes in the rainy season. I didn't bring any appliances to Guatemala except a hair dryer, a radio, and a computer. If you want radio news in English, bring a good shortwave radio. If you're renting, the homes are likely to come equipped with most of the appliances you'll need.

TVs, VCRs, radios, and stereos may be bought in Guatemala but are relatively expensive. A new color TV in Guatemala City starts at over $500; a small black-and-white starts at $125. The Almacen Archi in Antigua at 6a Avenida and 4a Calle has bikes, televisions, stereos, and other appliances. The store has a good reputation and has been around for years. Because of frequent surges in the power supply, all sensitive electronic equipment should be connected to surge protectors, which you should bring with you.

You should bring bed and table linens, and lots of film, from home if you're trying to save money. You may also want to bring flatware and glassware, although these can be purchased in Guatemala at a fairly high price. The locally made blankets and wool rugs are of good quality and reasonable in price.

Locally manufactured furniture is satisfactory, but there is little variety. Furniture made of tropical hardwood is usually unseasoned and may warp over time. However, the craftsmanship of locally made wooden furniture—chairs and tables—is generally quite good. Larger imported furnishings like couches and beds are very expensive.

There is good rattan and wicker furniture for sale at stands and shops along the road between Guatemala City and Antigua. You can also find good deals at garage sales—yes, garage sales—especially in

Guatemala City and Antigua. Look for ads in the *Classifieds Revue*—an English-language publication found at most hotels and restaurants—for furniture, televisions, scooters, cars, and all kinds of appliances, including washers and dryers.

CLOTHES YOU'LL WANT

High society in Guatemala is very fashion conscious, but most other people are quite casual in their dress. Since the temperature is generally warm and moderate, you should bring lightweight clothes, but have a few sweaters and jackets for cool nights. Big overcoats are seldom worn, but a raincoat might come in handy during the rainy season. More and more, Ladino women are starting to wear shorts, although it isn't a good idea if you're walking in downtown Guatemala City. Shorts are appropriate, however, in places like Panajachel and Antigua. Still, long shorts are better than short shorts. Some Guatemalans look down upon people who wear clothes that are too revealing.

BRINGING BOWSER AND BUTTONS WITH YOU

Dogs and cats must have a certificate of health signed by a licensed veterinarian to be accepted into Guatemala. If the pet is arriving from a rabies-infected area, the certificate must state that the animal has been vaccinated against rabies no less than thirty days and no more than one year prior to arrival. All dogs must have a certificate of vaccination against parvovirus.

The certificates must be notarized and the notarization certified by the Secretary of State of the state in which the pet's owner resides, and then must be certified by the Guatemalan consulate having jurisdiction over that state. The Guatemalan consulate can complete the necessary certifications within twenty-four hours. Only pedigreed pets may be imported duty free. Contact the Guatemalan Embassy in Washington, D.C., for the latest information on requirements involving pets.

THE QUEST FOR PEANUT BUTTER
AND OTHER NECESSITIES

Believe it or not, you can find peanut butter, French wines, pâté, Hamburger Helper, and Lean Cuisine frozen meals in Guatemala.

You can also find businesses that will train your dog to stop chewing, chasing, or barking. There are dress services that will make clothes or repair clothes for you. There's a place called the Dixi Deli in Zona 9 that will home-deliver spiral-cut honey-glazed ham and luncheon meats to your front door.

Cemaco Ace Hardware chains have five locations in Guatemala City and are the best hardware stores around. In Guatemala City, there's also a Hickory Farms, Chuck E' Cheese, Dunkin' Donuts, Taco Bell, Kids R Us, McDonalds, Wendy's, Rax (like Arby's), and KFC. Needless to say, American-style consumerism is alive and well in the Third World.

Here are just a few hints to help you get by, hints that we learned while living in Guatemala.

❑ In Guatemala City, Parma on 19 Calle in Zona 10 is a good place to buy milk, cheese, ice cream, and bread. In Antigua, Doña Luisa's (there's a shop adjacent to the popular restaurant) is a good place to buy the same types of items.

❑ In Antigua, La Cava del Marqués is where everyone goes to get wines from France, Spain, Germany, Chile, Italy, Mexico, Portugal, South Africa, and Argentina. They also sell imported liquors and cheese and milk items, as well as things like chips and luncheon meats and pâté. It's located at 3a Ave. Norte No. 1.

❑ Challos is the local supermarket in Panajachel, where you can get Bigelow English breakfast tea and almost anything else you might need. "It's pretty responsive to the community," said one retiree. Another Panajachel resident added that: "You have to go to the mercado for vegetables. Shopping is more time-consuming here. Canned goods are very expensive. There are no frozen foods. But the fruits and vegetables are very good." Still another Panajachel resident says: "They don't know how to cut meat here. They have only two cuts: filet mignon and the rest. There's very little pork and no lamb to be found in Pana."

❑ Paiz is the largest supermarket chain in Guatemala, with a well-stocked store on 11 Calle, Zona 13, in Guatemala City. Canned staples, breads, wine and beer, vegetables, fruits, meats, and toiletries are all available.

❑ If you want really good produce in Guatemala City, go around the corner from that Paiz to Primavera on 15 Avenida. A wide selection of imported foods is sold at Selectas on 9 Calle in Zona 14.

You can always find wonderful fruits and vegetables at any Indian market in towns outside Guatemala City.

❑ Quality, American-style cuts of beef, rare in Guatemalan super-markets, can be purchased at an American-owned butcher, Los Tres Cochinitos, on 20 Calle in Zona 10.

You can also get your laundry done in Guatemala; there are *lavenderias* everywhere, but they are expensive. In Guatemala City, you'll be charged about $1.75 per load. It's just slightly cheaper in Antigua and Panajachel.

One thing you must remember when going to almost any major store, shopping center, or even restaurant is that you'll likely have to pay someone to watch your car. These informal attendants, usually young Guatemalan boys—sometimes as young as five years old—will approach you when you get out of your vehicle. Simply nod that they can watch your car, and give them a bit of change when you leave. It's better to pay them than to not pay them because if you don't, they may wind up slashing a tire or breaking a window. Upon returning to your car, give them a handful of change or a quetzal and they'll be satisfied.

METRIC MEASURES

Guatemala operates on the metric system of weights and measurements. Here are some conversions to help you adjust.

1 gallon	equals	3.8 liters
1 quart	equals	.95 liter
1 pound	equals	.37 kilogram
1 ounce	equals	31.1 grams
1 mile	equals	1.61 kilometers
1 yard	equals	.91 meter
1 inch	equals	2.54 centimeters
1 kilogram	equals	2.2 pounds
1 liter	equals	1.06 quarts
1 gram	equals	.035 ounce
1 kilometer	equals	.62 mile
1 meter	equals	39.37 inches
1 centimeter	equals	.39 inch

HOUSEHOLD HELP

Stephanie Riegel lives just outside Panajachel and constantly brags about the good help she has in Guatemala. She says she pays her gardener $4 to come once a month to do all the windows in her house, and there are plenty. He gets paid less than $50 a month to come three times a week to tend to her spacious lawn and gardens. She pays $2 a day for a maid, who comes three times a week. "This is one of the nicest things about living in Guatemala," she said. "I could never afford so much help in the United States."

When we were renting an apartment in Guatemala City, we paid a maid $5 a week to come and clean every Tuesday. Her name was Delia and we got to be very good friends; we still write back and forth. She did a great job and often brought us cakes, casseroles, and other goodies she had cooked at home. We treated her like one of the family, often giving her a little extra money or presenting her with small gifts. She spent hours at our apartment, and would do ironing and anything else we asked. We still miss her, not because of her housekeeping duties but because of her sunny disposition. We even visited her home a few times for dinner.

Most expatriates hire Guatemalans to help them with cleaning, gardening, driving, laundry, and cooking. These helpers come in handy for security reasons as well. It's not always safe to leave your home unattended, even for a short period of time.

The best way to find a good maid is through word of mouth from other expatriates. It is preferable to seek a domestic worker who has been employed by other expatriates and who has references. Domestic workers employed by you full time, or almost full time, are entitled to fifteen days' paid vacation each year. On dismissal, employees are entitled to one month's salary for each year of service. A Christmas bonus equal to one month's salary is mandatory. The monthly salary for a live-in maid is from $100 to $300.

Getting Around

You'll want to explore Guatemala and visit the countryside as well as see its towns and cities. The options are public transportation and private cars.

PUBLIC TRANSPORTATION

Buses in Guatemala are an adventure unto themselves. Most of them are in a poor state of repair and breakdowns can occur. They are forever overloaded. Although recent government legislation has reduced problems of overcrowding, it is still difficult to get on buses in mid-route unless you're prepared to stand. Try always to arrive early to get a good seat on a bus going a long distance. Still, buses are undoubtedly the cheapest and easiest way to explore most of Guatemala.

Bus connections are regular. Tickets are bought on the bus, and usually cost less than 50 cents. To avoid paying a higher price, or gringo fare, it's always a good idea to ask a local passenger what the fare is before the ticket man gets to you.

On some routes, it's possible to travel by Pullman buses, which are more comfortable than the local chicken buses (old Blue Bird, or retired U.S. school buses, packed with people and often small livestock). Pullmans are a bit more expensive, but you get a reserved seat to yourself and it makes fewer stops.

While Antigua is an easy thirty-minute drive from Guatemala City, it's also an easy ride by bus. There are many places in the city where you can catch the bus as it makes its way toward Antigua, but it's best to board at the terminal at 18th Calle in Guatemala City. Buses leave every few minutes, and you'll want to go to the terminal so you can get a window seat. If you have luggage, the driver's helper will tie it securely on top of the bus. The trip takes between forty-five minutes and an hour and costs about 50 cents. The bus ride ends at either Antigua's terminal, the central square, or along one of the city's main streets. You can get out almost anywhere and simply walk or catch a cab to your destination. By the way, bus is pronounced "boose" in Spanish.

There are other ways to get from Guatemala City to Antigua, such as passenger vans that make the run from most hotels, but they are expensive. Taxis charge $50 or $60 to go from Guatemala City to Antigua, which isn't as bad as it sounds when the ride is shared with one or two other passengers.

Lots of private shuttle services operate in Guatemala and most begin at major hotels. A private shuttle will take you from Antigua to the airport for $7; from Panajachel to the airport for $20. Check postings on bulletin boards, or with travel agencies, for costs and schedules.

Taxis are easy to find in most areas frequented by Americans in

Guatemala, but they are expensive. They look like ordinary cars, except that the license plate begins with an A. The taxis are not metered, which is why you must always agree on a fare with the driver before he takes off for your destination. Once you have negotiated the fare, it is not necessary to tip. Cabbies tend to overcharge foreigners, whom they assume have money to burn. But taxis are not exorbitantly expensive if you find one that can be hired by the hour. The going rate should be about $10 or $20.

Guatemala has about 600 miles of railways—railways operate from the Atlantic to the Pacific and to the Mexican border—although few people ride trains. Service is far from luxurious or reliable, although it is quite cheap and less crowded than the buses. We once embarked on a nine-hour train ride to the east coast from Guatemala City, only to break down a few hours into the trip. We were left to fend for ourselves in the middle of nowhere.

DRIVING IN GUATEMALA

Although the country is small, getting around Guatemala can be a challenge, especially when you consider that there are about 12,000 miles of roads, of which only 16 percent are paved. However, getting around the places you'll most likely need to get around—Guatemala City, Antigua, and Panajachel—is a piece of cake.

The paved roads are generally good, although they can be pothole-ridden in some spots. The dirt roads in the country's most rural areas (where you won't likely be traveling much, if ever) are often very bad, although my husband and I have used them many a time. Be warned, though, that in some parts of the country, you'll encounter frequent police stops, especially near borders. Driving from the Mexican border to Guatemala City, my husband and I were once stopped seven times.

Stopping is usually compulsory, especially if you see an Alto sign. If police don't want you to stop, they'll wave you on. Unfortunately, if police do find you guilty of an infraction (if you don't have your passport or proof of insurance, for example—definite no-nos) they can impound your license, which can take some time to recover. To avoid this, a tip of $5 or so will help.

International licenses are not recognized in Guatemala, and foreign driver's licenses are good for only the first thirty days, although most expatriates drive with their U.S. licenses for several months. Technically, expatriates taking up residence in the country must obtain a Guatemalan driver's license. No examination is necessary if you have a valid license from the United States or another country.

Despite talk of potholes and policemen, you should encounter no problems if this is the way you decide to travel around Guatemala. But do take a few precautions. Carry a spare wheel and any other essential spare parts that you may not be able to find in Guatemala. The Guatemalan Tourist Office (Inguat) sells a reliable road map, which has all gas stations marked on it, and includes a mileage chart.

If you have to park, look for secure facilities whenever you can. Traffic outside the cities is generally sparse, so driving is relatively relaxed, barring the occasional hazardous driver or military checkpoint. Still, you should not travel the roads outside the cities at night. Also, watch out when driving in the countryside on Sunday afternoons, when the Indian men tend to drink a few too many and can often be found roaming drunk in the middle of the road.

Car Rentals

For those who want to rent a car, Guatemala City and Antigua have many car rental agencies, and good deals can be found. On our last trip to Guatemala, we rented a Volkswagon bug from Avis, located across the street from the El Dorado Hotel, for $20 a day with unlimited mileage.

Be certain before driving the car off, though, that a rental car employee makes a complete and accurate list of every scratch, dent, and anything else on the car so that you won't be stuck with a bill when you turn the car back in.

Rental car agencies have many locations, and most have an office at the airport, across the road from where you'll exit the airport with your bags.

Avis Rent-A-Car
12 Calle 2-73, Zona 9

Phone: 2-31-69-90

Budget Rent-A-Car
Avenida La Reforma 15-00,
Zona 9

Phone: 2-31-65-46

Hertz Rent-A-Car
7a Avenida 14-76, Zona 9

Phone: 2-32-22-42

National Car Rental
14 Calle 1-42,
Zona 10

Phone: 2-68-01-75

SECURITY CONCERNS

Everyone wants to know about security in Guatemala. If you listened to the U.S. media, you'd swear guerrillas were fighting the government on every street corner.

That's pure hogwash. But what is true is that crime is a problem, just as it's a problem in Miami, New York City, and Chicago. In fact, when you talk to Guatemalans, one of the first things they'll ask you about is crime in the United States. "How do you stand it?" they'll say. Raised on a diet of violent U.S. movies, they believe all high school students are shooting each other in the hallways. So there are a lot of misconceptions on both sides of the fence.

Serious crime against tourists is rare in Guatemala, although pickpocketing is not, which is why you should not walk alone at night, and why you should carry money, credit cards, and passport in a pouch around your neck or in a money belt under your shirt. Fortunately, pickpockets usually won't bother the wary and careful traveler; and they are rare to nonexistent in suburbs or on the fringes of the city. Pickpockets frequent local markets, holiday fiestas, sporting events, and other crowded areas.

To protect their homes against burglaries, many residents have dogs, employ security guards, or have high walls covered in broken glass to keep prowlers away.

Vehicles are often a target of criminals in Guatemala. Left unattended, they are at risk of being stolen. Driving after dark anywhere in Guatemala also puts your vehicle (and you, of course) in jeopardy. Incidents have been reported in which people have been robbed along roads in Guatemala by thieves posing as military or police officers. If confronted by armed

Importing Your Car

Most people consider a car a necessity in Guatemala City, although a car is not a necessity in either Antigua or Panajachel. In the capital, residential areas are located some distance from shops and businesses, so driving is a must if you want to avoid riding buses or tak-

bandits, those who go along with all requests without arguing are usually not harmed.

Typically, the U.S. Department of State issues travel advisories when they want to urge U.S. citizens to defer nonessential travel to Guatemala. There is good reason for this. Still, if you're cautious, you'll probably be safer in Guatemala than you would be in most parts of the United States, even when an advisory is in effect. Really.

So why does the U.S. government issue travel warnings? Well, one that was issued in early 1994 was the result of wild rumors that Americans were stealing Guatemalan babies for adoption and other reasons. These rumors led to riots and injuries involving three American tourists in the towns of Santa Lucia, Escuintla, and San Cristobal Verapaz. These rumors have died down, fortunately. Even during the most tension-filled days, anyone who wasn't carrying around a baby was safe.

Sometimes you'll hear about a flurry of terrorist incidents in Guatemala, especially during periods surrounding key political events, such as special elections. Explosives have been detonated at electrical, television, and radio towers near Guatemala City and in the departments of Santa Rosa, Escuintla, and Chimaltenango. Smaller explosive devices have been detonated or have been deactivated by police agents in various businesses, newspaper offices, and shopping malls in Guatemala City. While most of the explosions have occurred at night and have resulted in relatively few deaths and injuries, the timing and character of any future incidents can never be predicted with certainty. The U.S. Department of State issues an information sheet on all countries of the world. The U.S. government used to issue what were known as different warning levels; now it simply issues information that covers both political actions and street crimes.

ing cabs. You'll be able to figure out upon visiting Guatemala what will work best for you. We lived in Guatemala for several months without a car with no problem. We rented a vehicle when we wanted to travel for a few days, and took buses the rest of the time. But I will admit that it made things like carrying lots of groceries much easier once we did bring a car down.

You'll have no problem importing a car as long as you present the title and pay a 20 percent import duty levied on the blue book value of the vehicle. You will not have to pay the heavy import duty if you bring in your car as a tourist, as many people do. But you will have to take your car out of the country every time the visa expires.

There are advantages to importing smaller cars even if they won't hold as much. Small cars are easier to service and easier to maneuver in narrow, congested streets and limited parking areas. Large, eight-cylinder U.S. automobiles are impractical in Guatemala.

Unleaded gasoline is widely available in Guatemala and spare parts for most popular U.S., Japanese, and European models should be easily located, although at prices a lot higher than in the United States.

Car Insurance

Regular American automobile insurance isn't valid in Guatemala. This obviously is a concern, since Guatemalan law requires that all vehicles be covered by third-party liability insurance. And Guatemalan law can be harsh if you don't have insurance and are involved in an accident. You can be jailed, and the car impounded, until blame is determined in court. Therefore, many people flee the scene of accidents to avoid having to go to jail until a judge determines who is at fault and levies a fine. Of course, to flee is against the law, but it's done every day.

To find out more about insurance requirements, you might try contacting Guatemala's main automotive club:

Club de Automovilismo y   Phone: 83-030
Turismo de Guatemala/CATGUA   Fax: 83-897.
9a Avenida 18- 03, Zona 1,
Guatemala City

Local insurance rates for collision and comprehensive insurance coverage are higher than those offered by U.S. overseas insurance carriers ($1,200 per year). That's why many expatriates obtain special overseas collision and comprehensive coverage from U.S. firms. Check with your insurance agent to see if your company offers such coverage.

Many people purchase car insurance in U.S. border towns before crossing into Mexico. Sanborn's Insurance is popular. There are also several insurance companies in Guatemala offering coverage that's priced based on the type and value of your automobile.

Inguat suggests calling or writing the following insurance company for information:

AGISA   Phone: 2-51-45-73.
19 Calle 11- 34, Zona 1,
Embajador Offcina 203;

Staying Healthy

Guatemala is more healthful than it looks, or more healthful than books about Guatemala make it appear to be, especially for those who live there and know what to eat and drink, and what to avoid. It's also healthier than many other Third World countries. In some ways, Guatemala is even more health-conscious than some parts of the United States. There's no smoking allowed in many restaurants and no smoking allowed inside the U.S. Embassy, a prohibition that's been implemented only in the last few years.

A variety of natural food establishments have sprung up in all parts of Guatemala, particularly Panajachel and Antigua, home to a population of what I call "earthy" types. For example, the Natural Food Store on Lake Atitlán sells juices, granola, herbs, sushi, vitamins, and organic coffee. You can get a massage there, and participate in health-related classes and workshops. By the way, most thirty-minute massages in Guatemala cost less than $10.

One sixty-eight-year-old retiree in Panajachel said he moved from New Mexico, known for its healthful environment, to Guatemala for the benefit of his health. Suffering from heart troubles, he found the clear air around the lake and the moderate climate advantageous to his condition. "There are three doctors and I'm happy with them," he said. "If I need to go to a hospital, there are two in Sololá, about a ten-minute drive from here."

DON'T DRINK THE WATER AND
OTHER SAFEGUARDS

Many people drink the water in Guatemala City, Antigua, and Panajachel and suffer no ill effects. Still, tap water in Guatemala is purified by putting chlorine in the water supply so, while it's safe, it may be wiser to purchase boiled or bottled water. For many months, I drank the water from the tap and suffered no serious consequences. However, my husband preferred purified water—called *agua salvavidas* in Guatemala—and so eventually we had it delivered to our apartment, as most Americans do. The price for a container the size of an office water cooler was about $1, and we asked that a container be delivered once a week. Most restaurants with even a few North American clientele use water that has been boiled previously so it is perfectly safe. But in rural areas, either boil the water yourself or use water purification tablets.

Besides water, milk served in first-class restaurants is usually pasteurized, though milk and cheese sold in cheap restaurants, *comedores*, or markets usually are not. Parma brand dairy products are most often purchased and consumed by Americans and are perfectly safe. Boxed milk products are also available at local supermarkets and are considered safe.

Some items you should remember to avoid are uncooked vegetables and unpeeled fruits, and you should always wash such products thoroughly. Although the "street foods" sold at kiosks around the city look tempting, these items are only for those who have traveled extensively in Third World countries and are used to all kinds of foods, or maybe for those with iron stomachs. If you just can't resist, at least remember to avoid ceviches (raw seafood); stick to foods cooked on the spot, and check the hygiene of the person serving the food.

Many people envision a series of painful shots when they think of going to the Third World, but there are no required immunizations for Guatemala, although it's wise to check with the U.S. State Department before going, to find out what it suggests. Some health officials advise keeping the following vaccinations current: gamma globulin (every six months); typhoid (every three years); tetanus (every ten years); and diphtheria (every ten years). Malaria tablets and vaccination against rabies are advised for those traveling in very rural areas.

The Centers for Disease Control and Prevention operates a CDC International Traveler's Hotline: 404-332-4559. To obtain CDC documents, call the CDC at 404-332-4565, follow the instructions, and the system will automatically send the documents to your fax machine. A good first step is to request a copy of the system's international travel directory, which will be faxed to your machine immediately. The directory lists documents available, from vaccination recommendations to malarial medications.

One disease you're likely to hear about is cholera. An epidemic that was first recognized in Peru in 1991 and spread through South America, Mexico, and Central America has also reached Guatemala. Cholera causes watery diarrhea and vomiting, and can lead to severe dehydration and death if not properly treated. The epidemic died down after a couple of years, but periodically cases of cholera are reported.

The main sources of cholera infection are thought to be municipal water supplies, food bought from street vendors, and vegetables irrigated with fresh sewage. While this definitely sounds troublesome, the risk to travelers and city dwellers is almost nonexistent. If you're careful about what you eat and drink, you should have no problem.

One aspect of Guatemalan life that may initially give you some headaches—literally—is the altitude. Guatemala City is about 5,000 feet above sea level. While healthy individuals rarely suffer ill effects from this altitude, some people might require an initial adjustment of two to three days or longer. Excessive eating, drinking, or physical exercise during the adjustment period should be avoided as body processes frequently slow down. Also, the atmosphere at Guatemala City's altitude offers little protection from the sun. Hats and sunblocks should be used to protect against sunburn. Furthermore, be aware that flowers and dense greenery in most of the country, as well as serious pollution problems in Guatemala City, may aggravate hay fever, asthma, and allergies.

I have two more pieces of advice: All of your household help should be examined by a physician before they begin work. They should be trained properly and well supervised. Make certain they understand your health concerns and take the same precautions you do.

It's also a good idea to keep a first aid kit at home that includes items such as ace bandages, antacids like Rolaids, antibacterial ointments for minor cuts, antidiarrhea medications like Imodium (which works wonders), aspirin, calamine lotion, cotton, sunscreen, tweezers, insect repellent, and water purification tablets.

DOCTORS AND HOSPITALS: WHAT IF YOU GET SICK?

Having said all that I did in the above section, you're probably certain you're going to get sick as soon as you step on Guatemalan soil. The truth is that in all the time I've spent in Guatemala, I've never contracted any serious sickness, nor has any one I've known ever gotten really sick. But if you do, medical care is as inexpensive as other goods and services in Guatemala.

Guatemala has well-trained physicians, dentists, and health-care professionals. Many of these people have been trained at universities in the United States and Europe; therefore, often they speak English.

The other good news is that fewer paperwork requirements allow these doctors in Guatemala to spend more time with their patients than their U.S. counterparts. And the patient in Guatemala has the freedom to make more decisions related to his or her well-being. For example, your prescription is often returned to you when it is filled, and you can often go to a laboratory and have a blood test or other analysis without a doctor's referral.

Thirteen private and thirty-two public hospitals offer X-ray, laboratory analysis, diagnostic, and treatment facilities. In Guatemala City, you will find state-of-the-art medical technology, including computer tomography, ultra-sound, video endoscopy electro-video surgery, and lithotripsy. A complete list of English-speaking doctors and hospitals is available at Citizen Services at the U.S. Embassy, and a shorter list is available at Inguat's office for *pensionados*. If those sources don't offer you enough choice, and you want even more listings, a directory of hospitals and doctors abroad is available from Intercontinental Medical. The company's source is a database of 5,500 doctors and hospitals compiled from medical directories, U.S. consular lists, and hospital associations. Each directory is customized to the traveler's itinerary. Therefore, you can request information just on Guatemala. The database is updated daily to ensure that travelers receive the most accurate information just prior to departure. All booklets specify the languages doctors speak, as well as more general information. For more information call Intercontenental Medical at 800-426-8828.

You can also get a directory of physicians by joining, at no cost, the International Association for Medical Assistance to Travellers (IAMAT). The organization provides a directory of IAMAT physicians in 125 countries. Telephone numbers are included. IAMAT physicians agree to a set payment schedule for members. You can sign up by writing the association at the following address:

IAMAT
417 Center Street
Lewiston, New York 14092

In general, retirees living in or around Guatemala City and in Antigua will easily find excellent medical attention. And there are clinics and adequate physicians in Panajachel. However, health care in other parts of Guatemala is, in general, deficient. Although there are 1,040 health-care centers scattered throughout Guatemala, with some 7,687 doctors on the job, the doctor-to-patient ratio in the countryside remains dismally low—about 1 to 1,268.

Another word of caution, this one from an employee at the U.S. Embassy: "I'd be afraid to ever go to a public hospital in Guatemala. Some have no razors or bandages at all. You have to go to the private hospitals to get the really good care."

In Guatemala, fees may vary for the same type of treatment, doctor to doctor, just as one hospital may charge higher rates than another. It is advisable to discuss anticipated expenses and fees before engaging medical services. Most doctors, dentists, and veterinarians would prefer to arrive at a prior understanding than to be later faced with disputes or requests for adjustments of bills.

PRIVATE HOSPITALS AND THEIR COSTS

Hospital Bella Aurora
10a Calle 2-31, Zona 14
Guatemala City

Phone: 2-68-19-51, 2-37-32-04, 2-37-32-09, and 2-37-32-34

Private room with bath and phone, $52; semiprivate room with bath, $43.

Hospital Centro Médico
6a. Avenida 3-47, Zona 10
Guatemala City

Phone: 2-32-35-55, 2-34-21-57

Private room with bath and phone, $54; semiprivate room, $41.

Hospital Herrera-Llerandi
6a. Avenida 8-71, Zona 10
Guatemala City

Phone: 2-34-59-59

Private room with bath, $57; semiprivate room with bath, $48.

Hospital Los Arcos
6a. Avenida 20-88, Zona 10
Guatemala City

Phone: 2-68-21-43, 2-68-01-30, 2-33-52-94

Private room, $31; semiprivate room, $22.

Hospital Nuestra Señora Del Pilar
3a. Calle 10-71, Zona 15
Guatemala City

Phone: 2-35-69-80

DEALING WITH EMERGENCIES

While it may not seem like an emergency now, diarrhea will likely seem like one in Guatemala. Though you're not likely to get very sick, you may suffer—at least once—from diarrhea while living in Guatemala. Only those who have traveled extensively in Third World countries, or who have iron stomachs, are immune.

If you get diarrhea, try staying off solid foods for one or two days. Visit a pharmacist and ask him for the best of his stomach remedies. If diarrhea persists, see a doctor. If you have been eating fruit with the peels on, raw vegetables, or meat that has not been well cooked, you may get amoebic dysentery, in which case you should see a doctor immediately.

A prevalent disease among Americans is amoebiasis, which is endemic in Guatemala. It is a disease caused by the protozoan parasite *Entamoeba histolytica.* Cysts are passed in human stools. The symptoms vary and include fever, chills, and bloody diarrhea. See a doctor if these symptoms occur.

If you suffer from something that requires immediate emergency care at the hospital, most reputable hospitals in the city provide their own ambulance service. Make a note of your preferred hospital's twenty-four-hour emergency number and keep it handy. The first-response emergency service offered by the city—staffed by *bomberos,* who are usually poorly trained volunteers—should be relied on only if your hospital's emergency service cannot be reached.

The International SOS Assistance provides professional help worldwide to subscribers in any medical or personal emergency. Services range from telephone advice and referrals to full-scale

---

EMERGENCY PHONE NUMBERS

Emergency phone numbers in Guatemala include the following (check these with the emergency numbers listed in the front of a current Guatemala phone book because they change periodically):

> Ambulance: 128
> Fire: 123
> National Police: 120
> Red Cross: 125

international medical evacuations. SOS operates via a network of multilingual critical care and aeromedical specialists at SOS centers around the country. For information, call 215-244-1500.

INSURANCE FOR OVERSEAS HEALTH CARE

You always hear horror stories about someone suffering a heart attack, or injuries in a car accident, while traveling overseas. And how that person winds up with monstrous medical bills because he or she didn't have insurance.

Elderly travelers are particularly at risk. Medicare usually does not cover care outside the United States. Those younger than sixty-five will discover that many—but not all—health insurance policies cover emergency health services abroad. But except for limited cases in Mexico and Canada, Medicare does not.

To make matters worse, two of the ten packages of Medicare supplemental insurance also exclude foreign travel. Most health insurance policies fail to cover emergency evacuations, and the cost of these ranges from $5,000 to $20,000.

Because reading insurance policies can be as tough as programming your VCR, you should call your insurance company and get a representative to spell out coverage and restrictions. Some policies limit the length of stay in a foreign country. Others stipulate that you must return home for treatment. Most require travelers to pay at the time services are rendered. Blue Cross-Blue Shield requests that travelers pay their own bills and then submit a carefully itemized bill, preferably in English and billed in U.S. dollars.

A medical assistance insurance policy can be purchased if you plan just a short stay (such as when you're visiting Guatemala to see if it's a place you'd like to retire). These policies generally cover medical expenses, telephone consultation, reference to a nearby hospital, translation, and evacuation in case of sudden illnesses or accidents. You can buy this insurance by itself or as part of a package that includes trip cancellation, baggage insurance, and the like. Travel insurance companies and travel agents sell these products.

Subscribers to a medical travel insurance plan called TravMed are given a round-the-clock, worldwide toll-free telephone number to call in the event of illness or injury. TravMed helps locate appropriate medical aid, maintains contact with the family and personal physician back home, monitors treatment progress, and, if necessary, flies the patient back to the United States for treatment. The cost of the insurance, backed by Monumental General Insurance Company, is about $3.50 per travel day for travelers up to age 70, about $5 for those 71 to 80. There is a $25 deductible. For a brochure and application, contact Travel Insurance Services of Walnut Creek, California at 800-937-1387.

In general, the insurance situation is pretty gloomy, so since Medicare won't cover retirees in Guatemala, many North Americans simply pay cash for their medical services, which is possible considering it costs $3.50 to get a medical checkup in Panajachel. However, if that makes you uncomfortable, there is medical insurance available to U.S. retirees in Guatemala, contrary to popular belief. The Golden Years Plan is offered by a company called Salúd Total, S.A., which means "total health." (See address below.) There are two plans, one that has a maximum lifetime payout of $22,500 and a maximum annual payout of $4,500, and the other with a maximum lifetime payout of $45,000 and a maximum annual payout of $9,000.

Salud Total, S.A.   Phone: 2-31-32-67
6th Avenue 9-19 A, Zona 10   2-31-66-45
Guatemala City

MEDICINES, PHARMACIES, AND PRESCRIPTIONS

Just as in the United States, *farmácias*, as pharmacies are known in Guatemala, are stocked with all types of drugs, many available without a prescription and many that are banned in Europe and North America. They also sell beauty aids, personal care products, and local and U.S. magazines.

Clearly, you should bring your own prescription medicines with you, or have them mailed to you. I also brought my nonprescription Excedrin from home, as it is prohibitively expensive and hard to find in Guatemalan drugstores. However, if you don't bring all your drugstore items with you, you should be able to buy most things you need here in Guatemala. Two items you may have difficulty finding are earplugs and contact lens solution. But you'll find most other items. As is always the case, U.S. brands are more expensive than local ones. For example, U.S. hairspray is $2 and Ponds hand cream is $5. The local brands run about 50 cents and $1, respectively.

One frustrating thing about pharmacies in Guatemala is that you're likely to be waited on by several people. One person may ask what you want, another may get it for you, another will take your money, and another may bag your purchase. It can be a tedious process and you must have patience. Many of the workers—besides the pharmacists, of course—aren't well trained.

I used to purchase the Sunday edition of the *Miami Herald* at one particular pharmacy each week. Because the paper is much larger than the local papers, and much larger than the daily edition of the *Miami Herald*, the workers always tried to charge me for each section of the paper, as if it were five or six papers rolled into one. The manager would always have to be called to explain to the workers that it was just one newspaper. Granted, it's a minor inconvenience in the scheme of things, but tiresome nonetheless.

Pharmacies take turns staying open through the night. To find the nearest open pharmacy, look for the Farmácia de Turno sign in any pharmacy window or check the listing of pharmacies in the daily newspaper.

Klee drugstore has several branches in Guatemala City and is very popular. Pharmacies in Guatemala City that are usually open twenty-four hours include El Carmen, 9a. Avenida 17-01, Zona 1, and Medico Obelisco Super 24, Boulevard Liberación 7-45, Zona 9.

DENTAL CARE

Cheap dental care, by itself, draws many North Americans south of the border. Office visits usually cost no more than $15. One woman told of having root canal and cap—$27 for the root canal and $23 for the cap, or $50 for the whole procedure. Another told of getting a filling for $15, and $125 for a full crown or cap. Even better, dentists, like many doctors, will often give you a discount if a spouse or friend becomes a patient as well.

Dentists are more prevalent today than even a year ago. Many have studied in the United States, or Europe, use modern equipment, and speak English. They are looking for patients and advertise in many English publications. For example, in the American Society's newsletter, *Aqui Guatemala*, one dentist advertised a copy of his master's degree from the University of Alabama. As always, you should check with the U.S. Embassy for their recommended list of dentists.

In Guatemala City, there are several dentists, most charging $15 to $20 for a first visit. Some have twenty-four-hour emergency service and some make house calls. Even Panajachel has an English-speaking dentist.

Staying Busy and Happy

Before moving to Guatemala, retirees frantically gather information on auto insurance, health care, property availability, and the cost of living, but few wonder what they'll be doing once they get there. Fortunately, there's so much to do, you'll never want for companionship, entertainment, or stimulation.

LEISURE ACTIVITIES

The selection of leisure activities is especially broad in Antigua, where a solid network of English-speaking residents publishes newspapers, plans weekend trips, takes art classes, does yoga, and holds dinner parties. There's also just the time spent enjoying all that Guatemala has to offer, like the culture of the Maya people.

Guatemala is rightly famous for its traditional Indian festivals, times when the air is thick with incense and resounds to the constant pops of earsplitting firecrackers. You'll see the Maya heritage at its most vibrant, with people decked out in their best native costumes, marching in candle-lit processions. While the most famous Indian festival in the country is the one that's held Easter week in Antigua, festivals occur seemingly all the time. You may be driving or walking down the street in Antigua or Guatemala City, and all of a sudden you'll come upon a massive crowd of somber, slow-stepping people. There will be little to do but stop and enjoy the scenery.

If you have any doubts that you won't have enough to do, just check the bulletin board at the popular restaurant Doña Luisa's in Antigua. Here's a sampling of postings the last time I checked it:

Aerobics classes	$2 a class
Salsa and merengue classes	$15 a week
Volcano climb with a guide	$5
Horseback riding instruction	less than $10 an hour

And just because you're staying in the Third World it doesn't mean you have to give up movies (they show up here about six weeks after they open in the United States, but they cost only a dollar or so), golf (there's an eighteen-hole golf course at the Guatemala Country Club and a nine-hole course at the Mayan Club), or even scuba diving (yes, there's an Escuela de Buceo on 16 Calle around the corner from the El Dorado Hotel).

There's also bowling, swimming pools, hot baths, motor bike rentals, putt-putt golf (just $1.25), and concerts by a symphony orchestra. If you're looking for something on the plush side, Guatemala has its share of spas, too. The Antigua Spa Resort offers facials, hair treatments, manicures, massages, specialized baths, and soaks to restore skin. You can rent a suite at this spa for $30 a night.

English-language bookstores and book exchanges abound. One of the most popular is El Establo in Guatemala City on Avenida Reforma between 14 and 15 calles—and lots of museums to browse through. Consider taking a look at the National Museum of Popular Art and Industries in Zona 1, the Popol Vuh Museum in Zona 9, the Ixchel Museum of Indian Costumes in Zona 10, the Natural Museum of History in Zona 1, and the National Museum of Modern Art in Zona 13.

While Guatemala City does have the most to offer in the way of museums, nightlife, and bookstores, Antigua is the spot to live if you have any fear at all of being stuck on a Saturday night alone. El Sereno restaurant hosts art exhibits and cocktail parties, usually on a weekly basis. These free events were a wonderful way for my husband and myself to meet people. The Cultural Association of Antigua has art exhibits. There's a Democrats Abroad group that meets at Doña Luisa's (I'm sure there must be a Republicans Abroad group as well). There are English-speaking Christian services in Antigua on Sundays and Bible studies on Wednesdays. There's a class in applied metaphysics. There's the Institutional Science of Yoga offering yoga classes. There's English-language AA Meetings at Doña Luisa's. And meetings for worship after the manner of Friends (Quakers). And if that's not enough to wear you out, La Asociación Cultural offers individual instruction in Antigua for adults in piano, drawing, painting, and theater. The Alianza Francesa Cultural Center in Antigua offers French classes and French films. There's even private training sessions for training your dog for just $6

Unlike Antigua, you have to make your own fun in Panajachel, especially if lake-related activities don't appeal to you. "We see too many people here who just drink a lot and eventually wither away. It's not a place where you can get away with that. You need to have something to do, to find things to do. Social life can be a big deal here and you can easily be a part of it," said Wally Johnson, sixty-eight, who paints and restores pre-Columbian pottery in his spare time.

Check the bulletin board at Al Chisme for the week's activities. Video centers have sprung up in recent years where you can enjoy movies on large-screen televisions with a usually raucous crowd of American viewers. Because you do have one of the world's most beautiful lakes at your fingertips, you can spend a lot of time kayaking (for about $1.70 per hour), fishing, and boating. Exploring the beautiful villages around the lake is enjoyable. You can hire boats for trips to other points on the lake for a few dollars. The lake is some 30 miles in circumference, and you can walk on or near the shore for most of it. Here and there the cliffs are too steep to allow for easy walking and you may have to move inland a bit. You can also rent a bike to make this trip. I did this once and, because of the hills and the poor shape I was in, I got a workout that I haven't forgotten.

HOW TO MAKE FRIENDS

One of the things I enjoyed most about living overseas is that Americans there always seem friendlier than they are in America. Maybe it's being away from home that just naturally makes people reach out more to each other. Or maybe it's because Americans are usually curious as to why you're there. Whatever the reason, conversations are easily struck up in the most unlikely of places: a crowded bus, an Indian market, a grocery store.

The American Society is a group of U.S. citizens living in Guatemala that sponsors social events like annual Fourth of July picnics and Christmas parties. I never joined this group, but I have heard nothing but good things about it. It also holds bridge and craft classes for members. In addition to the American Society, there is a Lions Club, Rotary Club, an English-speaking Masonic Lodge, and Toastmasters International.

The American Chamber of Commerce of Guatemala, although primarily business- and investment-oriented, is also a good place to engage in social networking. Its monthly luncheons are frequently open to the public and its programs and service activities promote excellent, broad-based relationships.

In general, Guatemalans are a vivacious people, and meeting them is not difficult. Many speak excellent English, having been educated in the United States. Others study English at Guatemalan institutions and are anxious to practice what they learn. Still, a knowledge of Spanish will greatly enhance your social life in Guatemala.

However, while it's easy to get to know Guatemalans on a casual basis, it's much more difficult to get into their inner circles, if that's what you're looking for. Guatemala is a class-conscious society, and the country lacks a real middle class, although one is growing. Above anything else, Guatemalans put family first, which means weekends and evenings are often set aside for birthday parties and other family get-togethers from which you may be excluded.

But if it's North Americans you're looking to meet, I think it's easier to do this in Guatemala than it would be if you moved to a new town in the United States. English-speaking residents aren't nearly as numerous in Guatemala as they are in Costa Rica or Mexico, but they do have their own networks and established social groups. The North American Society publishes a weekly newspaper called *Aquí Guatemala*, which is full of information about upcoming events and is a good place to start in your search for companionship.

It's more difficult to meet retirees in Guatemala City than it is in Antigua and Panajachel, where you'll likely be invited to social gatherings within a matter of days of your arrival. However, a worker in Inguat's pensionado office tells me that American retirees meet for breakfast at the Pan American Hotel in Guatemala City's Zona 1.

There's also the Union Church in Guatemala City, which has English language services and lots of activities to choose from. And there's the Instituto Guatemalteco Americano (called IGA), which offers Spanish classes, concerts, art exhibits, and cocktail parties. But Guatemala City's still not Antigua, where you can meet people just sitting on a park bench in the town's central square. And if you meet one long-time resident, you'll be quickly introduced to the entire community.

For example, Maria Elena Streicher, manager of Jades, S.A. at 4a Calle Oriente No. 34, has lived in Antigua for years and knows absolutely everyone. She's very friendly and loves to meet newcomers. So drop by!

There are two groups of residents in Antigua, the ones who live there year-round, and the ones who arrive every fall and head back to the United States every spring. Doña Luisa's restaurant is the "in" place for both groups, known not so much for its food or service as for its bulletin board and atmosphere. Americans gather here just for a cup of coffee in the afternoon, and to play poker on Sunday nights. The setting is the patio of an old mansion that has a balcony overlooking the dining area. Try the fruit, granola, and yogurt breakfast. It's great!

Across the street is Mistral's, a restaurant-bar that features a large-screen television and satellite dish. This is an extremely popular place during major sporting events or when something hot is happening in the news.

Overlooking the central park, under an arcade near the southeast corner of the square, the San Carlos restaurant is well known to tourists and residents as a place to meet newcomers, have a beer, or plan sightseeing trips. A long table in the restaurant's front-and-center is traditionally reserved for Americans and is generally filled by noon.

It's also easy to meet English speakers in Panajachel. According to one American woman in her fifties: "They have a large women's network here. We have a free exercise class, three mornings a week. If you want to find out anything that's going on in town, come to the class. The women here are strong and not petty. The oldest in the class is seventy-three and the youngest is in her twenties."

As in Antigua, there are really two groups of Americans here. One is committed to fun, learning, and staying active. But Panajachel also attracts a crowd of Americans who simply want to watch the world go by with a drink in their hand.

LANGUAGE SCHOOLS:
HOW MUCH SHOULD YOU KNOW?

There are about thirty-five language schools in Antigua, and many others in Guatemala City, Panajachel, and Quetzaltenango. The rate depends on how many hours of education you have a week, and varies from school to school. You will benefit more from the classes if you have done some study before you arrive. And you'll especially benefit if you make a conscious effort to speak Spanish outside class.

One difficulty in learning Spanish while living in Antigua, Guatemala City, or Panajachel is that there's just so many Americans around, it's easy to fall into the habit of speaking English. That's why I tell people who really want to learn Spanish—and you should learn Spanish if you want to make the most of your new life—to go spend a few weeks in Quetzaltenango before settling in at Antigua or elsewhere.

Quetzaltenango, commonly known as Xela (pronounced *shay-la*), has over 100,000 people, but not many foreigners. Set among a group of high mountains and volcanoes, it's about a three-hour drive west of Guatemala City. Spanish schools are cheaper in Xela than in other more touristy cities, and you'll be forced to practice your Spanish.

Almost all schools offer one-on-one education. Many allow you to live with a family if that's what you want. Actually, this is the best deal—in terms of price. You can sometimes study Spanish, live with a family, and receive meals for just $300 a month. That's a car payment back in the United States!

To find a school, all you need to do is check out bulletin boards or guidebooks, or simply walk the streets. In Antigua, there is practically one school located on each corner.

The atmosphere at the schools is conducive to learning. They're quiet and pleasant. Students usually sit face-to-face with their teachers at tables surrounding flower-filled gardens. On top of the tables is a pile of blank pieces of paper, which serve as blackboards. Students study from books sold by the schools, and an emphasis is placed on conversation.

The most popular, and one of the oldest, schools in Antigua is the Proyecto Linguistico Francisco Marroquin. This school, which I attended, provides up to seven hours of individual instruction a day and places students with local families, although you don't have to stay with a local family. The fee for one week including seven hours study, board, and lodging is about $150. Because of the school's popularity—it's also where the U.S. government sends its employees and big-name newspapers send their reporters—it charges more than other schools.

Here's a sampling of what some other Spanish schools in Antigua have to offer. You'll need to check out the Spanish schools that interest you and ask around once you get there. You can check with the tourist office that's located on the main central square in Antigua and someone there should be able to recommend some options.

Centro de Español
Don Pedro de Alvarado
1 Calle Poniente No. 24

Offers four hours of instruction a day for $35 a week. If you choose to study and live with a family, plus receive three meals a day, the cost is $65 a week.

Sevilla Academia de Español
6a. Calle Oriente No. 3

The cost is $60 per week for four hours of daily instruction. The price goes up to $75 per week for five hours of daily instruction, and $90 per week for six hours. A private room with a Guatemalan family, plus three meals a day, costs an extra $40 per week.

ALM Internacional
Spanish School
2a Calle Oriente #2
(They also have a school
in Quetzaltenango)

You can learn Spanish for $55 a week for four hours of daily instruction, or $85 a week for seven hours of daily instruction. Room and board cost an additional $40 a week.

VOLUNTEER OPPORTUNITIES

Living in Guatemala, surrounded by very poor people—people who eat beans and rice three times a day and nothing else—you'll find it's hard not to want to help. Fortunately, it's easy to do so. Postings on bulletin boards in all cities populated by Americans speak of golden opportunities for lending a hand. When I was in Guatemala recently, a group of Americans was requesting help in initiating a program to provide food for indigenous girls. A new school for handicapped children in Antigua was looking for volunteers to participate in recreational activities, in addition to material donations. A facility for the mentally ill was searching for volunteers to read and play games with patients. A children's kitchen and school for indigenous students in Panajachel was looking for Americans skilled in art, sports, math, and other subjects.

If it's other Americans you want to help, you can do that too. Several U.S. citizens are currently jailed in various parts of the country, including Guatemala City. They have been convicted of drug smuggling, drug use, or various criminal acts. Most of these prisoners speak little or no Spanish and have limited contact with friends and relatives back home. You can provide a service by volunteering to visit one or more. To do this, contact Citizens Services at the U.S. Embassy.

The Peace Corps provides a wonderful opportunity to explore the country and put your expertise and energy to use. While most of the volunteers are college age, about 20 percent of the volunteers are people over fifty who are just as excited about their posts as their younger counterparts. The Peace Corps has an impressive branch in Guatemala, and its training headquarters is located on a mountainside not far outside Antigua, in a small village called Santa Lucia Milpa Alta. Many volunteers are married couples, and most make a two-year commitment to the country. Volunteers receive about $200 a month (plus a vacation allowance) and a bonus at the end of the tour of duty that averages about $5,500. By the way, this is also a wonderful way to learn Spanish. To locate the Peace Corps nearest you, call 800-424-8580.

You may also sign up and volunteer with the International Executive Service Corps. They are looking for people with experience in business, hotel operation, tourism, education, health, judi-

---

EXPATRIATE ORGANIZATIONS: A USER'S GUIDE

Guatemala offers a range of expatriate associations—organizations that assist U.S. citizens living or traveling in Guatemala. These groups can both smooth your adjustment and help you meet other Americans.

Alianza Francesa
Cultural Center
3a Calle Oriente #19a
Antigua

American Society
Edificio Rodriguez
Diagonal 6, 13-08, Zona 10
Guatemala City, Office 408

Phone: 2-37-14-16

El Sereno restaurant
6a Calle P. No. 30
Antigua

El Sereno hosts cocktail parties and art showings.

Guatemalan American
Chamber of Commerce
7a. Avenida 14-44, Zona 9
Edificio La Galeria,
2nd Floor, Office 10
Guatemala City

Phone: 2-31-22-35

Instituto Guatemalteco
Americano (IGA)
Ruta 1, 4-05, Zona 4
Guatemala City

Phone: 2-31-00-22, 2-34-43-93.

IGA offers Spanish-language classes and lots of cultural activities, as well as a great library where you can read the previous week's newspapers from various cities in the United States.

Union Church of Guatemala
Plazuela Espana, Zona 9
Guatemala City

This church has English services, as well as lots of activities for Americans.

U.S. Embassy
7-01 Avenida la Reforma,
Zona 10
Guatemala City

Phone: 2-31-15-41

ciary, government operations, and finance to work in a wide range of countries, including Guatemala. The projects are usually only a few months long, but I hear the experience is very rewarding. Participants receive no salary, but their expenses are paid and insurance is provided. Spouses are welcome, and some of their expenses are covered as well. You could wind up doing anything from assisting nurses to helping convert state-owned enterprisees into private operations. To sign up or receive more information, contact:

IESC   Phone: 800-243-4372
P.O. Box 10005
Stamford, Connecticut 06904-2005.

Your Exploratory Trip

Anyone considering retiring to Guatemala should first visit the country. Most Americans start a tour of Guatemala in Guatemala City. If making your first tour of Guatemala, you should also definitely spend a few days checking out Antigua, and plan to visit Panajachel, both popular spots for retirees.

ADVANCE PREPARATION

You need make no earth-shattering or permanent decisions to begin your quest for the good life in Guatemala.

You need only a simple tourist card in order to fly or drive into the country, as well as an abundance of curiosity, and a sense of humor and adventure. The tourist card is good for ninety days and should be carried on you at all times.

Tourist cards are available from the airlines—you'll be given one to fill out just before boarding or when you're on the plane—or from the consulate in border towns. They cost $5. To get a tourist card, all you need is proof of citizenship, usually a valid passport.

To apply for a passport for the first time, you must present, in person, a completed passport application at a U.S. State Department Passport Agency (located in major cities) or at one of the several thousand federal or state courts or U.S. Post Offices authorized to accept passport applications. Along with your application, bring proof of U.S. citizenship (such as a certified copy of your birth certificate), an ID that includes your signature and photo, and two identical 2-inch photos. The fee is $65 and the adult passport is valid for ten years. If you need to renew your passport, you can renew by mail by picking up an application at U.S. Post Offices or at a Passport Agency. The mail-in procedure costs $55 and can take up to four weeks.

Also before you go, you might want to consider getting certain vaccinations. Those which should be kept current include the following: gamma globulin (every six months); typhoid (every three years); tetanus (every ten years); and diphtheria (every ten years). You might want to take some malaria tablets if you plan to travel into very rural areas. Check with the U.S. State Department weeks before leaving for up-to-the-minute advisories about the health situation.

Heavy coats, jackets, and suits are not necessary. However, you might want to bring a light jacket and a few sweaters as it sometimes gets chilly at night in Antigua and Panajachel. Dress is basically informal all across the country. A light raincoat might come in handy during the rainy season (May to November).

There are many books on Guatemala that you may want to read before you go, including many on Guatemala's fascinating history and culture. Good travel guides include the *Mexico & Central America Handbook* and *The Real Guide: Guatemala and Belize.* Other books worth taking a look at include *Time Among the Maya* and *The Maya.*

Most major newspapers have published travel articles about Guatemala, and you might want to research these at your local library or via your computer on-line service. *Travel & Leisure* magazine has printed articles about Guatemala, as has *National Geographic.*

FLYING TO GUATEMALA

The quickest and easiest way to get to Central America is by air. A number of airlines provide service to Guatemala: American Airlines, United, and Continental, among others. Many stop in Miami or Dallas before heading on to Guatemala.

Guatemala City's international airport is a small facility, and it's not very complicated to maneuver your way through customs.

You'll see a branch of the Guatemalan Bank when you embark where you can change money or traveler's checks, although sometimes it's not open late at night. As always, when you change money in public places, tuck it into a secure place on your person and be especially cautious in a crowd.

Taxis are always lined up at the exit of the airport, so you'll have no problem getting to your hotel or even to Antigua or Panajachel. Make sure the driver agrees with you on the amount before you enter the cab. You'll also find rental car offices located next to where the taxis are waiting, but be aware that they close by 9:00 p.m. or so, and sometimes don't have any cars available.

DRIVING TO GUATEMALA

If you want the convenience of your own car while you tour Guatemala, you will want to drive there. The recommended place to cross into Guatemala is near Tapachula, Mexico, at the Guatemalan town of Tecun Uman. There are many entry points into Mexico from the United States. Most experts recommend driving the route through Mexico along the Gulf Coast, primarily because it involves 1,400 fewer miles over Mexican roads (San José, Costa Rica, is 3,700 miles from Tijuana and 2,300 miles from Brownsville). If you opt for the Gulf Coast Highway, passing through the port city of Vera Cruz, you will likely arrive at the southern Mexican border city of Tapachula after an easy five-day drive, depending on how often you stop. Most of the roads are in excellent shape, although you'll likely have to pay a lot of what can be hefty tolls. Be sure to get a mile-by-mile guide from Sanborn's in one of the Texas border cities before heading into Mexico. It is invaluable. When driving through Mexico, try to avoid Mexico City at all costs. The traffic is a nightmare and driving anywhere near the city can be very confusing. You might consider a stop in Oaxaca on your way through, though, because it is a lovely place to spend a few days.

Just south of Tapachula, the highway divides between the mountain and coastal routes before entering Guatemala. It's easier and faster to travel the coastal route and to head directly to Guatemala City. Nearing the border into Guatemala, you'll follow a steady stream of cars and trucks down a potholed highway. You'll be deluged with young men wanting to change money and lead you through the maze of admittance procedures for Guatemala. The whole process is likely to take more than an hour.

Once you get through the border crossing, be prepared to be stopped several times at roadblocks by the army and police, who are supposedly in search of stolen vehicles, drugs, and weapons. The roadblocks will usually be marked with orange cones, and several officers will be standing alongside the road. Cars are singled out for closer examination by an officer who points at your vehicle and blows a whistle. Do not drive through if asked to stop; in tenser times, people have been shot for such infractions.

Usually these stops entail no more than a quick search of the car and an examination of the passengers' and vehicle's papers. It shouldn't take more than a few minutes to get through one of these roadblocks.

However, always carry your passport with you when driving: it will be the first thing you're asked for in the event you are stopped, along with the car's papers and a driver's license.

If the police claim that something is wrong at a roadblock, they might be looking for a bribe. If you know you are in the right, insist on being taken to the station to see the commanding officer. They will almost always back off. Bribes are the normal way of dealing with blatant traffic violations, but be discreet. Ask if you can pay the "fine" (25 to 50 quetzales) directly to the police officer.

Will You Be Retiring in Guatemala?

One of the most colorful and beautiful countries south of the U.S. border, Guatemala offers endless possibilities for an interesting and exciting retirement. Its warm climate, slow pace, and low prices are only part of what makes this tiny country appealing to retirees. A gracious country, Guatemala offers a big welcome to the more adventurous souls who choose to retire south of the border.

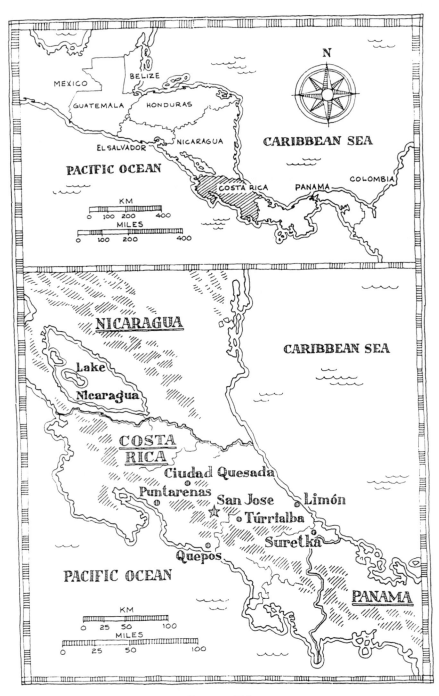

Costa Rica

Costa Rica

It's too good to be true. That's how many retirees describe life in Costa Rica. There are light-years of difference between Costa Rica and its Central American neighbors, for many reasons. While living in Guatemala, I made several sojourns to Costa Rica, and have visited the country many times since returning to the United States a few years ago. In short, Costa Rica is captivating, and I'm sure it will captivate you.

Why Here and Not Arizona?

A manageable size, Costa Rica is no bigger than West Virginia. From one end to the other, the country stretches only 200 miles. The shortest distance between the Pacific Ocean and the Caribbean is seventy-five miles. Costa Rica occupies an area of 20,000 square miles and has a population of just over 3 million. Three mountain ranges define the country, forming five distinct areas. These areas are the tropical lowlands along the Pacific and Caribbean coasts, the north central plains, the Meseta Central—also known as the Central Valley—and the northwest peninsula.

The capital city of San José is centrally located, and it is an ideal base from which to explore the rest of the country. With its parks, museums, cinemas, delis, spas, and health clubs, you might easily mistake San José, Costa Rica, for San Jose, California. The city of about 300,000 people is ringed by dozens of what you and I would call suburban towns, all of which rise from the Meseta Central. The Meseta Central sits in a wide depression about halfway down the

Cordillera, a mountain range that starts near the country's border with Nicaragua, extends the length of Costa Rica, and ends across the border in Panama. San José is the business center of Costa Rica and a mecca for Americans, despite its rising costs, hustle and bustle, and big-city pollution. Unlike the downtowns of many U.S. cities, San José comes alive with people on the weekends. Residents of nearby towns often come here to do their shopping. Teenagers gather in San José to do their partying. Business people visit to do their networking.

Costa Rica stands apart from the rest of Central America in that it has no army. Instead of pumping money into defense, the government has splurged on infrastructure, health care, and education. As a result, Costa Rica has a network of paved roads that are easily navigable, a health-care system respected around the world, and one of the highest literacy rates in the Western Hemisphere— 95 percent. And that's not all.

Violent crime here is rare, the people are astonishingly friendly, and more than 27 percent of the country's territory has been set aside as national parks.

Temperatures are usually pleasant, averaging 72 degrees year-round. The landscape is breathtaking, the wildlife abundant, and the diverse scenery includes everything from cloud forests to jungle swamps. Costa Rica has some 774 miles of Caribbean and Pacific coast studded with clean white beaches. In fact, with its two long coastlines, the country is much like the state of Florida, although Costa Rica is more often compared to Hawaii because of its abundance of green mountains and forests.

The secret of this jewel, embedded between Nicaragua and Panama, leaked out years ago. Today, the country attracts hundreds of thousands of tourists each year and is home to more than 30,000 U.S. citizens, many of whom are retired. You'll have no problem finding friends or ways to keep yourself occupied in Costa Rica. Highly cultured, Costa Rica is said to have more theater companies per capita than any other country in the world. Retirees here have formed a wide range of clubs—everything from the Coffee Pickin' Square Dancers, to the Bridge Club, to the Women's Club, to the Amateur Fishing Club.

Because of Costa Rica's excellent health care, lower cost of living, good weather, decent telecommunications system, and pleasant people, retirees consider the quality of life here to be among the highest in this hemisphere. But there is one downside: because this country has become so popular with foreigners, prices have been on the rise for the past few years. In some parts of the country, real estate values have been escalating by 100 percent a year.

Still, there are good deals on rentals and purchases outside San José and in the Pacific beach areas. And the costs for food and household help are still low. Medical fees are a fraction of what you'd pay in the United States; facelifts and other plastic surgeries cost only a small percentage of what they would back home. Because residents don't need central air conditioning or heat, monthly utility bills total next to nothing.

To become a *pensionado*, or government-approved retiree, you must prove a steady income of only $600 a month. According to retirees already living in Costa Rica, you won't need much more than that to live here comfortably! If you don't want to become a *pensionado*, the red tape for entering Costa Rica as a tourist is fortunately not the hassle it can be in other Latin American countries. A passport is all you need to spend an entire winter or summer in Costa Rica, and extensions are easily obtained.

Pensionados cannot hold salaried jobs in Costa Rica, but they are free, and even encouraged, to start businesses. The government offers tax incentives and duty-free imports to stimulate investment. The Costa Rican government also doesn't require you to be a citizen or legal resident to own property here. You don't even have to be a resident to own or manage a business.

Despite all the positives, I don't recommend a hasty decision when it comes to moving permanently to Costa Rica. You should spend several months in the country before deciding anything. Talk to other U.S. citizens, explore neighborhoods, go grocery shopping, learn some Spanish, drive through the countryside. In a word, investigate. The best time to visit the country is between November and April, the dry season. Keep an open mind, maintain a sense of humor, and have some fun, too.

The People and the Culture

Costa Ricans playfully call themselves "Ticos," just as they often use the name "Gringos" when describing Americans. Costa Ricans are friendly and are used to foreigners, both those who come as tourists and those who choose to make their country home. Many speak at least some English, and you should have no problem developing friendships with this warm and genuine population.

FACTS AT A GLANCE

Population:	3.5 million
Ethnic groups:	Most people are of European descent, usually from Spain, tiny Indian and black populations
Religion:	95 percent Roman Catholic
Languages:	Spanish
Monetary unit:	Colón
Head of state:	President
Political system:	Independent democratic republic
Industries:	Textiles, plastics, cement
Literacy rate:	95 percent
Capital:	San José
Provinces:	7
Crops:	Coffee, bananas, and sugar
Average temperature:	72 degrees
Square mileage:	20,000 square miles
Rainy season:	May through October
American population:	30,000

SOME BACKGROUND INFORMATION

Costa Ricans are, for the most part, middle class and highly literate. More often than not, they are proud, well traveled, and interested in how life is lived in the United States. They are hard working, conscientious, and dedicated to their jobs. They are also religious—about 95 percent of the population is Roman Catholic—although many do not attend mass regularly.

Most Costa Ricans are of European descent, primarily from Spain. The country has a small indigenous Indian population of about 20,000 people—less than lived in the country when the Spanish first arrived. Blacks, mostly descendants of nineteenth-century Jamaican immigrant workers, make up a significant English-speaking minority of about 30,000, who live mainly around Puerto Limón on the Caribbean coast.

You'll find that family means everything to the people of Latin America, and residents of Costa Rica are no exception.

On Sunday afternoons, you'll pass parks that are packed with extended families—grandparents, aunts and uncles, cousins, and siblings—enjoying time together by picnicking, playing, and lounging on huge blankets. In fact, if anything makes you feel like an outsider here, it is the country's strong sense of family. Family gatherings take up a lot of a Tico's time, and foreigners won't likely be included, no matter how close they become to a Costa Rican family.

Most couples are married in the church. Divorce is legal, but it is frowned upon. Elders are respected, and many older people live with their sons or daughters. Employers find that if they can instill a sense of belonging to a "professional family" in their employees, they will see higher productivity.

THE LOCAL CUSTOMS

Although I said earlier that, at first glance, one might easily mistake San José, Costa Rica for San Jose, California, you'll definitely find some differences regarding local customs.

First and foremost is the concept of punctuality. Although Costa Ricans tend to honor appointments more so than their Central American neighbors, don't be surprised if you ask someone for dinner at 7:00 p.m. and he or she fails to show up until 8:00 p.m. or later. You may be kept waiting at business appointments as well. And if a business is supposed to open at 9:00 a.m., it might not open until 9:45. You just have to be patient and keep in mind that many people are attracted to Costa Rica because of its slow pace and lack of regard for punctuality.

Another equally annoying custom is the ingrained sexism that permeates most Latin American countries. Costa Rican men tend to be more flirtatious and aggressive than men at home. Blame it on machismo. If you're single, keep in mind that Costa Ricans tend to believe that North Americans are rich and loose, or, in other words, easy prey for unscrupulous Ticos in search of easy money. Spend a lot of time with a Costa Rican before entering into a romantic relationship.

If you do business in Costa Rica, personal relationships will be the key to your success. You must spend a lot of time networking, and this means a lot of time discussing your family, yourself, and your history. Being able to say that "Mr. or Ms. so-and-so referred me to you" is far better than contacting somebody cold.

Titles are very important here, as are business cards. It seems that everybody in Costa Rica has both. Principal titles are *licenciado* for a person with a bachelor's degree; *doctor* for a person with a Ph.D.; *arquitecto* for a person who's an architect; and *ingeniero* for a person who's an engineer.

A good way to start a conversation when trying to get to know someone is by asking what to do and see in Costa Rica. When you are introduced to someone, you should always shake hands. The hugging and kissing that's so common in places such as Guatemala are not as common in Costa Rica. Women who are very good friends will sometimes kiss each other on the cheek, and men who are very good friends will sometimes hug each other briefly.

Never just drop in on someone; wait to be invited. If you are invited to someone's house, it is a good idea to bring a gift, such as a bouquet of flowers.

A BRIEF HISTORY OF THE COUNTRY

Costa Rica's earliest people arrived around the thirteenth century from southern Mexico. These settlers, called the Chorotegas—their name means "fleeing people"—were trying to get away from enemies who wanted to enslave them. Other early settlers include Indians from the jungles of Brazil and Ecuador and the Chibchas from Colombia.

It wasn't until 1502 that Christopher Columbus anchored for eighteen days in what is now Puerto Limón. He named the country Costa Rica—which means "rich coast"—because he was left with the impression that there were vast amounts of gold, and a gentle Indian population that could be easily conquered. Unfortunately, he would become deeply disappointed. He never found any riches, and the country's small Indian population was later mostly wiped out by disease. Still, the Spanish managed to successfully colonize the country in the mid-1500s, when settlers moved into the Cartago Valley, attractive because of its pleasant climate and rich soil. But because disease had decimated the native population, there was no large workforce to exploit. Therefore, Costa Rica's Spanish population remained small, and its lifestyle remained humble through the seventeenth century.

Costa Rica remained a colony of Spain governed from Guatemala City until 1821, when all the Central American nations, including Costa Rica, signed a joint statement declaring their independence. The nations formed a federation, but border disputes caused some hostility, and Costa Rica withdrew from the federation in 1838, proclaiming itself an independent nation.

Juan Mora Fernández was the first president of Costa Rica following independence. A popular leader, he constructed roads and schools and gave away land grants to anyone who would plant coffee. By the mid-1800s, coffee was the country's most important export. (It remains one of the country's top generators of revenue, along with bananas and tourism.) Coffee growers became the wealthy elite. Soon Costa Rica built an Atlantic port to accommodate rising coffee exports to Europe. Thousands of Jamaican, Italian, and Chinese workers were brought to Costa Rica to work in the coffee fields.

Costa Rica's democratic tradition began in 1889, ushered in by free and honest elections. One of the only breaks in this tradition came in 1917, when Federico Tinoco overthrew the president and ruled as a dictator for thirty months before democracy was restored. Another came in 1948, when José Figueres led a popular revolt following a disputed presidential election. A civil war ensued, and more than two thousand people died. Following the forty-day skirmish, Figueres held on long enough as president to draft a new constitution declaring communist parties and labor unions illegal, abolishing the army, and giving women and blacks the right to vote. Costa Rica now has nearly fifty years of democracy under its belt and it has survived all this time without an army.

Today, a 5,000-man police force, under control of the civilian government, maintains order. Because the country has not had to pour huge amounts of money into its defense, the government has been able to spend more on its communication systems, medical services, and public education.

GOVERNMENT AND POLITICS

The government of Costa Rica is divided into four branches: the executive branch, which consists of the president, two vice-presidents, and the presidential cabinet; the legislative branch, composed of the Legislative Assembly with fifty-seven elected representatives; the judicial branch, with a Supreme Court and civil and special courts; and the electoral tribunal, which is responsible for organizing and supervising elections.

The president and legislators are elected to four-year terms and cannot be reelected. The country's seven provinces are headed by governors appointed by the president, but they exercise little power. There are no provincial legislatures. The two main parties are the United Social Christian Party (PUSC) and the National Liberation Party (PLN). In the February 1994 presidential elections, the PLN's José Maria Figueres barely won election with 51 percent of the vote. Costa Rica is known around the world as a peaceful paradise with a high regard for human rights. The country cemented its reputation when, in 1987, its former president, Oscar Arias Sánchez, was awarded the Nobel Peace Prize for his efforts to encourage peace throughout war-torn Central America.

Indeed, Costa Ricans are enthusiastic about their democratic system. Politicians tend to be very accessible, and election day is cause for celebration. Voting is mandatory, and stores and businesses are closed. Transportation is free and everywhere people wave their party's flag, cheer, and blast car horns. The day is often marked by festive parties that last well into the night. Costa Ricans like to talk politics and are proud of their Democratic traditions.

A Look at Living Costs

Although prices are on the rise, your dollar still buys you more in Costa Rica than it does in the United States. Because of the constant springlike climate, heating and cooling bills are nonexistent. Taxis are cheap, costing about a fourth of what they would in the United States. Household help is a bargain. Health care is very affordable. Fruits and vegetables grown locally are a steal. Property taxes are low; taxes on an average three-bedroom, two-bath house run from $150 to $200 a year.

On the flip side of the coin, housing costs—and I'm speaking of those in urban areas like San José—run nearly what they do at home in some cases. Buying a car is expensive owing to high import taxes. Almost any item that's imported—things like cameras, telephones, and watches—are double their price in the United States. Computers are the only technological item whose price is quite low because of low import taxes that are the government's attempt to improve technology.

To maintain a good standard of living for a single person, you'll probably need $750 to $1,000 a month, although many people live on much more or much less. A couple can live well on $1,200 to $1,500 a month, and live like kings for $2,000 a month. Keep in mind that the average Costa Rican earns less than $300 a month!

You can probably find a full-time, live-in maid for $150 to $200 a month. Telephone service is about $10 a month. Coffee is about half the cost it is in the United States. Hotel rooms run from $20 to $120. An eye examination costs less than $5, and you can have a cavity filled by a dentist for $7 to $12.

PRICES AT A MAS X MENOS GROCERY STORE

Toothpaste, local brand (1 tube)	$1.04
Soap, local brand (1 bar)	$0.64
Large shrimp (1 kilogram)	$9.68
Chicken	$2.00
Lean ground beef (1 kilogram)	$4.31
Macaroni and cheese (1 box)	$0.54
Cornflakes (1 box)	$1.78
Ketchup (1 bottle)	$1.15
Tuna (1 can)	$0.50
Soup, local brand (1 can)	$0.44
Kraft dressing (1 bottle)	$1.90
Vegetable oil (1 liter)	$1.45
Milk (1 liter)	$0.71
Coffee (250 grams)	$0.64

OTHER PRICES

Gas (1 gallon)	$1.29
Copy of *Miami Herald*	$1.85
Arcedol headache medicine (1 tablet)	$0.30
Cinema ticket	$2.58
Bus ride across town	$0.18

Immigration Rules and Regulations

If you want to settle permanently in Costa Rica, there are many ways to establish legal residency. You can reside here as a *pensionado* (retiree), or a *rentista* (a foreigner with a guaranteed income), or an investor. These are all temporary residencies. After several years as a temporary resident, you can apply for permanent residency.

For assistance with residency, and for help in getting settled, you should consider joining or at least visiting the Asociación de Residentes de Costa Rica, or the Association of Residents of Costa Rica. The phone number is 506-233-8068. This association, which used to be only for retirees, now serves all foreigners living in Costa Rica. Membership fees are $100 for the first year and $50 for subsequent years.

The cost is well worth it. Not only is the association's office a one-stop shop for information, but members get use of the association's attorney (for a fee, of course), which can come in handy when you're trying to establish residency. The association charges $900 to process a residency application.

The *pensionado* and *rentista* programs have always been popular, especially before the Costa Rican government did away with benefits in April 1992 allowing *pensionados* and *rentistas* to import household goods and one car into the country duty-free. But despite this change in the law, *pensionado-rentista* status remains the quickest and cheapest way to become a temporary resident of Costa Rica.

Pensionados must be retired with a pension of at least $600 a month. *Rentistas* must have investments that will generate at least $1,000 a month for five years. Investor status is granted to people who invest at least $50,000 in projects like tourism or exports or $200,000 in any other kind of business.

To become a *pensionado,* you must submit your application to the Director of Intelligence and Security. You can get this application from the Costa Rican Tourism Institute or from the Asociación de Residentes de Costa Rica. With the application, you must include four photocopies, a certified copy of all pages of your passport, and two passport-size photos.

To get investor status, which benefits those who decide to invest in Costa Rican business (more about this in the section on local investment opportunities), you must do the following:

❑ Swear before a notary to abide by certain conditions, such as the country's laws.

❑ Submit a certificate proving no police record, issued by a qualified police official near your home.

❑ Go for an INTERPOL check—including fingerprints—in Costa Rica.

❑ Submit birth and marriage certificates.

❑ Submit a certified copy of your entire passport.

❑ Submit twelve passport-size photos, six front view and six profile.

As you can see, it isn't easy to become a resident of Costa Rica, which is why I recommend seeking the help of the attorney working for the association for foreign residents. The association can help make certain your papers are always up-to-date, and it will translate and notarize your documents. The application process can take anywhere from a few weeks to a year, but on the average takes about two to four months.

When deciding on your form of residency, be aware that some retirees report little benefit to obtaining legal *pensionado* or *rentista* status now that the tax breaks have been abolished. This is especially true since you can now stay in the country for ninety days upon arrival, and then easily get extensions so that you can stay in Costa Rica for several months at a time as a tourist.

If you get legal status as a *pensionado* or *rentista*, you have the hassle of having to prove your monthly income and other red tape. The only advantage to becoming a legal resident is that it allows you to spend all year in Costa Rica with little trouble, and it might make it easier to do things like get a bank account or a loan. Still, anyone in Costa Rica—whether a resident or not—can own a business or own property.

But whether you become a legal resident or not, joining the residents' association is something that definitely does have its benefits. The organization will make certain your papers are in order, translate and notarize your documents, help you get your driver's license and other permits, and assist you in buying a car. It's also a way to meet people and to become eligible for medical care.

Financial Matters

Costa Rica's currency is called the colón, and it is divided into 100 centavos.

Credit cards are widely accepted in Costa Rica, including

American Express, MasterCard, Diners Club and Visa. Credomatic S.A. is the representative of Visa and MasterCard in Costa Rica. It's located on Ave. 1, Calle 3/5 in San José; phone 233-2156. If you lose your Visa or MasterCard, call 253-2155. American Express is located on Calle 1, Ave. Central and 1, at Agéncia de Viajes in San José; phone 233-0044 during office hours, or 223-0116 in case of emergencies, losses, or robberies.

A retiree who lives outside the country can receive Social Security benefits at the U.S. Embassy. Social Security has a pamphlet called "Your Social Security Checks While You Are Outside the United States." For information call 800-772-1213. You can arrange to receive distributions from your 401(k) plan while living in Costa Rica, and you might be able to begin distributions earlier in Costa Rica than if you were living in the United States. Distributions normally begin at age 59 years 6 months, when the recipient becomes disabled, or when the individual leaves the company that established the plan or dies. But distributions may begin earlier in case of a hardship. Some experts say that simply living abroad may be considered a hardship, believe it or not.

CURRENCY EXCHANGE

At the time of this writing, a U.S. dollar was worth about 192 colones. The value of the colón fluctuates against the dollar according to supply and demand. The exchange rate, which you can always find printed in the newspaper, has remained fairly stable in recent years. For example, the rate was 140 to the dollar in early 1992, not too big a difference from what it is now. You'll get a better rate outside San José than you will inside San José. You'll also find the exchange rate to be better at banks than at upscale hotels.

You can change money at the airport, at the banks, at the *casas de cambios* (which usually charge a 1 percent commission), or on the black market, headquartered in the streets around the Banco Nacionál in San José.

Changing money on the black market is supposed to be illegal, although many people do it and it's widely tolerated. It's much easier and faster than changing money in the banks. Black market dealers usually take both currency and traveler's checks. Not all dealers are honest, though, which is why you should have a rough idea of the amount of money you should get back for your dollars before handing them over. You can also change money at most hotels, and cash can be drawn on a Visa card from any branch of the Banco Nacionál.

When you leave the country, you can change no more than $50 back into U.S. dollars at the airport, so keep that in mind.

BANKING

Although in many ways Costa Rica is the model of efficiency when compared with other Latin countries, the maze of banking can still be a difficult one to navigate. Unfortunately, you'll find yourself spending lots of time in Costa Rican banks, since they are where you pay traffic tickets, utility bills, and Social Security payments for your domestic help. It's not unusual to go to the bank, stand in line for 30 minutes, then find out from the teller that you've been standing in the wrong line and that you need to start all over again in another! This inefficiency will likely improve, though, as the country's banking system opens up and more competition comes in.

The good news is that Costa Rica's banking system is stable. Investors feel confident enough to leave money in the country. The Central Bank's reserves are more than $1 billion. The government insures deposits at both state-owned and private banks.

There are dozens of private banks in Costa Rica. State-owned banks include the Banco Nacional, Banco Anglo Costarricense, Banco de Costa Rica, and Banco Crédito Agricola de Cartago, all of which operate several branches throughout the country. The banks offer savings accounts and checking accounts, which are accepted at supermarkets and elsewhere. These accounts can be in either colones or U.S. dollars. The following U.S. bank has a branch in Costa Rica:

Citicorp S.A.
Edificio Plaza La Arillería   Phone: 222-9494
5 piso, Calle 4, Avenida Centro y Primera
San José

As in the United States, some banks offer twenty-four-hour automatic teller machines that will dispense money from your checking or savings account. Banks also offer certificates of deposit in colones or U.S. dollars. Most experts recommend keeping as little money as possible in your savings account and buying certificates of deposit because they usually carry better rates. It's hard to get a loan at any bank for foreigners, and loans are not very appealing anyway, since they usually have interest rates of 20 to 30 percent. Most private banks are "on line" to American banks and credit institutions, so that transferred funds can be made available instantly.

Most banks are open daily from 9:00 a.m. to 3:00 p.m., although some in San José stay open later. The Banco Nacional de Costa Rica, Avenida 4, Calle 0-2, is open until 6:30 p.m. and on Saturday mornings until noon.

Costa Rica also has what are called finance companies, which can provide you with a wide range of services, such as paying your utility bills and obtaining small lines of credit. Many finance companies promote investments at attractive rates.

TAXES: U.S. AND COSTA RICAN

You don't have to pay Costa Rican income tax on foreign-source income. You also don't have to pay taxes on interest earned from bank deposits. And you can transfer money in and out of the country without any restrictions.

However, you will have to pay Costa Rican income tax on locally derived income, no matter what your resident status is. Nonresidents are usually liable only for withholding taxes on such income. Anyone who has been living in Costa Rica for six months or longer during a taxable year is considered a resident for tax purposes and must file a regular tax return.

Here are some other Costa Rican tax facts:

❑ There is no capital gains tax on the sale of real estate or securities.

❑ A sales tax of 12 percent is applied on the sale of merchandise or the billing of a service, such as that rendered in restaurants, auto-repair shops, and dry-cleaning establishments.

❑ Any household belongings imported into the country are taxed at a rate of 100 percent. An imported car here costs five times what it does in most other countries because of the exorbitant automobile tax of 520 percent. (I have heard that the residents' association in Costa Rica has challenged the new law in court, and a decision is soon expected as to whether benefits will be restored to pensionados. Check with the association for the latest information on this issue.)

❑ Income taxes can be 50 percent and higher.

Any U.S. citizen, no matter where he or she resides in the world, is subject to the same Uncle Sam tax laws as when living in the United States. But there are some important exceptions. For example, the U.S. government grants a $80,000 exemption on earned income to anyone who is out of the United States for 330 days during a 365-day period. Also, if you pay taxes to a foreign country, those taxes can be exempted from your U.S. taxes.

In general, dealing with U.S. taxes while living overseas can be a major headache. Rules are constantly changing. Therefore, before you move permanently to Costa Rica, you may want to contact a special department at the U.S. Internal Revenue Service called IRS International, which serves Americans who are living overseas and filing income-tax returns. This fairly helpful department offers assistance over the phone and in person. It provides tax guides and hosts workshops. For further information, contact:

Internal Revenue Service
Assistant Commissioner (International)   Phone: 202-874-1460
Attn: IN:C:TPS
950 L'Enfant Plaza South, S.W.
Washington, D.C. 20024

You can also receive help from sources in Costa Rica. I noticed advertisements by several tax attorneys and an H & R Block office in recent issues of the *Tico Times*. U.S. taxpayers who are living overseas should mail their completed returns to the Internal Revenue Service, Philadelphia, Pennsylvania 19255.

LOCAL INVESTMENT OPPORTUNITIES

The word on Costa Rica is out, and investors are scrambling to make their fortune. Lured by the country's strategic location, its inexpensive labor force, its tax incentives, and its overall stability, North Americans by the thousands have set up shop in Costa Rica and are making money in all kinds of businesses.

The Costa Rican government encourages foreign investment, and looks at it as a way to spur development. Depending on the type of business, the government may issue lines of credit, eliminate customs duties on the importation of certain materials and equipment, and/or give a twelve-year exemption from income taxes. A free trade zone program provides foreign-owned firms with generous tax exemptions such as a 100 percent exemption on profits or other taxable income for the first eight years of operation.

Foreigners are not allowed to hold a salaried job in Costa Rica, but they are allowed to own a business through the establishment of a company. There are several types of companies. The most common is called *sociedad anonima*, whose structure is quite similar to that of corporations in the United States. Before establishing a company, you must contact a lawyer. Once registered, the company can engage in any type of legal business, except for buying state properties. The cost to set up a business ranges from $400 to $1,000.

North Americans have found success in all kinds of areas, but especially in the areas of tourism, the export of nontraditional fruits and vegetables, and the import of textiles and other raw materials which can be assembled and then exported.

Tourism has surpassed bananas as the number-one industry in Costa Rica, making this an area you might want to investigate. Most of the hotels and tourist facilities going up in Costa Rica have been built with outside investment.

Many foreigners have found the bed-and-breakfast business a profitable one. Investment in the area of ecotourism, or tourism that emphasizes the country's natural environment, has grown by leaps and bounds. Meanwhile, Costa Rica offers good opportunities for people who want to export items such as ornamental plants, winter fruits and vegetables, and exotic woods. With its rich soil and spectacular climate, almost anything grows. The export of textiles has also risen steadily over the last several years. Many textile plants operate in the country's free-trade zones.

Some foreigners who choose to do business in Costa Rica seek what's called *inversionista-rentista* (investor) status. To obtain this status, you must invest at least $50,000 in special projects such as tourism or exports, or $200,000 in any other kind of enterprise. The government requires foreigners who obtain this status to live in Costa Rica six months of the year. It also requires nationals to make up 90 percent of a company's workforce. If you decide to obtain this status, you should seek help from a reliable attorney and from the residents' association of Costa Rica.

While there are definitely ways to make money in Costa Rica, there are also lots of ways to be swindled. Scam artists, many of whom are foreigners themselves, prey upon unsuspecting newcomers, so you have to be wary. Some Americans have lost their life savings by investing in nonexistent gold mines, tourist resorts that were never constructed, real estate that doesn't exist, phony banks, and bogus mutual funds.

The best way to avoid getting cheated is to check all offerings carefully, and to contact offices, like those listed below, for advice.

If you are serious about investing in Costa Rica, here are some places to turn for help and for more information. Also, the Costa Rican-American Chamber of Commerce publishes "The Guide to Investing and Doing Business in Costa Rica," which you should be able to find at most English-language bookstores or by contacting the chamber.

Cámara de Comercio
de Costa Rica
Calles 1A/3A, Avenida Central
Apartado 1114
San José

Phone: 221-0005

Cámara de Indústrias
de Costa Rica
Calles 13/15, Avenida 6
Apartado 10003
San José

Phone: 223-2411

Centro de Promoción
de Exportaciones y
Inversiones (CENPRO)
Apartado 5418
San José

Phone: 221-7166

Costa Rican Investment
Promotion Program (CINDE)
Apartado 7170-1000
San José

Phone: 233-1711

TIPPING GUIDE

On all hotel bills, a 10 percent sales tax is charged as well as a 3 percent tourist tax. In cafés and restaurants, there is a 10 percent gratuity and a 10 percent tax included as well. Tipping above this amount is not necessary.

However, you can leave something extra if service was especially outstanding.

Often, people will tip maids at hotels, especially if they perform a special service such as laundry service. Employees such as bellhops and taxi drivers are appreciative of any additional gratuity for excellent service. Store clerks are never tipped, but kids who carry your packages to the car are usually given a bit of change, as are the kids who volunteer to watch your car while you shop. (By the way, when a child offers to watch your car, it's usually a good idea to say yes in order to secure the safety of your car.)

Rentals and Real Estate

Costa Rica has it all. Nice homes and cabins sit on pine-covered mountains. Sky-high apartment complexes tower over the frenetic big city of San José. Chic town houses stand in the middle of quiet and elegant suburbs, such as Escazú. Condominiums and apartments face clean white beaches and palm trees.

No matter what you're looking for, you won't have any problem finding it in Costa Rica, whether it's an apartment, house, or condominium. There is a plentiful supply of all three throughout the country. Rents remain fairly reasonable, although the price of property has skyrocketed in recent years. Still, it's still possible to buy a home in Costa Rica for $40,000 and, to most North Americans, that's pretty cheap.

HOUSES, APARTMENTS, AND CONDOS

Most homes and apartments have all the amenities: large bedrooms, bathrooms with hot water, dining rooms, kitchens, laundry rooms, and so forth. Most houses have three bedrooms and two bathrooms. Make certain you find a place with a phone and a garage (to prevent theft if you have a car). It's not unusual for houses to have enclosed or covered patios or porches, and indoor sun rooms for plants.

Most unfurnished houses don't have stoves or refrigerators, although most apartments will come with all necessary appliances. Most homes have showers rather than bathtubs. Really nice homes have walls or fences around them. Furnished housing is not always easy to find, and won't likely include lamps, linens, silverware, small appliances, and dishes.

THE PLACES WHERE RETIREES LIVE

Costa Rica is divided into seven provinces: San José, Alajuela, Cartago, Heredia, Guanacaste, Puntarenas, and Limón. The first four are landlocked, while Guanacaste and Puntarenas enjoy the warmth of the tropical Pacific, and Limón, the splendor of the Caribbean. The last three are well known for their miles of clean, white beaches. Deciding where to live or stay in Costa Rica depends on your own personal lifestyle.

If you like a pleasant climate and the hustle and bustle of big-city life, then you'll probably enjoy living in San José or in one of the adjacent suburbs that ring the capital city in what's called the Meseta Central, or the Central Valley.

In San José, where rentals tend to be more expensive, a nice unfurnished one-bedroom apartment is likely to rent for $350 to $475; a two-bedroom apartment for $450 to $775; and a three-bedroom apartment or larger for $600 to $1,300. Furnished apartments will run $500 to $600; $600 to $875; and $900 to $1,600, respectively. Nice unfurnished two-bedroom houses in San José are likely to rent for $600 to $800; three-bedroom houses for $950 to $1,750; and four-bedroom houses or larger for $1,500 to $2,500. Furnished houses will run $800 to $1,000; $1,600 to $2,000; and $2,000 or more, respectively. If you wish for a more tranquil setting, you might choose a home or cabin on a pine tree-covered mountain surrounding the Central Valley. If you want warmer weather, and still want to hold on to urban life, you might choose a condominium or town house in the small city of Alajuela, near the airport and a short drive from San José. Keep in mind that the farther you go from San José, the cheaper the price of property.

Retirees also love the beach. Many choose the area along the Caribbean coast that's just below Limón, south of Cahuita. But because of the area's high amount of rainfall, others prefer the Pacific coast. Retirees can be found living along the many beautiful beaches located along the Nicoya Peninsula and in Guanacaste to the north. Still other retirees choose the area farther south on the west coast between Punta Arenas and Dominical beaches. Manuel Antonio, considered by many to be the most splendid beach in Costa Rica, is located in this area.

Considering all the choices, I would say that the most popular places for retirees to live are in the residential suburbs surrounding San José, where the price of property has rapidly escalated in recent years primarily because of that popularity. Escazú is one of San José's most desirable neighborhoods. Ten minutes from San José, Escazú has a wide range of houses—many of which are surrounded by messy, overgrown yet lovely gardens—in all price ranges. Town houses and detached homes with spacious yards are going up all over the place. New developments such as Trejos Montealegre, Bello Horizonte, and Los Laureles offer town houses and detached homes with large yards. Rents in the district range from $500 to $4,000 per month. The price of homes runs the gamut from $80,000 to $1 million.

Escazú is home to the Costa Rica Country Club, and to lots of English-speaking schools and churches. To give you an idea of how Americanized Escazú has become, you'll find that there's a McDonald's across the street from a Benetton, which is down the street from a Shell service station, a Circle K, an Exxon service station, and a 24-hour Mobil service station. The Super Pet pet store in Escazú even sells Iams! The area is still semirural, but is quickly becoming a flourishing commercial center famous for its good restaurants and trendy shops. The population of Escazú is said to be about 40,000, although it really feels much smaller, with its cobblestone streets and quaint adobe buildings.

Escazú is a good place to stay while exploring the rest of Costa Rica. Bus service to San José is reliable and convenient, and hotels are abundant. We stayed in Escazú at a bed and breakfast during our last visit to Costa Rica for $30 a night. The food was great and we were within walking distance of major shopping centers, cinemas, and restaurants.

A little farther west than Escazú is the community of Santa Ana, a town of about 20,000 people that is cheaper and more rural than Escazú. While still inhabited mainly by locals, it is growing in popularity as an out-of-town neighborhood for foreigners. Larger homes and estates are more reasonably priced than in Escazú—$400 to $2,000 per month—and shopping is plentiful. Here, there's plenty of room for development and new homes, and condomimiums are going up all over the place.

Indeed, a popular suburb, Santa Ana is about five minutes farther from San José than Escazú, but homes there are more reasonably priced and the atmosphere is more peaceful. And there is a lively mix of foreigners and locals. The last time I was in Costa Rica, I noticed dozens of new homes and condominiums being constructed on the road between Santa Ana and Escazú.

Much closer to town but still on the west end are the neighborhoods of Rohrmoser and La Sabana—areas popular among the Costa Rican upper crust. Prices are in the middle range—$300 to $3,000 per month—and the area is within walking distance of downtown San José. There are a number of restaurants, health clubs, bars, and discos in these two middle- to upper-class areas.

Ciudad Cariari is east of town closer to the airport and a development of mainly newer homes. The neighborhoods of Cariari, Bosques de Doña Rosa, and Los Arcos are all part of the Hotel and Club Cariari Resort Development near the Herradura Hotel and Conference Center. It's also home to Costa Rica's most famous championship golf course. Monthly rentals range from $800 to $3,000 per month. The Costa Rican Academy, one of the better English-language schools in the country, is located within the development. Also on the east end of San José is San Pedro, about five minutes from downtown San José. The area has a mix of middle- and upper-class housing surrounding the University of Costa Rica. Because of all the foreign exchange students, this suburb has a definite cosmopolitan feel. Apartment rentals start at around $220 a month.

In San Rafael de Heredia, which is about 35 minutes from San José and which attracts middle- to upper-class locals and foreigners, rentals run from $200 to $1,500 a month. Heredia is a relaxed and pleasant place to live filled with commuters who work in San José. To me, Heredia looks almost like Miami, with lots of palm trees, houses built over two-car garages with second-story balconies and tin roofs, and clean wide streets.

If you don't want to live near San José, but are looking for something on or near the beach, you'd better hurry because property with access to reasonable roads, reliable electricity and other services is going fast. Property near Tamarindo, Sámara, or Flamingo in Guanacaste; in the Nosara area of Nicoya Peninsula; and in the Manuel Antonio area in Quepos are most popular with foreigners. Homes in the Flamingo area go for $50,000 to $750,000, depending on the property. Prices are more reasonable for properties along the Atlantic coast. There, Cahuita, Puerto Viejo, Punta Uva, and Manzanillo are among the most sought-after spots.

In this area, as well as in some spots along the Pacific Coast, you can get a 2.47-acre lot for less than $20,000.

RENTING: WHAT IT WILL COST

As you can see, you may have to do a lot of exploring before deciding on a place to rent because there's simply so much to choose from at such a wide range of prices. In Costa Rica, apartments and houses are usually rented through agents or directly from landlords. Often, foreigners find rental properties by word-of-mouth, or simply by driving around and spotting "for rent" signs in windows. All of the major newspapers, including the *Tico Times*, have massive real estate listings.

When you rent a property, you will generally be asked to pay one month's rent in advance and another month's rent as a security deposit. Leases legally have no expiration term other than the one stipulated by the parties involved. If you use an agent, you will usually be charged a month's rent as a fee. Moving-in time after signing a lease is usually ten to thirty days. You should be able to find housing in just a few weeks.

If you are in Costa Rica looking for property to buy—a process that should not be rushed!—you might want to stay in an "apartotel," a small apartment complete with phone, television, cooking supplies, and everything else you need to live. You can pay anywhere from $200 to $1,000 a month for an apartment in an apartotel, depending on its size and amenities.

If you want something cheaper, you might want to stay with a Costa Rican family. This likely will cost you $100 a week or so, maybe higher, which usually includes meals and laundry service. Living with a family is an excellent way to learn Spanish; most Spanish schools will be able to recommend families to you.

BUYING PROPERTY AND FINANCING THE DEAL

Although rentals are still pretty reasonable in Costa Rica, the price of property has jumped considerably in the last few years—by as much as 100 percent a year in some parts. Fortunately, good deals are still to be had outside San José and in some areas along the Pacific beach. But they're going fast. Improvements in the country's infrastructure, as well as a huge influx of foreigners in recent years and a general shortage of land, have contributed to the making of what's considered to be the hottest real estate market in Central America.

Foreigners enjoy the same protections as Costa Ricans under the law as it applies to property ownership. Neither citizenship nor residence, nor even a presence in the country, is required for property ownership. While people in many Latin countries resent the fact that U.S. residents appear to be moving in on their territory, that's not the case in Costa Rica. People here are used to foreigners—tourism has been one of the top industries for several years—and they are both welcoming and friendly.

Here are a few things you should know before purchasing property in Costa Rica:

❑ There is very little bank financing at decent rates available for the purchase of property in Costa Rica. You must either pay for your property in cash or arrange financing with the owner.

❑ Closing costs for a sale include a transfer land tax, a stamp tax, and legal fees. Closing costs generally run 5 to 6 percent of the sales price and are usually split equally between the buyer and seller.

❑ The transfer and land taxes are assessed based on the declared value, while legal fees are charged based on the sales price of the property.

❑ It is now possible to have contracts in dollars, rather than only in colones. This has been a great change, beneficial to foreign buyers, because it does away with any worries regarding the devaluation of the colón.

❑ Before purchasing a piece of property, check the National Registry, which has registered almost every plot of land in the country. By doing this, you'll be able to determine whether the land is really registered to the person who's selling it to you; whether there are any liens against the property; and whether the land has been surveyed.

❑ Real estate agents usually receive 5 percent of the purchase price—generally paid for by the seller—while lawyers are paid 1.5 percent.

❑ Before closing on a deal, always talk to neighbors in the area about potential problems, such as crime. Make certain the property is not a national park or reserve.

❑ Land here is sold in square meters or sometimes in *manzanas,* an old measurement that equals about two acres.

❑ Be aware of problems concerning squatters and legitimate land owners. In Costa Rica, there are laws that say that unowned or abandoned property is open for homesteading. This is why you must make certain a friend or attorney stops by your property periodically if you are out of the country.

In general, *never* buy property in Costa Rica without the advice and assistance of a competent, English-speaking attorney. There are many reasons why. For example, matters such as making earnest money deposits are fairly complicated in Costa Rica, which is why it is advisable to make deposits through a trusted lawyer. A good lawyer will also be familiar with the country's zoning regulations, such as the fact that all building plans must be signed by a registered local engineer and approved by the local municipality.

A lawyer will be able to help when it comes to a search of the title registration in the country's registry, so as to confirm that there are no liens on the property and to establish its proper ownership.

Once a deal is complete, it's your attorney who will provide documents proving that the sale was registered. If you buy a beach property, a lawyer will be able to help you decipher regulations regarding these properties. For example, by law, the first fifty meters above the high tide line along Costa Rica's beaches are public.

You can get recommendations of reputable attorneys from the U.S. Embassy or from the Costa Rican-American Chamber of Commerce.

Yearly property taxes in Costa Rica are not high, ranging from 0.5 percent to 1.5 percent of the declared value of the property. This declared value is a common law practice in which a property's value according to the government is very low, almost always lower than the sales price.

UTILITIES: WHAT YOU'LL PAY

One of the benefits of living in Costa Rica is that utility costs are low. Electricity averages about $15 a month since heating and air conditioning are not necessary. Basic phone service usually costs between $5 and $10 a month. Water and garbage service total $4 to $5 a month. Utilities are usually paid for by the tenant, who should arrange with the landlord how payments should be made.

Telephone bills, as well as other utility bills, must be paid at the ICE (Instituto Costarricense de Electricidad, with offices in downtown San José at Calle 1 and Avenida 5 as well as in La Sabana and San Pedro) or at banks or most Mas X Menos and Perifico supermarkets.

Telephone service will be shut off if you fail to pay a bill within one week of the *fecha de vencimiento* (expiration date) written on the bill. If you don't receive a bill in the mail, it's your job to hunt it down or call the utility to find out how much you owe. Bill or no bill, you must make regular payments for service or face cutoff.

The electrical current in Costa Rica is 110V/120V, just as it is in the United States, and U.S.-type plugs are used.

Setting Up, Settling In

Of the countries described in this book, Costa Rica is perhaps the easiest to settle into and establish a comfortable home. You'll quickly feel right at home.

NEWSPAPERS, MAGAZINES, TELEVISION, MOVIES

North Americans living in Costa Rica have no problem keeping up with news from home. Racks at bookstores and newsstands are stuffed with a wide range of U.S. newspapers and magazines. You can buy the *Miami Herald, USA Today,* and *The New York Times,* as well as news weeklies like *Time* and *Newsweek.* They'll be more expensive than they would be back home—they are flown in on a daily basis—but the money's usually well worth it for those of us news junkies.

The most popular and widely circulated English-language newspaper published in Central America is the *Tico Times,* and you can find it everywhere. Reading it is another good way to keep up with the news, especially what's happening in Costa Rica and throughout Central America. The *Tico Times* also publishes a huge listing of classified ads, so it's *the* place to find information on North American clubs and social groups, churches, restaurants, movies, and even companionship. The *Tico Times* comes out every Friday. To subscribe if you live in the United States, write:

Tico Times
Dept. 717
P.O. Box 025216
Miami, Florida 33102

Another well-regarded English-language publication, along the same line as the *Tico Times,* is *Costa Rica Today,* which is also widely available. To subscribe, write:

Costa Rica Today 117
P.O. Box 0025216
Miami, Florida 33102.

English-language publications are available at many bookstores, including the Candy Shop of the Gran Hotel Costa Rica at Calle 3, Avenida Central/2; The Bookshop at Avenida 1, Calle 1/3, and the Hotel Amstel Shop at Calle 7, Avenida 1.

About 90 percent of households in Costa Rica have televisions, and there are several local stations and foreign cable networks to choose from. Costa Rica has six local channels, one of them being a government-operated cultural channel. CNN is shown in many hotels and bars, as is HBO and some other popular U.S. channels. Many local stations broadcast U.S. programs dubbed in Spanish.

(Watching these programs is an excellent way to learn the language.) In addition to television, you can watch your favorite movies rented from one of many video rental stores if you have a VCR. Most movies you rent are in English with Spanish subtitles.

MAIL SERVICE

Just as in the United States, mail is sent and received from the post office, called *correo* or *casa de correos*, and although service is not as reliable as it is in the United States, it is more reliable than service in other Central American countries. The main post office is located in downtown San José at Calle 2, Avenida 1-3. Other cities and towns throughout the country have their own post offices, which are usually open from 7:30 a.m. to 11:30 a.m., and from 1:30 p.m. to 5:30 p.m., Mondays through Fridays. Airmail between the United States and Costa Rica usually takes five to ten days.

It's probably a good idea to use the post office when you have to mail something, rather than using mail boxes along the streets, because pickups from these boxes tend to be less reliable. Because of the uncertainty of mail service, it's not a good idea to have money mailed to you. Instead, you should have money sent to you in an international money order via a courier service such as DHL. Or you should have money wired to you via U.S. banks or Western Union. You can have your Social Security checks mailed to you directly through the U.S. Embassy in San José.

A word of warning: Try to avoid having anything larger than a letter or a magazine mailed to you in Costa Rica, because large items will be forwarded to the customs warehouse (*aduana*) and it will take you several trips, and a lot of patience, to get them out of customs. Plus, you'll probably have to pay sky-high duty fees to retrieve them.

Because of the unreliability of mail service, some Americans pay for special service. For example, if you join the Asociación de Residentes de Costa Rica, you can use its mail service; a letter costs $1, coming in or going out. Other residents use services based in Miami that allow your mail to be delivered to a post office box there, then flown to you in San José on a daily basis. These services generally cost $20 to $30 a month, and are advertised in publications such as the *Tico Times*. Other residents pay a small yearly fee for post office boxes in San José, called *apartados*, which means you have to pick up your mail each day at the post office. If you are worried about receiving your mail from home, there's a mail service that can help you by picking it up and forwarding it to you weekly. For further information contact:

Personal Mail International (PMI)
P.O. Box 311   Phone: 201-543-6001
Mendham, New Jersey 07945-0311

Growing in popularity are businesses that offer access to faxes and E-mail. You'll find ads for these businesses in English-language publications. A fax to the United States costs $1.50 to $2.00.

TELEPHONE SERVICE

As in most of Latin America, telephone service is not as efficient in Costa Rica as it is in the United States, but it's not too bad, either. For one thing, pay phones actually work in this Central American country. They take coins in denominations of 5, 10, or 20 colones. Slide a coin into the groove at the top of the phone and dial. If you hear a rapid beeping noise while talking, you must insert more money.

To call Costa Rica from the United States, you must dial 011, then the country code, 506, and then the number. There are no city codes. To call the United States from Costa Rica, you must dial 00, then 1, then the area code and local number. To get an English-speaking operator inside Costa Rica, dial 116. You don't have to deposit any coins; this operator can place your collect or credit-card calls. To use an AT&T card, dial 114 to be connected with an AT&T operator. To use MCI, dial 162 to be connected with an MCI operator. Sprint customers must dial 163.

If you rent, your telephone will probably not be listed under your name, since the directory lists only the name of the owner of the line, who is usually the landlord. If you want any extension phones, you should bring these with you since phones purchased locally are usually quite expensive and not very good.

The installation of a phone line can take several months, depending on the availability of lines in the area. A new seven-digit system became operational in spring 1994, and this is supposed to allow for quicker installation in the future. Still, you should try to rent a house or apartment with a telephone already installed to avoid any delays. If you are waiting for phone installation and just can't wait any longer, you might try checking the classified ads in local newspapers for people who want to sell their phone lines. Basic phone service costs about $10 a month.

FURNISHING A HOME,
FROM SILVERWARE TO APPLIANCES

When trying to decide what to bring to Costa Rica to furnish your home, keep in mind that appliances and many consumer goods are expensive if purchased in Costa Rica. Clocks, telephones, and almost all imported manufactured items are usually double their price in the United States. Computers are the only technological item whose price is quite low, because taxes on them are minimal as a result of efforts by the Costa Rican government to improve technology in the country.

But despite the cost, it's probably a better idea to buy items in Costa Rica than to ship everything in, owing to high import duties. (Before April 1992, retirees were allowed to import household goods duty-free. The benefit was repealed, making the import of belongings not nearly as desirable as it once was.) For example, towels are taxed at 99 percent of their value; refrigerators and other appliances are taxed at 60 percent; compact discs are taxed at 42 percent. And the value of your items for tax purposes is determined by Costa Rican customs agents, so no two shipments of, say, towels or anything else will ever be valued the same. Customs clearance of household goods usually takes four to five weeks or longer following arrival of the items in the country.

According to the association for residents of Costa Rica, you'd likely pay an estimated tax of $6,000 to $7,000 if you moved an entire three-bedroom house full of furnishings. And, in addition to these taxes, you would also be taxed on your shipping costs. This is why moving experts recommend shipping your things domestically to a U.S. city close to Costa Rica, such as Houston or Miami, since the government can tax you only on shipping charged from that city to Costa Rica.

My advice is to take only what you absolutely can't live without. Fortunately, you can buy all the appliances you need locally, although, as I said, it will cost you. You can buy all types of furniture in Costa Rica, and come across some pretty good deals. Curtains can be custom-made locally of good fabric at decent prices.

Also, anyone entering Costa Rica on a tourist visa is allowed to bring in various small electrical appliances, such as hair dryers and radios. Some items you might consider bringing with you if you have the space is a portable heater or an electric blanket, since there's no central air conditioning or heating in Costa Rica and the nights can get chilly.

You should carry valuable, personal items, such as jewelry or silverware, on the plane with you. These personal items will not be taxed at the airport. You should also take items with you that you'll need right away, since cargo goods can be held up a long time in customs.

CLOTHES YOU'LL WANT

Costa Ricans consider themselves a very fashionable people so it's a good idea to bring along some nice clothes for your evenings out. In general, you'll want to dress in Costa Rica just as you would at home. Sleeveless shirts and blouses, lightweight sweaters and slacks are good year-round.

For men, heavy winter clothing and coats are not necessary, but a raincoat and umbrella will come in handy. For women, pants are appropriate for both formal and casual wear, but shorts should be reserved for the beach or sports. Both men and women should pack a good supply of shoes since large sizes can be hard to find in Costa Rica.

BRINGING BOWSER AND BUTTONS WITH YOU

Since I have two dogs that are just like children to me, I always place great importance on the issue of importing pets. Yes, you can bring pets with you to Costa Rica, but you've got to do a little bit of paperwork and maintain a high level of patience.

If you want to take an animal into Costa Rica, you must get a health certificate from your local veterinarian that states that your pet is free of internal and external parasites. Your pet's vaccinations against rabies, distemper, leptospirosis, hepatitis, and parvovirus must be up to date. The rabies vaccination must be at least three months old, but no older than three years.

Other vaccinations should be administered at least 30 days prior to departure, but not longer than 180 days. Once you get these documents, they must be certified by the Costa Rican consulate closest to you. You also will need an import permit, which may be obtained at the time of entry of the pet into San José if the pet is accompanying the passenger.

Fortunately, there are no quarantine requirements, although the Costa Rican government can require a quarantine period if you don't have the proper documents. It's best to have your pet arrive with you and declare it as luggage instead of cargo. All of this probably seems rather complicated, but it's really not too bad.

Since rules in Latin America seem to change all the time, you might contact the Departamento de Zoonosis for the most up-to-date information before you go. The departamento can be reached at:

Ministerio de Salúd   Phone: 223-0333
Apartado Postal 10123
San José, Costa Rica

There is also a pet-moving company that can give you some help, if you so desire. For information, contact:

Air Animal Inc.   Phone: 813-879-3210,
Pet Moving Services   or 800-635-3448
4120 West Cypress Street
Tampa, Florida 33607-2358

THE QUEST FOR PEANUT BUTTER AND OTHER NECESSITIES

Depending on how you look at it, you may be either disappointed or delighted to find that grocery stores in Costa Rica are almost exactly like those in the United States. Mas X Menos and other popular grocery stores carry everything from Pringles to SlimFast to Niagara spray starch. You can buy Iams pet food at the Super Pet pet store. You can buy select cuts of meat at Tega in Escazú. You can buy Max Factor mascara and almost any other kind of make-up you can think of at most pharmacies.

San José supermarkets have a good supply of packaged foods, pasta, canned meats, soft drinks, and snack foods. Dry cereals are available at relatively high prices. Some frozen foods are available, but the selection is not very good. A decent selection of wine is available, and bottles of Chilean wine are an especially good deal.

METRIC MEASURES

Costa Rica operates on the metric system of weights and measurements. Here are some conversions to help you adjust.

1 gallon	equals	3.8 liters
1 quart	equals	.95 liter
1 pound	equals	.37 kilogram
1 ounce	equals	31.1 grams
1 mile	equals	1.61 kilometers
1 yard	equals	.91 meter
1 inch	equals	2.54 centimeters
1 kilogram	equals	2.2 pounds
1 liter	equals	1.06 quarts
1 gram	equals	.035 ounce
1 kilometer	equals	.62 mile
1 meter	equals	39.37 inches
1 centimeter	equals	.39 inch

Keep in mind that you'll pay a lot more for imported items, and that local products are often better than their U.S. counterparts. You can buy Kraft dressings, Campbell's soup, and Hyde Park macaroni and cheese. But you could buy local brands, which I think are just as tasty, at a fraction of the cost. (By the way, at most grocery stores in Costa Rica, you'll be asked to check belongings like umbrellas or shopping bags—not purses—before entering the store.)

Says one long-time North American resident in San José: "You couldn't buy turkey or canned goods when I moved here eighteen years ago, but now Dr. Pepper is the only thing I miss. Products are coming in from Mexico because of increased trade and, because of NAFTA, we get almost everything here now."

In general, you can find a good supply of quality fresh meats at all times, including beef, pork, chicken, and fish. Costa Rica is known for its fresh seafood, including sea bass, corvina, and lobster, as well as its local grass-fed beef. Since cattle is such a big industry here, steaks and roasts are quite cheap; pork and chicken is often higher priced. Another plus is that you can buy what's considered to be some of the best coffee in the world in Costa Rica.

Instead of buying all your goods at the grocery store, you should check out San José's Central Market, where fruits, vegetables, shrimp, lobster, and other goodies are available seven days a week at incredibly low prices. In addition to the Central Market, you can buy fruits and vegetables—I remember seeing mangos the size of cantaloupes—at sidewalk stands. There is a big open-air market on Saturdays in Escazú, near the main square. Other markets are held Sundays in Zapote; Saturdays in Pavas; and every day in Heredia. Some good local items to look out for include the yucca root, which is often substituted for potatoes here; batidas, a popular drink made from fresh fruit, milk, and ice; and exotic tropical fruits such as carambolas, guayabas, and tamarindos.

HOUSEHOLD HELP

Employing full-time domestic help in the United States can cost you an arm and a leg. A young woman cleans my house in Atlanta—a process that takes about three hours—and charges $50. In Costa Rica, the charge for a live-in maid is usually less than $200 a month! And maids in Costa Rica will not only clean but some will cook, do laundry, and iron clothes. They also act as a great theft deterrent. Day and live-in help is easy to find through the classifieds or through word-of-mouth, but you should always ask for references and check these references out thoroughly.

If you do decide to hire domestic help, there are some local labor laws you must follow. All domestic help has the right to Social Security benefits from the Caja Costarricense de Seguro Social, as well as maternity benefits, an annual bonus, and severance pay. Live-in help cannot be asked to work more than twelve hours a day; day workers, eight hours. The employee must be given at least one-half day off each week, a fifteen-day paid vacation after fifty weeks of continuous service, and half-days on New Year's Day, Christmas, Holy Thursday, Good Friday, May 1, and September 15. If the employee works on these days, an additional half-day's salary must be paid.

A pregnant employee is entitled to one-month leave before the birth and three months after, at half her usual monthly wage. An annual bonus equivalent to two weeks' salary is paid to employees who have worked from December 1 through November 30, usually around Christmastime. A dismissed employee is allowed all wages due, payment for unused vacation time, and the proportionate yearly bonus. An employee who leaves of his or her own accord is not entitled to severance pay.

Domestic help should be registered with the Caja, or the Department of Inspections. The employer must bring identification such as a passport, as well as the employee's *cedula* (an identification card issued by the government) and a description of the job and wages. The employer is supposed to pay 19.5 percent of monthly wages to the Caja.

Getting Around

Costa Rica has the advantages of both a good public transportation system and ample services for those choosing to drive their own cars.

PUBLIC TRANSPORTATION

Probably the most popular way to get around Costa Rica is by bus. An excellent service of well-maintained modern buses connects San José with all main towns, and connects all parts of San José. You can probably get almost anywhere in the country by bus for as little as from $2 to $6. Bus stands and the buses themselves are marked with the service's ultimate destination.

Since most Costa Ricans don't have cars and rely on buses for transportation, buses can be quite crowded during rush hours and on weekends. San José has no central bus station and each line departs from its own terminal. Most tourist guides will list bus lines, terminal addresses, and trip fares. While many buses in Costa Rica are rickety old school buses purchased from U.S. companies, others are quite nice. Some luxury buses used for long-distance journeys come equipped with air conditioning, color TV, and roomy bathrooms.

Despite the popularity of buses, I actually prefer getting around by cab. There appear to be zillions of taxis in Costa Rica, and they are an easy and inexpensive way to travel. Costa Rican law requires all taxi cabs to have working meters, a novelty in Latin America. (Still, always make sure the taxi driver is *using* his meter, and be sure to ask for a cost estimate before getting into a taxi.) The taxi system here is quite organized in that, if you feel you've been overcharged, you can write down the taxi driver's permit number or his license number and complain to the Ministério de Obras Públicas y Transporte. Taxis are red with yellow taxi signs on top. It costs about $2.50 to get from downtown San José to the neighborhood of Escazú. Taxi drivers are allowed under the law to charge 20 percent more from 10:00 p.m. to 5:00 a.m.

Despite the convenience of taxis and buses in Costa Rica, some people are addicted to train travel. Unfortunately, the country's train system is not what it used to be. Thanks to the earthquake of 1991, passenger trains no longer journey from San José to Limón. Still, there remains what is called "the banana train," a daily three-hour train ride between the Caribbean coastal banana towns of Guápiles and Siquirres. Other train trips take you to Cartago and to Turrialba.

Costa Rica is served by an extensive network of inexpensive internal flights operated by SANSA, the national airline. SANSA serves many beach cities including Sámara, Golfito, and Quepos. All these flights leave from a small airport west of the main terminal at the Santamaría airport.

If you do choose to fly, make certain you reconfirm reservations, whether you have tickets or not. Try to make your reservations in person at a SANSA office. Don't rely on travel agents to make reservations or get your tickets. Flights can be crowded, especially during dry season, so you should make reservations at least two weeks in advance.

DRIVING IN COSTA RICA

If public transportation doesn't suit you, and you prefer to go at your own pace, where you want and when you want, you should rent a car. I agree that this is the best way to see the country, especially if you are trying to make a decision about where to retire.

Compared with other Central American countries, driving around Costa Rica is a breeze. The main roads are well maintained and traffic is not particularly heavy or hair-raising, although off the main roads conditions can be rough, particularly during the rainy season. Gas stations are well distributed; obtain a copy of the International Travel Map Productions map, which marks all petrol stations. Gas is sold by the liter, and unleaded gasoline, called "super," is widely available.

If you are driving, it shouldn't be too difficult to find your way around the country's towns and cities. Almost all are built on a strict grid pattern and use the same numbering system. Streets (*calles*) run one way and avenues (*avenidas*) the other. Number 0 is the central street or avenue and running parallel to this on one side are the even numbers, with the odd numbers moving away in the other direction. So walking a block from Calle 2 brings you to Calle 4, and Calle 3 is six blocks away on the other side of Calle 0. Addresses are given with the street or avenue that they are on and then the two streets or avenues that they are between, leaving you to look along that block. So Avenida 1, Calles 3-5, is on Avenida 1 between Calles 3 and 5. It may sound confusing but you'll get the hang of it.

Small tolls are charged on the main roads leaving the capital. The speed limit is 75 kilometers an hour, or 60 miles per hour, unless otherwise specified, and police speed traps are sometimes used. You can also get a ticket for not wearing a seat belt. Tickets are issued by the police, and fines have to be paid at a bank. You should never, ever, give a police officer money when he gives you a traffic ticket. Crooked police offiers are not the problem they once were, but you may run across one that insists it's easier to pay him the fine rather than pay the fine at the bank. Just smile, be polite, and say you'd prefer paying at the bank. If you haven't paid by the time you leave, it's just possible that you will be detained at the airport. If you're involved in a serious accident, the police might confiscate your number plates, preventing you from driving until the matter is resolved.

If you plan to do much driving in Costa Rica, you might consider getting an International Driving Permit before you go. Basically, this is a translation of your driver's license. It may come in handy should you get a traffic ticket or be involved in an accident by reassuring the police officer that your driver's license is valid. For more information, contact the national headquarters of the American Automobile Association at:

American Automobile Association
1000 AAA Drive
Heathrow, Florida 32746-5080.

As a *pensionado*, you will have to get a Costa Rican driver's license if you want to drive here. Your U.S. license is good for only three months. Fortunately, it's not that difficult to get a new license. Just go to the Dirección de Transporte Automotor, Avenida 18, Calle 5,

San José; phone 227-2188 or 223-4626. You must present your U.S. license, bring along some photos of yourself, pay a small fee, and pass an eye exam; then you should have your license in a few hours. If you don't have a U.S. license, you'll have to take a driving test, just as you would have to in the United States.

Car Rentals

Many rental-car companies have offices in San José, including Avis, Budget, Dollar, and National. Most of these offices are located at the Juan Santamaría International Airport and at major hotels. Car rental prices run the gamut. I rented a car in San José from Budget for $38 a day, or $228 a week, with unlimited mileage.

To rent a car in Costa Rica, you must be at least twenty-five years old and have a valid driver's license, passport, and credit card. Insurance may be an additional charge, and rentals are subject to a 6 percent tax. Always be sure to give rental cars a careful once-over before leaving the lot. Make certain an agency employee documents every scratch and dent so that you won't be charged for damages when you return the car. Check to make sure the car has a good spare tire.

For reliable rentals, try the following agencies:

Avis
Calle 42,   Phone: 222-6066
Avenue las Américas

Budget
Calle 30, Paseo Colón   Phone: 223-3284

Hertz
Calle 38, Paseo Colón   Phone: 223-5959

Importing Your Car

As mentioned earlier, retirees used to enjoy zero import duties on automobiles, but no more, making the option of bringing a new car with you a less than desirable one. Duties on cars from 1986 to the present can be as high as 427 percent of the car's value.

Better options might be to either import an older car, and enjoy

SECURITY CONCERNS

When I lived in Central America, friends and family back home asked me time and time again: Aren't you afraid living down there? My answer was always the same: I'm less afraid here than I would be living in the United States. And I still feel that way, especially now that I reside in Atlanta, which has one of the highest murder rates in the United States and where houses in my neighborhood are routinely burglarized.

This is not to say you shouldn't be careful when living or traveling in Costa Rica. Although the rate of violent crime is extremely low, there is a problem with thieves and pickpockets. Therefore, it would be wise to look for a house or apartment with steel bars on the windows, or to look for a neighborhood or complex that employs twenty-four-hour security personnel. You should also park in lots that employ a security officer, and never wear expensive jewelry or carry cash in your back pocket. It's best to use traveler's checks, to avoid carrying original documents, such as passports, and to tightly clutch your purse at all times. If you do carry a copy of your passport, be sure to make copies of the first several pages, including the number, your photo, and your entry visa stamped at the airport.

Immigration officials may ask to see your passport at any time or place. Don't leave valuables in your car unless it is parked in a very secure place. Try not to leave cars out overnight except if, once again, they are parked in a very secure place. Record credit card numbers and keep them separate so that you can report stolen cards if need be. Try using a traveler's pouch, worn inside your shirt or around your waist, instead of carrying a purse or wallet.

The U.S. State Department has not issued any travel advisories for Costa Rica, but you can contact the Citizens Emergency Center at 202-647-5225 for the latest information.

a 70 percent reduction in the normal import duty, or buy a car locally, should you decide to make Costa Rica your home. Used cars can be shipped from Miami for an estimated $400 to $1,200. And many U.S. citizens enjoy the adventure of driving their cars to Central America (see the section on border crossings, page 187).

If you do decide to import your car, be aware that the tariff schedule for imports is highly complex, based on both the age of the car and other factors. Also be aware that owning a car in Costa Rica can be frustrating, since finding a trustworthy mechanic is not always easy and repairs and replacement parts can be quite expensive. All cars driven into Costa Rica must be registered at the Customs House in San José within forty-eight hours of entry. A car is really not a must if you live in San José or nearby.

Car Insurance

In Costa Rica, all insurance, including car insurance, is sold by the National Insurance Institute (INS), a state monopoly (see address below). Car insurance will cover drivers who have a valid license, or one that was issued in Costa Rica, as well as those who have a foreign license if the driver entered the country less than ninety days before and is over eighteen. For cars with foreign license plates, the INS will issue coverage only for personal liability and property damage to third parties, and only for the exact period covered by the official permit for the car to be driven in Costa Rica.

There are two types of optional auto insurance sold in Costa Rica: obligatory and supplementary. Obligatory insurance covers injury to anyone in an accident involving the insured vehicle. Supplementary covers personal liability.

Foreign liability insurance isn't legal in Costa Rica. But several U.S. companies sell comprehensive policies for coverage in Costa Rica, although few have local offices or claims adjusters, so you should check with your agent to see what's available.

National Insurance Institute (INS)   Phone: 223-5800
Avenida 7, Calle 9/11
San José

Staying Healthy

Maybe the best thing about living in Costa Rica is its top-quality yet inexpensive health-care system. Unlike hospitals in the United States, government hospitals in Costa Rica don't ask you to flash an insurance card the minute you walk in the door. Emergency rooms will treat you no matter who you are. And the level of care matches that in the United States. Infant mortality is lower in Costa Rica than in the United States, and the average life expectancy is seventy-four years for men, or about the same as in the United States.

Recent studies conducted by the Costa Rican government have shown that, in fact, 10 to 20 percent of North Americans visiting Costa Rica do so to receive some kind of medical care, lured by the high quality and low costs. A visit to a private doctor's office costs no more than $25 to $55. A day in a modern, first-class private hospital is less than $90. The price is even less if you're willing to share a room and bathroom. That's a far cry from the $1,000 or more you'll pay in many U.S. hospitals.

WATER AND FOOD SAFEGUARDS

Fortunately, most Americans in Costa Rica don't have to fear Montezuma's revenge. Intestinal problems are not nearly as widespread as they are elsewhere in Latin America, primarily because Costa Rica's water supply is good and perfectly safe to drink in San José and in most of the country's other cities and towns. Still, even in Costa Rica you should be careful not to drink water in very rural areas. To be on the safe side, drink bottled water.

Although Costa Rica is considered to have a high standard of sanitation and health care, it's always a good idea to take some of the same simple precautions as you'd take if you were traveling in any other Central American country. For example, don't eat fresh fruits or vegetables unless they are thoroughly washed with a supply of safe water. Peel raw fruits and vegetables. Avoid lesser-known brands of dairy products. Instead, try pasteurized products from Dos Piños and Borden, two reputable companies. Milk sold in boxes or cartons is safe. Avoid fruit drinks sold in plastic bags, homemade popsicles, and—in rural areas—fresh fruit drinks made with water. If water is suspect, order soft drinks and bottled water *sin hielo*, pronounced "seen yellow," meaning without ice.

When it comes to immunizations, none are required to enter Costa Rica. However, if you'll be traveling to rural areas, some doctors may advise a tetanus booster, and polio and typhoid-paratyphoid vaccinations. I've traveled throughout Costa Rica, was never told to get any immunizations, and made it just fine. Still, you might want to call the Centers for Disease Control and Prevention

(CDC) before you go to get an up-to-date account regarding diseases and vaccinations; phone 404-332-4555. The CDC International Traveler's Hotline is another good source; phone 404-332-4559.

DOCTORS AND HOSPITALS:
WHAT IF YOU GET SICK?

No matter how good the year-round temperatures, the water supply, and the sanitation, it's almost impossible to avoid getting sick no matter where in Latin America you choose to retire. In Costa Rica, the altitude in some parts of the country, coupled with a high pollen count at certain times of the year, could affect those people plagued with sinusitis, hay fever, or asthma. Colds could also be bothersome during the rainy season. No matter how careful you are, you might eventually suffer from some intestinal problems.

At least you can take comfort in the fact that Costa Rica is known for its quality medical care, well-trained doctors, and competent private clinics. A list of English-speaking, U.S.-trained doctors and their specialties is available from the U.S. Embassy in San José. You can also find a good doctor through word-of-mouth simply by asking other retirees. Or you can locate a physician by looking in the Yellow Pages under "Medicos."

Many of the doctors on staff at major hospitals in San José speak English and have been trained in the United States or Europe. Obviously, hospitals in areas outside San José may not always have such capable staff members on hand.

No matter where you go, doctors and hospitals usually expect immediate cash payment for health services, although a few hospitals now take credit cards. Many Americans prefer this way of paying for health care, and are able to do so since costs are much lower than in industrialized countries. In fact, many Americans come to Costa Rica for plastic surgery, dental work, cataract operations, sessions at health spas, and other procedures because they are so inexpensive here. Liposuction ranges in price from $1,500 to $2,500, plus $300 to $500 for the hospital stay. Facelifts range from $2,000 to $3,500, with $700 to $900 for hospital costs. An eye examination costs less than $4.

The low cost of health care and labor also make custodial care of the elderly less expensive. Golden Valley Hacienda offers specialized care for Alzheimer's patients, and Villa Comfort

Geriatric Hotel provides a comfortable atmosphere for the elderly who just need help in everyday living. The cost is about $1,500 a month for around-the-clock care; phone 221-6381, 433-8191, or 433-8575.

Clínicas are private hospitals, available to foreigners at decent rates. The others are social-security hospitals that provide emergency service to everyone, including foreigners. All have X-ray facilities, laboratories, and pharmacies, although the social-security hospitals will be cheaper than private facilities. However, the social-security hospitals will not accept insurance from the National Insurance Institute.

Many Americans like the Clínica Bíblica or Clínica Católica, both private facilities, because of the high quality of care. English-speaking medical professional can be found in the Yellow Pages, and many advertise in tourist guides and English-language magazines. Although doctors in social-security hospitals are well qualified, lines and paperwork at these facilities can be time-consuming, especially for someone who is not feeling well.

Hospitals and clinics in San José include:

Calderón Guardia
Avenida 9, Calle 17

Phone: 224-4133

This is a social-security facility.

Clínica Americana
Calle Central/1, Avenida 14

Phone: 222-1010

This is a private facility that does not accept insurance or credit cards.

Clínica Bíblica
Calle Central/1, Avenida 14

Phone: 223-6422

This is a private facility that offers emergency service, mammograms, cardiology, pathology, etc. It accepts

INS insurance and some credit cards.

Clínica Católica
Guadalupe

Phone: 225-9095

This is a private facility that offers emergency service, respiratory therapy, ultrasound, etc. It accepts INS insurance and most credit cards.

San Juan de Diós
Paseo Colón, Calle 14

Phone: 222-0166

This is a social-security facility.

DEALING WITH EMERGENCIES

In a medical emergency you might want to head for the Hospital San Juan de Diós, Paseo Colón, Calle 14; phone 222-0166.

If it's not an emergency, you might try one of the private clinics such as the Clínica Bíblica, Calle Central/1, Avenida 14; phone 223-6422, where many of the staff members speak English.

If you do come down with something resembling Montezuma's revenge, marked by diarrhea and nausea, you should take a stool sample to a local laboratory and have it analyzed for a small fee. The lab doctor or pharmacist can tell you what kind of medicine you should take.

EMERGENCY PHONE NUMBERS

Emergency phone numbers in Costa Rica include the following (check these with the emergency numbers listed in the current Costa Rica phone book because they change periodically):

Ambulance: 221-5858
Burn Unit: 257-0180
Poison Center: 223-1028

If you are really concerned about having an emergency while out of the United States, you might consider contacting the following services that offer assistance to foreigners in an emergency:

❑ International SOS Assistance: Provides telephone assistance and referrals, as well as worldwide medical evacuations. Subscribers are given professional help in any medical or personal emergency from specialists at SOS centers around the world. P.O. Box 11568, Philadelphia, Pennsylvania 19116; phone 215-244-1500.

❑ Medex Assistance Corporation: Provides services that are similar to those offered by International SOS Assistance. It operates with a network of multilingual specialists who answer calls directly. Medex has a list of 10,000 providers worldwide. P.O. Box 10623, Baltimore, Maryland 21285-0623; phone 410-296-2530.

INSURANCE FOR OVERSEAS HEALTH CARE

Each year, about 23,000 Americans are hospitalized abroad. While being hospitalized in a strange country can be an ordeal in itself, many of these people also suffer financially because some health insurance policies do not cover medical care overseas.

U.S. medical insurance will not likely be accepted in Costa Rica, although some insurers do offer specific overseas coverage. Medicare does not cover any health services in Costa Rica, and some of the Medicare supplemental insurance packages also exclude foreign travel. You should check with your insurance agent and ask him or her to spell out your coverage. However, as I said earlier in this section, many foreigners prefer to pay cash for health services because of the low cost. Furthermore, the country's social-security system makes low-cost medical care available to anyone who wants it, including North American *pensionados*.

It is possible that the Clínica Biblica, a private facility, will become a branch of a U.S. hospital so that retirees and tourists can use their Medicare coverage to pay for medical expenses there. You should contact the Asociación de Residentes de Costa Rica, or the Association of Residents of Costa Rica, at 233-8068 for the latest information on this situation and on insurance issues in general. The association also offers its own group health insurance policy for its members.

Tourists can purchase a policy that will cover medical or dental emergencies from the International Cultural Exchange Organization and the Tourist Homestay Program in the form of a blue "convenience card." Card holders can go to any social-security hospital for treatment. The card costs about $45 and is good for one month. For more information, write to Apdo, 687-1011, San José, or send a fax to Carlos Cortes at 222-7867; phone 257-0680.

The National Insurance Institute (INS), which is the Costa Rican government's insurance company, offers a policy to anyone who wants it, including *pensionados*. The policy covers medical expenses due to accident, and due to acute illness and permanent disability resulting from an accident. The last time I checked, policies were being sold for $170 a year for adults; there is a discount if more than one person is insured under the same policy.

These policies pay 80 percent of the costs of hospitalization, medicines, and various tests. Apparently, people over seventy years of age are not eligible, although that rule may change. When you buy a policy, INS supplies you with an identification card and a booklet that lists the names of affiliated groups, such as hospitals, doctors, and pharmacies. You pay for the services yourself, and then submit a claim for reimbursement by the INS. For information, go to the National Insurance Institute, Mezzanine 2, Calle 7 & 9, Avenida 7; phone 223-5800. Or contact an insurance agent in Costa Rica about the INS plan.

For more information on insurance, you might try contacting the following:

AIU North America, Inc.
Personal Lines Division
503 Carr Road R23-7A
Wilmington, DE 19809

Phone: 302-761-3107

Contact: Susan Schmidt

Amex Travel Protection Plan
P.O. Box 919010
San Diego, CA 92191-9970

Phone: 800-234-0375

You can get a policy without being a cardholder.

Henry Ward Johnson & Co., Inc.
125 Broad Street
New York, NY 10004

Phone: 212-574-8977

Contact: Leonora Burgess

Travel Insurance Services
2930 Camino Diablo
Suite 200
Miami, FL 33131

Phone: 800-327-7033

MEDICINES, PHARMACIES, AND PRESCRIPTIONS

Many pharmacies stay open twenty-four hours a day and even deliver medicines and prescriptions to your home! Medications available only by prescription in the United States often can be purchased over-the-counter at Costa Rican pharmacies. Still, if you require long-term medications, you might want to arrange to have prescriptions filled in the United States just to be on the safe side.

In addition to medicines, you can find all sorts of products at pharmacies—everything from hairspray to make-up to magazines. As is usual, contact lens solutions can be difficult to find. In Costa Rica, pharmacists are allowed to prescribe medicines, as well as administer on-the-spot injections.

DENTAL CARE

Many dentists in Costa Rica speak English and were trained in the United States. You can get a list of English-speaking dentists from the U.S. Embassy.

Most dental procedures cost one- to two-thirds of what they would in the United States. A routine examination is likely to cost about $35. Here are some estimates of other charges:

Single root canal	$110
Wisdom tooth surgery	$150
Tooth extraction	$30
Complete prosthesis	$200
Porcelain laminate	$130

Staying Busy and Happy

You will have no problem whatsoever filling your time in Costa Rica. There's so much to keep you busy that your only problem will be finding a moment to relax! You can choose from hiking, football, running, hang gliding, bridge, libraries, movies, social clubs, museums, parks, wind surfing, bowling, tennis, ceramics classes, camping, bird watching, dancing, racquetball, bicycling, sun bathing, horseback riding, art galleries, and scores of other activities. For such a tiny country, there is an astonishing number of ways to keep you going.

You can take Latin dance lessons at places such as the Academy of Latin Dances, the Danza Viva, or the Merecumbe Research and Training Center of Popular Dance. You can meditate, do yoga, and enjoy "physical and emotional harmony" at New Age centers such as the Costa Rica Rainbow Connection, Centro Creativo, and the Hearty Hands Health Home. You can join a country club, such as the Cariari Country Club, the Costa Rica Country Club, or the Los Reyes Country Club, and play golf, swim, and exercise. You can ride horses at Hípico La Carana, about fifteen miles west of San José, and at the Cariari Country Club. You can watch soccer, the national sport, or basketball, which is growing in popularity.

HAVING FUN OUTDOORS

Costa Rica has become a mecca for the nature lover and the conservationist. As of 1992, Costa Rica is the world headquarters for the Earth Council because of its natural resource conservation activities. Currently, the National Parks Service is responsible for the care and conservation of twenty natural parks, eight wildlife refuges, and one area declared a national archeological monument. At the same time, the Forestry Service is in charge of twenty-six protected areas, nine forest reserves, seven fauna sanctuaries, and a national forest. These protected areas total about 26 percent of Costa Rica's territory, meaning that Costa Rica has a larger percentage of its total area set aside in parks and preserves than any other country in the world.

Tortuguero National Park on the Atlantic coast is one of the most important nesting sites for the green turtle. A natural system of canals and navigable lagoons cross the park, forming the habitat for seven species of land turtles, the sea cow, and the crocodile. This is one of the rainiest and most biologically diverse regions in the country.

Turning to the Pacific coast, the main attractions of the Manuel Antonio National Park are two white, sandy beaches called Espadilla Sur and Manuel Antonio. The park includes twelve islands located a short distance from shore that serve as seabird sanctuaries. The seas contain dolphins and, occasionally, migrating whales.

Back on the Atlantic coast is Cahuita National Park, one of the most beautiful areas in the country. Cahuita's pluses are its white sands, miles of coconut groves, coral reef, and tranquil clear seas. Some of the reef's most beautiful fish include the French angelfish, rock beauty, and blue parrotfish. The area is full of howler monkeys and many species of endemic birds.

If you love water sports, you've come to the right place. Costa Rica is a paradise of lakes, natural water basins, coasts, and rivers. You can enjoy some of the best fishing in the world here. You can enjoy both kayaking and river rafting along more than sixty miles of navigable rivers. You can enjoy boating, windsurfing, water-skiing, and skin diving along the coastline and in crystal-clear lakes. Whatever you desire to do, you can do it here.

Costa Rica has 767 miles of coastline on two coasts beckoning the surfer, snorkeler, swimmer, sheller, and sunbather. There's Plaza Blanca in Santa Rosa National Park, which may be the most isolated beach in Costa Rica. There's Playa Nosara, a lovely white-sand beach surrounded by lush hills and a residential community of foreigners. There are playas Blanco and Flamingo, which look like Hawaii with their posh resorts and gourmet restaurants.

There are many businesses that cater to both the highly skilled and the novice fishing enthusiast. Many companies rent boats, provide charters, and organize fishing excursions. Sportfishing along the Pacific coast is best from facilities in Golfito, Drake Bay, and Sierpe, where snook, snapper, roosterfish, and corvina are caught. The Caribbean coast has a season from January to June for tarpon and snook, with a shorter season from September to October, mainly for snook. Inland, freshwater fishing is mainly for rainbow trout, bass, tarpon, and snook. A fishing license is required to fish in Costa Rica. Local tackle shops, fishing camps, and professional guides can provide these licenses for you.

HAVING FUN ELSEWHERE, TOO

Costa Rica is certainly more than a nature lover's paradise. It is also a country known for its culture. There are more than thirty museums scattered around Costa Rica—everything from the Costa Rican Art Museum to the Entomological Museum to the Gold Museum. Art galleries are opening all over San José. Costa Rica's theatrical tradition is well established in the capital, and its fine theaters are complemented by a vibrant fringe group that performs in small theaters across San José. The performing arts scene includes an annual concert series by the National Symphony Orchestra and the Costa Rican Youth Symphony. Dozens of movie theaters feature U.S. films—usually in English with Spanish subtitles—for just a dollar or two.

In addition to the cultural activities, San José has a fairly active nightlife, offering everything from the National Lyric Opera Company to sleazy strip joints. There's no shortage of seedy bars, loud Western music, and video screens. Serious drinkers frequent Nashville South. An impressive mariachi band makes Bar Mexico a popular hangout. Other bars popular with North Americans include Risas, Lucky's Piano Bar, Tropical Tiny's, and Marley's. If you enjoy gambling, Costa Rica has more than twenty casinos to choose from. Most casinos serve free drinks while you play, and are open from about 6:00 p.m. to 3:00 or 4:00 a.m.

HOW TO MAKE FRIENDS

Every time I go to Costa Rica, I'm surprised again by how many clubs there are for North Americans living in Costa Rica. If you flip through the pages of the *Tico Times* or *Costa Rica Today*, you'll see column after column of clubs such as the Investment Club, the Bridge Club, the Personal Computer Club, the Women's Club, the English-speaking Kiwanis Club, the Association of People Who've Had Brain Surgery, the Rotary Club, and Alcoholics Anonymous. And this doesn't even begin to scratch the surface. In other words, you will have no trouble meeting at least some of the 30,000 North Americans currently living in Costa Rica.

Probably the best way to meet people is to attend one of the weekly Newcomer's Seminars. These seminars are held each Tuesday morning at the Hotel Irazu, except for the last Tuesday of the month, when they are held at the Hotel Cariari. These seminars not only provide a meeting place, but are a great way to keep up with the latest on issues such as tax laws, health insurance, *pensionado* benefits, and the like. For more information, call Terry Ennis at 220-4988. You can find advertisements for these seminars in both the *Tico Times* and *Costa Rica Today*.

You can also meet people at church. Several churches hold services in English and are a gathering place for North Americans who make their home in Costa Rica or are just passing through on vacation. Some of the churches with English services include the Episcopal Church of the Good Shepherd, the Escazú Christian Fellowship, the International Baptist Church, the Union Church, and the Church of Jesus Christ of Latter-Day Saints.

Costa Rica has also become known as a place for singles to meet each other. Several singles clubs advertise excursions and parties in the English-language publications. Hotels are constantly sponsoring singles dances. Personal ads pepper the pages of local newspapers.

Should you decide to start dating a Costa Rican, there are a few things to remember. Costa Rican men tend to be more flirtatious and aggressive than North American men. Costa Rican women tend to be more flirtatious and accessible than North American women. You should give any relationship a lot of time because many Costa Ricans, unfortunately, are on the lookout for North Americans with money.

LANGUAGE SCHOOLS: HOW MUCH SHOULD YOU KNOW?

Although many people in Costa Rica speak at least a little English, you should still learn at least a few basic phrases in Spanish before heading to Costa Rica, at least enough so that you can order food in a restaurant, take a cab to your hotel, and rent a car. A good way to learn Spanish is to purchase a Spanish-language cassette tape and listen to it at home and in your car.

Fortunately, Spanish is not a difficult language to learn. With a little self-discipline, you ought to be able to pick up a vocabulary of a few hundred words within a few weeks. Many Spanish words are so similar to their English counterparts that you can figure out their meanings just by looking at them. Spanish pronunciation is easier than English, because words are pronounced as they are spelled. The Spanish alphabet is almost the same as the English one.

Like Guatemala and Mexico, Costa Rica has established a reputation as one of the best places in the world to learn Spanish. The country boasts dozens of Spanish schools that vary widely when it comes to price and quality.

Take some time when choosing a Spanish school. Decide if you want one that offers field trips for students or one that sticks to rigid one-on-one instruction. Decide if you want to study for eight hours a day or only four. Decide if you want to live with a Costa Rican family while studying, or simply in an apartment or hotel.

When I attended Spanish schools in Guatemala, I found eight hours a day to be too tiresome. By the end of the day, I couldn't stand to hear another word in Spanish, let alone practice my Spanish. I think it is a better idea, at least at the outset, to study for four or five hours a day. That way you can ease into the routine, and you won't be too worn out on evenings and weekends to practice what you've learned. And you must practice if you are serious about learning. I recommend attending a school with one-on-one instruction that emphasizes conversation. It's much more important to speak Spanish than it is to write gramatically correct sentences in Spanish.

Although I haven't attended Spanish schools in Costa Rica, here are a few that come recommended by other North Americans:

Central American Institute for International Affairs
P.O. Box 10302
Barrio Otoya, 1000
San José

Phone: 233-8571

Created in 1984, this school offers programs that combine Spanish-language study with cultural events. A two-week program, with four hours of classroom study a day, costs $595, which includes accommodations with a Costa Rican family.

Centro Cultural Costarricense-Nortemericano (CCCN)
Spanish Program
Apartado 1489-1000
San José

Phone: 225-9433

CCCN was founded in 1945, and offers sessions that are two to five weeks long, two to nine hours daily. A twenty-hour two-week program costs $245. Accommodations with a family can also be arranged for $79 a week.

Forester Instituto Internacional
Apartado 6945
Los Yoses, del Costas Rica
P.O. Box 6945, 1000
San José

Phone: 225-3155

This school was founded in 1979. Four 50-minute Spanish lessons are offered daily, and class time includes field trips. There is a $100 registration fee, $50 of which is applied to tuition. You can choose from among two-, three-, and four-week sessions. Prices are $415 to $500, including accommodations with a family.

Intensa
P.O. Box 8110-1000
Calle 33, Avenidas 5 y 7
Barrio Escalante, 1000
San José

Phone: 224-6353/6009

More than any other school, Intensa emphasizes speaking the language. Classes here are limited to no more than six students. A two-week program with four hours of class time a day costs $315. Accommodations with a family costs $200 a week.

Mesoamerica Language Institute
Apartado 1524
Avenida 2
Calle 5
San José, 2050 San Pedro

Phone: 234-7682

This school offers instruction solely in Spanish. Teachers also take students on field trips. A one-week program costs $110; a four-week program, $390. Accommodations with a family cost $85 a week.

If you grow tired of school—I did after a few months—you might want to hone your Spanish skills by joining a Spanish conversation group. Many such groups have been organized by North Americans and advertise meetings in the newspaper.

VOLUNTEER OPPORTUNITIES

Because Costa Rica is such a haven for naturalists, there are plenty of groups that need volunteers to help fight deforestation, pollution, and threats to wildlife. Here are just a few:

**The Association of Volunteers
for Service in Protected Areas**

Phone: 222-5085

This group has an extensive program for volunteers, from writing newsletters to helping park guards search for poachers.

**The Costa Rican Association
for the Conservation of Nature**

Phone: 235-9856

This is one of the country's oldest environmental groups.

The Costa Rican Ecology Association

Phone: 233-3013

This association has all sorts of field projects and works with indigenous people.

You can find volunteer opportunities advertised in the *Tico Times* and in *Costa Rica Today*. Many schools and other facilities are looking for English speakers to help Costa Ricans learn English. (This is a great way to meet the locals and to learn Spanish.)

Here are some other organizations that coordinate volunteer programs throughout the world, and may be able to tell you about such programs in Costa Rica:

The Coordinating Committee for International Voluntary Service
UNESCO
1 rue Miollis
75015 Paris
France

Phone: 331-45-68-1000

This agency is in charge of non-governmental voluntary service programs in many countries.

The Council on International Educational Exchange (CIEE)
205 E. 42nd Street
New York, N.Y. 10017

Phone: 212-661-1414, ext. 1139

This organization seeks volunteers for programs ranging from conservation projects to projects that work with children.

The International Executive Service Corps
P.O. Box 10005
Stamford, CT 06904-2005

Phone: 800-243-4372

This organization places mostly retired executives in countries around the world. It provides opportunities for everyone from lawyers and judges to skilled technicians. There are no age restrictions, and the organization pays for round-trip airfare, expenses, and usually a per diem to cover housing and meals.

The Peace Corps
1190 K Street, N.W.
Washington, DC 20526

Phone: 202-606-3000 or 800-424-8580

The Peace Corps is now made up of many volunteers who are over the age of sixty. All participants are required to serve for two years.

EXPATRIATE ORGANIZATIONS: A USER'S GUIDE

In Costa Rica, you'll find a range of expatriate organizations—organizations designed to assist U.S. citizens living or traveling in Costa Rica. These groups will help smooth your adjustment to your new home.

BUSINESS SOURCES

American Chamber of Commerce of Costa Rica
P.O. Box 4946
San José

Phone: 332-1033

Chamber of Commerce of Costa Rica
Calles 1A/3A, Avenida Central, Apartado 1114
San José

Phone: 221-0005

Costa Rica Agricultural Trade Development Program
7200 N.W. 19th Street, Suite 303
Miami, FL 33126

Phone: 305-477-4121

CLUBS

The Association of Residents of Costa Rica
ICT Building, Calle 5, Avenida 4
San José

Phone: 233-8068

EMBASSIES AND CONSULATES

Costa Rican Consulate General
80 Wall Street, Suite 718-719
New York, NY 10005

Phone: 212-425-2620

Costa Rican Embassy/Consulate
1825 Connecticut Ave. N.W., Suite 211
Washington, DC 20009

Phone: 202-234-2945

TOURIST OFFICES

Costa Rica National Tourist Bureau
1101 Brickell Avenue
BIV Tower, Suite 801
Miami, FL 33131

Phone: 800-327-7033

Instituto Costarricense de Turismo (ICT)
Office of Tourist Information
Plaza de la Cultura, Calle 5, Avenida ctl./2
San José

Phone: 223-1733

Your Exploratory Trip

Many people hear about Costa Rica—the slow pace, the low cost of living, the friendly people—and think that, yes, this is the life for me. However, the Third World is not always the easiest place to get used to, especially if you haven't traveled much before.

Costa Rica can be truly wonderful. Still, you shouldn't jump into anything without checking it out thoroughly first. That's why I recommend an extended visit to Costa Rica before deciding whether to make a permanent move. Visit for a few weeks or, better yet, a few months. Check out different neighborhoods. Meet with other U.S. retirees. Visit grocery stores, gas stations, and post offices. I'm sure you'll fall in love with the place, as I did and as thousands of other U.S. retirees have done.

ADVANCE PREPARATION

Even if you decide to visit Costa Rica for only a few days, you must have a valid passport. This will allow you to stay in the country for ninety days, a stay which can be extended by another sixty days. If do you decide to stay longer, you can apply at the Departamento de Permisos Temporales y Prorrogas, at the Dirección de Migración y Extranjera. However, this can involve some heavy-duty paperwork. To avoid this, you might try simply leaving the country for a few days for a visit to Panama, Nicaragua, or elsewhere. You can then return to Costa Rica seventy-two hours later for another sixty- or ninety-day visit.

To apply for a passport for the first time, you must present, in person, a completed passport application at a U.S. State Department Passport Agency or at almost any U.S. Post Office or federal or state courthouse. Along with your application, you must present proof of U.S. citizenship such as a certified copy of your birth certificate, an ID that includes your signature and photo such as a driver's license, and two identical 2-inch photos. The fee is $65 and the passport is valid for ten years. You can renew your passport by mail for $55, a process that can take up to four weeks during peak travel periods.

Even if you're in the "just thinking about it" stage of trying to decide where to retire, definitely consider getting a subscription to the *Tico Times*, an informative and popular English-language weekly newspaper based in San José. Not only does it cover the news in Central America but it provides all kinds of information for foreigners living in Costa Rica, including a wide range of classified advertising and a long list of organizations catering to North Americans. To subscribe, contact:

Tico Times   Phone: 222-8952
Avenida 8, Calle 15
Apartado 4632
San José

Other things you might consider before taking off for Costa Rica include:

❑ Getting a calling card (AT&T, MCI, or Sprint) so that you can easily make long-distance calls from Costa Rica with no hassles.

❑ Purchasing a few good travel guidebooks on Costa Rica such as the *New Key to Costa Rica* by Beatrice Blake and Anne Becher, or the *Central American Handbook.*

❑ Obtaining some kind of health insurance (see section on insurance) to cover you while outside the country.

❑ Deciding who's going to collect your mail while you're gone; you might consider paying for a post office box in the United States. There are plenty of services that will fly your mail to you in Costa Rica on a daily basis.

❑ How much money you'll need. Be sure to take most of your money in traveler's checks.

❑ Reservations at a hotel in San José where you can stay upon arrival. You might want to send for information from the Costa Rica National Tourist Bureau in Miami.

FLYING TO COSTA RICA

You'll likely be flying the first time you visit Costa Rica. American Airlines, United, LACSA (the Costa Rican airline), and Iberia fly direct from Miami to San José. Many nonstop flights are available. American and LACSA also provide direct service from New York, and American flies direct from Dallas. (This is subject to change, of course.)

From Miami, it takes about two and a half hours to reach San José; from New York, about five and a half hours. When flying, you'll arrive in San José at the Juan Santamaría International Airport, about twelve miles from downtown San José. There's a tourist office and money-changing booths at the airport, and taxis are available outside. A taxi ride to the city costs $2 to $3. There are many rental-car offices at or near the airport, including Hertz, Avis, and Budget.

DRIVING TO COSTA RICA

To get to Costa Rica from Texas will likely take several days, if not a lot longer. Of course, if you stop along the way you can stretch such a journey out for weeks, even months. During the drive, you'll pass through Mexico, Guatemala, Honduras, and Nicaragua. That means a lot of border crossings, which in turn means a lot of major headaches, even for the most adventurous of souls.

Before you even set out for your trip, make certain your car is in good mechanical shape, preferably with a new set of tires and a decent spare or two. Make sure you carry a good tool kit and a flashlight. The Inter-American Highway is paved, but there are a couple of spots in Guatemala and Nicaragua that can place some wear and tear on your shock absorbers.

You should also carry a good supply of maps; a good source for these is the American Automobile Association (AAA). If you enter Mexico through McAllen, Texas, stop by Sanborn's Travel (there are plenty of signs to lead you there) to pick up some maps. While there, you can also buy auto insurance that's valid in Mexico and Central America, as well as an entertaining and informative travel-og to lead you along your journey.

Obviously, there are lots of spots to enter Mexico along the 1,700-mile U.S.-Mexico border. Most experts recommend driving the route along the Gulf Coast, primarily because it involves 1,400 fewer miles of driving over Mexican roads (San José, Costa Rica, is 3,700 miles from Tijuana and 2,300 miles from Brownsville), plus it allows you to stop by Sanborn's in McAllen, which is right next to Brownsville.

Experts also recommend not taking more belongings than absolutely necessary, and to not advise the Mexican customs and immigration officials that you are planning anything other than an every-day tourist visit to Mexico, to no particular destination. Why? Because if you say you're traveling to Central America, you probably will find yourself assigned to an officially escorted caravan through Mexico. This is something that's just come about in the last few years and is imposed in order to make sure you don't illegally sell any contraband merchandise in Mexico. I've heard plenty of horror stories about escorted trips through Mexico. They can be quite time-consuming and allow you no control over your travels.

If you take the Gulf Coast highway, passing through the port city of Veracruz, you should arrive at the southern Mexican border city of Tapachula after an easy five-day drive, depending on how many stops you make. Remember, never drive at night. The roads, with their stretches of gravel and strings of potholes, can be treacherous in the dark.

Just south of Tapachula, the highway divides between the mountain and coastal routes before entering Guatemala. It's faster and easier to take the coastal route and to head directly to Guatemala City, then on directly to San Pedro Sula, Honduras, skipping El Salvador. From San Pedro Sula, it's an uneventful one-day drive to Danll, via the mountain-ringed capital of Tegucigalpa, from where an early start the next day will allow you to get through Nicaragua to the Costa Rican border in one day. From there it's an easy six-hour drive to San José.

Be prepared for long waits at the borders. Sometimes it takes an hour or longer to get through. A modest tip to one of the many children who will undoubtedly bombard you, hoping to assist in guiding you through the maze of customs-immigration footwork, is a good investment and will save you some time. These children are especially useful if you don't speak Spanish.

The Honduran border is renowned as the worst crossing in Central America. When entering Honduras, be prepared to pass around money to various officials. Be sure to get a *transito*, or traffic permit, at the Honduran border, as this is the piece of paper that says you have permission to drive through Honduras. If you don't have one, you'll have to pay off police officers at stops all through the country. Also in Honduras, don't drive too fast, watch for traffic-control roadblocks, and be prepared to pay cops for absolutely no reason at all. Don't argue. Just hand $5 to anyone who gives you trouble.

Besides title of ownership, at most borders, you will need to show insurance coverage effective for the country you are entering. You will also likely be asked to pay a departure tax when leaving most countries.

Will You Be Retiring in Costa Rica?

Though Costa Rica is a very small country, it extends a generous welcome to Americans who want to spend their leisure years in a lovely and warm climate, away from the problems and stress of big-city life. Noted for its stability and economic progress, Costa Rica is an especially comfortable place to retire, with all the amenities of life in the United States. And the country's national parks and reserves make this an especially good destination for the nature lover. Prices in Costa Rica may be higher than they used to be, but this country south of the border remains a very desirable retirement destination.

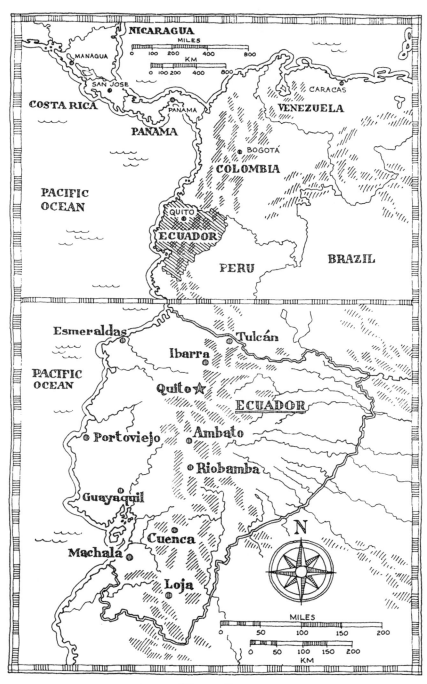

Ecuador

Ecuador

Each year, a magazine for travelers called *International Living* rates the world's top retirement havens. In 1994, Ecuador ranked eleventh overall. But it ranked first when it came to cost of living, taking into account the cost of property, utilities, groceries, and so on. And the magazine was right. Of all the countries discussed in this book, Ecuador is the cheapest. (By the way, Ecuador had been ranked the best retirement spot in 1993, but it lost first place because the country now imposes an import duty on personal belongings brought into the country by foreign retirees.) In fact, employees at the U.S. Embassy in Quito claim a person can live on $400 to $500 a month in Ecuador.

Why Here and Not Nevada?

I fell in love with Ecuador while visiting the town of Otavalo, just north of Quito, where master weavers were at their looms long before the Spaniards—or even the Incas—arrived. I had the most scrumptious lunch at a lovely restaurant with a name that doesn't do it justice—the Sisa Cafeteria. For less than $3, I ate grilled sea bass, bread, green beans, potatoes, and dessert—and it was a meal accompanied by the sound of seven talented men playing various Ecuadorean instruments.

In addition to the low cost, other reasons to retire in Ecuador include the climate, the country's stability, and its citizens. I think the people of Ecuador are friendlier than in any other Latin country I've visited, and that's saying a lot. When you ask people for directions, for example, they answer politely, and with the correct response! In other countries, Latins will often tell you anything just to keep from admitting they don't know the answer.

Besides that, the service is better, although not as good as in the United States. At a sidewalk café in Quito, I asked for a *pastel*, or a piece of cake. The waiter apologized, saying the restaurant was out. I grimaced. Immediately, the manager came over, insisting that they did have *pastel* after all. I had chocolate cake only because the waiter was told to run out and buy some for me at a nearby store.

In general, Ecuador's climate is comfortable, with maximum highs and lows that are pretty well static: about 72 to 80 degrees for the highs, and 45 to 50 for the lows. The dry months are May through October, and you can expect at least some mild afternoon showers the rest of the year.

Another lure of this Colorado-sized country is the comparative security it offers, as its Latin American neighbors increasingly scare off tourists with headlines of terrorism, drugs, and economic troubles. Although Ecuador's history in the twentieth century has been spotted with military coups, the country has sustained a democracy since 1979.

Ecuador is in the northwest corner of South America. It straddles the equator, which gives the country its name. Ecuador is located south of Colombia. Peru is to the south and east, with the Pacific Ocean to the west. Ecuador has three different zones, each marked by its own ecology: Costa (coast), Sierra (highlands), and Oriente (jungle). Most of the population lives along the coast or in the Sierra. And you could consider the Galápagos Islands another ecological region. Located about 600 miles from the mainland, these islands are popular with tourists and are known for their unusual animal life, including the giant tortoises. The finches of the Galápagos were studied by Charles Darwin and formed the basis for his theory of natural selection.

The country has beautiful beaches that aren't nearly as developed with condominiums and hotels as they are in places such as Mexico or Costa Rica. Salinas and Playas, both beach towns, are a short drive from the large seaport of Guayaquil. Punta Carnero Inn, near Salinas, is a paradise for those who like deep-sea fishing, with black marlin in abundance. From Quito, you can reach beaches such as Atacamés, Súa, Playa Ancha, and Tonsupa by car in five hours or less.

FACTS AT A GLANCE

Population:	12 million
Ethnic groups:	Indians 25 percent, Mestizos 65 percent, Spanish 7 percent, Africans and Asians make up the rest
Religion:	95 percent Roman Catholic
Languages:	Spanish and Quechua
Monetary unit:	Sucre
Head of state:	President
Political system:	Constitutional democracy
Industries:	Petroleum, pharmaceuticals, balsa wood
Literacy rate:	90 percent
Capital:	Quito
Crops:	Bananas, coffee, rice, sugar, and corn
Average temperature:	60 to 70 degrees
Square mileage:	109,500 square miles
Rainy season:	November through May
American population:	2,000 to 3,000

One negative aspect of the country may be its altitude. Quito is more than 9,000 feet above sea level, and it could take some time to acclimate. High altitudes mean the sun is particularly strong, so you have to be extra careful of sunburn and sunstroke. But this is a minor consideration when you take into account the attractions of this country, which hasn't yet been visited by many U.S. retirees. It can be your own personal discovery!

The People and the Culture

Ecuador is home to some 12 million people, half of whom live in the country's Costa region west of the Andes, and nearly half of whom live in the Andean Sierra. Very few people live in the Oriente, or the jungles. In the city, the people dress just like you or I would at home in the United States. But in the rural areas, Ecuadorean women wear beautiful panchos or blankets draped around the upper halves of their bodies, and on their heads they almost always wear hats. The women usually wear strings of necklaces, sometimes covering their whole neck. Apparently, this is considered a status symbol; the more you wear, the richer you are considered to be.

SOME BACKGROUND INFORMATION

About 65 percent of Ecuador's population is mestizo, or mixed Spanish and Indian, and 25 percent is Indian. About 7 percent is Caucasian and the remainder is of African and Asian descent. Alas, the country suffers sharp racial divisions. White Ecuadorans sometimes regard themselves as being better than Indians, and they've held sway over the economy and politics for centuries without serious challenge. In general, though, Ecuadorans are very friendly and will invariably go out of their way to help strangers. In the major cities, you'll find many Ecuadorans to be well educated and well traveled, and very welcoming toward North Americans.

Ecuador has two official languages: Spanish and Quechua, the language of the former Inca empire. English is spoken, though, in hotels and tourist shops and in major visitor centers.

Families in Ecuador are very close-knit. The elderly are respected and cared for by family members, with many generations sometimes living under the same roof. Dating begins later here, at around age eighteen, and couples usually marry in their early twenties. Young people often hold jobs, and frequently both parents work.

There is a large disparity in the income distribution in Ecuador. More than 40 percent of the national income goes to the richest 5 percent of the population, one of the highest ratios in the world. About 12 percent of the people live in abject poverty. Yet no matter how poor the people, almost everyone tries to keep his or her home clean and nicely furnished on the inside, while placing less emphasis on the appearance of the outside.

THE LOCAL CUSTOMS

Like all countries, Ecuador has its idiosyncrasies, and anyone who plans to make this country his or her home should be aware of them.

These aren't hard and fast rules, and Ecuador has seen its share of foreigners who don't know local custom, but you might try being a bit "Ecuadorean" while in Ecuador. A handshake is usually used when meeting someone for the first time, and is always used in subsequent greetings, as in the United States. Women who are friends may kiss each other on the cheek, while men often embrace. When calling out a greeting, one will usually say "Hola," meaning hello.

Excessive gesturing with the hands is considered impolite. You should not motion with your head to indicate a yes or no. Touching another person of the same sex is acceptable and shows friendly concern.

When visiting someone, it is considered polite for visitors to sincerely compliment the host or hostess on his or her family and home. After a meal or when receiving a gift, it is common for the recipient to thank the host or hostess profusely. Also, don't play the Hollywood movie star. Remove your sunglasses when talking.

You can dress casually, but always dress neatly and conservatively. Clothes are very important to Ecuadorans, and even the poor often buy one good outfit so that they can be well dressed in public.

Most stores close daily at siesta time, which lasts about three hours during the lunch period, as is the custom in most of Latin America. Ecuadorans usually eat at home on Sunday evenings, so you'll find many restaurants are closed. If you do eat out on Sunday, find a restaurant early. When trying to catch a taxi, stand on the street and raise your hand. Ask the fare before boarding.

A BRIEF HISTORY OF THE COUNTRY

Because Ecuadorans consider their history a source of pride, it is something you should be familiar with. You'll see evidence of this history everywhere, from the Inca artifacts at museums, to the popular Indian tapestries, to the superb churches whose interiors shine with the glitter of gold.

The nation was part of the Inca empire until it fell to Spanish conquistadors in 1533. Like its counterparts in Mexico and Guatemala—the Aztec and Maya civilizations—the Inca culture was as sophisticated as that of the Europeans who conquered them. It wasn't until the early nineteenth century that Simón Bolívar, "The Great Liberator," helped to free Ecuador from the Spanish, and statues depicting this well-loved man can be found all over Latin America.

When the Spaniards departed, they left behind a vast collection of colonial art and architectural treaures, the most impressive of which may be the La Compañía Church, whose richly carved facade is the most ornate in Quito and whose interior is a dazzle of golden altars, gilded columns, and intricate balconies.

Following an unsuccessful federation with Peru, Colombia, and Venezuela, Ecuador began the long, difficult road toward political stability and real democracy. In this period, there wasn't much job security in being leader of Ecuador. In its first ninety-five years of independence (1822-1917), Ecuador had forty presidents, dictators, and juntas. And from 1925 to 1948, none of the twenty-two presidents or chiefs of state was able to complete his term in office. Meanwhile, as the result of a 1942 war with Peru, Ecuador lost a significant portion of its Amazon territory—the border change is still a source of friction.

With the election of Sixto Durán Ballen in 1992, the fourth democratically elected president since the military relinquished power and permanently returned to the barracks in 1979, Ecuador has slowly emerged from its economic shell. Inflation has been tamed, tariffs have been lowered, and government spending has been slashed. Durán ran for president as a candidate of the United Republican Party coalition. After the election, he made peace with the Social Christian Party and was able to enjoy a working majority in the congress.

GOVERNMENT

There are twenty-one provinces in Ecuador, including the Galápagos Islands. The provinces are like states, divided into cantons and parishes for administration. The president and vice-president are elected for four-year terms. The president may not stand for reelection. The legislative branch consists of a single Chamber of Representatives of seventy-seven members, of which sixty-five are provincial representatives elected for a two-year term and twelve are national representatives elected for a four-year term.

A Look at Living Costs

Living costs in Ecuador depend largely on where you live and how you live. If you live in Otavalo, you can rent a bedroom and bathroom in a house for $50 a month and shop in the local Indian market; your expenses will barely dent your wallet. If you live in a swanky section of Quito, you can rent a condominium for $1,000 a month and shop at supermarkets for imported products; your expenses can total more than what you would live on in the United States.

In Ecuador, you'll spend a lot to purchase a car, but taxis and buses are cheap. Medical care is inexpensive, as is food. But appliances are costly, and so is private laundry service. U.S. brands of consumer goods always cost a lot more than local brands, yet sometimes the local brands are better. Local soups, for example, are superior to some American brands. So it's up to you as to what your retirement budget will allow you to buy. As is usually the case, the farther you live from Quito, the lower the cost of living. But life in Quito is still very inexpensive compared with life in Miami or Phoenix.

TIPPING GUIDE

Not only are taxis cheap in Ecuador, but you don't have to tip the taxi drivers. At least it's not the custom, although some tourists pay a little extra when they are especially happy with the service received.

Restaurants usually include a 10 percent surcharge for service in the bill. However, another 3 to 5 percent extra is expected as a tip in nicer places. When dining or shopping, you'll be approached by Ecuadorans, usually young boys, who want to watch your parked car. Allow them to do so—it's better than taking the chance that something might happen to the car. You'll have to give them some change for a tip, maybe 50 cents or so.

You should also tip bellboys or the hotel doorman who takes luggage to your room—once again, just some change is ample—as well as the person who provides room service.

At a service station, the usual tip for checking the oil, tires, water, and so on and for washing the windshield is about 50 cents. The carry-out boy at the supermarket could be given the equivalent of a quarter. The hairdresser, too, should receive a small tip.

In general, tipping in Ecuador is a flexible matter, and common sense should be your guide. One thing to note: in Ecuador, Christmas bonuses to those people who provide services are the norm, so you might want to consider giving a few dollars to people such as the postman, guard, gardener, garbage collector, and/or caretaker.

COSTS AT A SUPERMAXI GROCERY STORE IN QUITO

Butter (4 sticks)	$0.59
Cheerios (1 box)	$2.82
Fab detergent (1 kilogram)	$2.00
Cat Chow (3$^1/_2$ pounds)	$6.56
Ponds cream (180 grams)	$4.04
Palmolive soap (1 bar)	$0.49
Colgate toothpaste (1 tube)	$1.47
Chicken legs (1 package)	$3.21
Ketchup (1 bottle)	$1.01
Lean ground beef (1 pound)	$1.00
Local coffee (1 pound)	$1.33
Paper towels (1 roll)	$0.90
Rice (2 kilos)	$1.28
Sugar (2 kilos)	$0.94
Campbell's chicken noodle soup (1 can)	$1.03
Kraft macaroni and cheese (1 box)	$0.92
Vegetable oil (1 liter)	$1.25

Immigration Rules and Regulations

If you want to stay in Ecuador just for a short time—three months or less—all you need is a valid passport and a return ticket. No visa is necessary for stays of less than ninety days. You will be issued a tourist card on arrival, which you need to hang on to throughout your stay. When you're issued the tourist card, you'll be asked how long you plan to stay in Ecuador. It's better to over-state your departure date than to understate it, if you're unsure, because you will be fined if you stay over the time limit on your tourist card.

Although this probably won't apply to you, foreigners who want to remain more than ninety days in Ecuador to do business

Tuna, local brand (1 can)	$0.59
Other Costs	
Super unleaded gas (1 gallon)	$1.40 to $1.50
Panasonic color 21-inch TV	$523.00
Taxi rides within cities	$1.00 to $3.00
Round-trip airfare between Quito and Cuenca	$60.00
Ten pounds of laundry done in Quito	$7.00
Doctor's visit	$20.00 to $40.00
Telephone (monthly base rate)	$0.21
Utilities (monthly range)	$30.00 to $70.00
Live-in maid (month)	$51.00
Auto insurance (annual premium)	$177.00
Taxi fare for 2-kilometer trip	$0.61
Meal (w/wine, 1 person) in Quito	$12.00
Cinema ticket	$1.00
Camera film (35 mm color prints, 36 exp.)	$4.96
Oil change and minor maintenance	$22.00

must submit a letter requesting a six-month visa, along with a valid passport, six passport-size photos, proof of round-trip transportation, a financial statement from their bank proving financial responsibility, and a letter from their firm showing terms of employment. The last two items must be translated into Spanish and notarized by the county clerk. There is no visa fee, but there is a $25 charge for document legalization. Visa applications can be processed within one day. Visas can be renewed for additional six-month periods once in Ecuador by applying to the country's Interior Ministry.

Regulations affecting foreign retirees have changed somewhat in recent years, and may change again at any time. Currently, retirees must obtain an immigrant visa if they want to live in Ecuador. It usually takes six months to a year to get one. You must show proof that you have enough money to live on, although no regulation establishes what that amount should be. You must also present a birth certificate, a health certificate, a copy of your police record, a marriage certificate, if applicable, and a copy of your passport. All presented documents have to be translated into Spanish and notarized.

If you want to work in Ecuador, you must do so legally with a proper visa. If you have only a tourist visa, you won't be allowed to be involved in any commercial activity or to be employed by any company.

There are several different kinds of visas, and each allows you to be engaged in a different activity. One type of visa is issued to those people who live on income from abroad. Another is issued to those people who invest in the purchase of real estate. Yet another is issued to people who invest in industry, agriculture, or the export trade. You can get more information about visas from the consulate nearest your U.S. city of residence before you go.

My advice is to go to Ecuador on a tourist visa, and then, if you decide to stay, visit the Citizens Services section of the U.S. Embassy in Quito for information about visas. You'll have to go by there anyway to discuss the distribution of your Social Security and pension checks, should you decide to live in Ecuador. It's also recommended that all U.S. citizens living or traveling in Ecuador register at the U.S. Embassy upon arrival. Once you fill out a registration card, it can be used as proof of U.S. citizenship should you lose your passport.

If you need help with the immigration process, or for more thorough, up-to-date information, seek assistance from an attorney. The U.S. Embassy can provide a list of English-speaking attorneys in Ecuador, as well as a list of reputable accounting firms. You should also seek information about visas at the consulate nearest your city of residence before leaving for Ecuador.

Financial Matters

The sucre is Ecuador's unit of currency, abbreviated "S/." There are 5, 10, 20, 50, 100, 500, 1,000, and 5,000-sucre bills, and coins for the lower denominations. One sucre has one hundred centavos, or cents, but inflation has made even one-sucre coins inconsequential. Mastercard, Visa, American Express, and Diner's Club credit cards are honored in many shops and restaurants.

CURRRENCY EXCHANGE

Cambios, or exchange houses, are located in all of Ecuador's major cities. Rodrigo Paz and M.M. Jaramillo *cambios* are recommended by North Americans because you might be able to bargain a better rate. In addition, there are plenty of money-changing booths at the airport in Quito, including one that will change traveler's checks. These booths stay open until the last flight comes in each day.

It's easy in Ecuador to change U.S. traveler's checks into U.S. currency. In addition to *cambios,* you can exchange money at most hotels and banks. Traveler's checks can be changed at most places within major cities as well, but a surcharge may be collected. It can be difficult, however, to change traveler's checks and foreign currency outside the main cities. (In Otavalo, the Inti-Express is a good place to change money.) Visa checks seem to be easier to cash than American Express checks. (Just the opposite of the way it is in most countries.) No currency controls exist in Ecuador, and the sucre is traded freely.

Credit card purchases will be converted at the time your bill is processed, rather than when the charge is made. With steady devaluation of the sucre, credit card purchases will likely become less expensive.

BANKING

It can be extremely difficult to juggle finances when making a move overseas, or even when trying out a new country for a few months' time. My advice is to maintain your U.S. accounts, at least for a while, until you figure out if you like Ecuador and how the banking system works.

One helpful source in dealing with your finances is Citizens Services at the U.S. Embassy in Quito. The Embassy collects about 1,180 pension and Social Security checks each month for U.S. citizens living in Ecuador. Employees at the Embassy assured me that you can have a bank account in Ecuador, including a dollar account, so you'll have somewhere to deposit your pension and/or Social Security checks. Many Americans purchase certificates of deposit in Ecuador, on which they earn about 30 percent interest.

The U.S. Social Security Administration now offers its most popular publications in electronic format via the Retirement Living

Forum, available on CompuServe. Or you can contact the Social Security Administration via phone or mail to get a copy of available publications, which include one on getting checks overseas. You should do this well in advance of your move. The agency maintains a toll-free phone number, 1-800-772-1213, to reply to individual questions about Social Security benefits.

  Banks in Ecuador are open to the public from 9:00 a.m. to 1:30 p.m., and some banks stay open until 6:00 p.m. to receive payments, cash checks, and provide financial advice or counseling. The following U.S. banks have branches in Quito and will be able to offer assistance:

Bank of America   Phone: 2-56-48-34
Avenida Amazonas y Patria,   Fax: 2-56-49-57
Casilla 344
Quito

Citibank   Phone: 2-56-33-00
Juan Leon Mera 130   Fax: 2-56-68-95
y Patria
Quito

Also, Avenida 9 de Octubre 416 Phone: 4-31-17-80
y Chile   Fax: 4-32-87-76
Guayaquil

TAXES: U.S. AND ECUADOREAN

Remember that Americans residing in foreign countries are exempt from U.S. tax on the first $80,000 of income. Nevertheless, you are required to file an income tax return. The U.S. Internal Revenue Service has a special department, called IRS-International, for expatriates filing income-tax returns. The office offers tax assistance over the phone and in person, publishes tax guides, and holds workshops. For more information contact:

Internal Revenue Service   Phone: 202-874-1460.
Assistant Commissioner (International)
Attn: IN:C:TPS
950 L'Enfant Plaza South, S.W.
Washington, DC 20024

The Consular Section of the U.S. Embassy in Quito has federal income tax forms but no state income tax forms. The consular employees can assist you in finding forms and answering basic questions, but keep in mind that they are not trained tax advisors.

Ecuador has a value-added and service tax of 10 percent. It is charged on most goods, imported or made locally, and on a number of specified services. Municipal real estate taxes vary from 0.3 percent to 3.0 percent. There is a $25 airport tax that must be paid upon leaving the country via plane.

There used to be special tax breaks in Latin countries for retirees, but little by little, governments have done away with these breaks in an effort to bring in money. At one time, Ecuador placed no import duties on belongings brought in by retirees, but that eventually changed. Now, just like everyone else, you have to pay import taxes, which vary according to item. However, this could change at any time if the government decides that it needs to attract more North Americans.

LOCAL INVESTMENT OPPORTUNITIES

In developing countries, especially small ones like Ecuador, few efforts are more important than that of exporting new products. Therefore, the government is very supportive of investments in this area. If you're the type of person who just has to be dabbling financially in something to keep you happy, you will find a good number of investment opportunities in Ecuador. The government has implemented a substantial program to promote Ecuadorean and foreign investment in the export of a wide variety of products.

For example, asparagus production has grown significantly in the last few years. In addition, Ecuador cultivates more than 3,000 species of orchids—about 10 percent of the world's total species—making this another popular item for export. (The largest orchid importers are Germany and the United States.) Other items exported from this South American country include handicrafts, woven goods, fine woods, tea, strawberries, and potatoes, as well as a number of other fruits and vegetables.

For more information about business opportunities in Ecuador, contact the following associations:

**Cámara de Comercio
de Quito**
(Quito Chamber of Commerce)
Avenida Amazonas y de la
República
Quito

Phone: 2-45-27-30

**Departamento de Promoción
de Exportaciones**
(Export Promotion Board)
Avenidas Juan Leon Mera and
Roca
Quito

Phone: 2-54-89-80

**Dirección Nacional
de Comercio Exterior**
(Foreign Trade Office)
Avenidas Juan Leon Mera
and Roca
Quito

Phone: 2-54-18-54

**Ecuadoran-American
Association**
150 Nassau Street, Suite 2015
New York, NY 10038

Phone: 212-233-7776

**Federación Ecuatoriana
de Exportadores**
(Exporter's Association)
Apartado 187-B
Quito

Phone: 2-45-27-69
Fax: 2-44-05-74

**Federación Nacional de
Cámaras de Comercio**
(Nacional Federation of
Chambers of Commerce)
Apartado 202, Avenida Olmedo
Guayaquil

Phone: 2-45-30-11

Rentals and Real Estate

One of your most important concerns, and rightly so, is where
you're going to live, should you decide to retire to Ecuador. Is it better to rent a house or apartment, or stay in a hotel while you try to
find a place to buy? I recommend renting for several months, if not
years, before purchasing property unless you're used to life overseas. Everyone needs time to get adjusted to new surroundings and
to make certain that a new, very different lifestyle is right for him or
her. There are plenty of houses, apartments, and condominiums in
Quito, as well as in Guayaquil, Otavalo, and Cuenca. You will just
have to spend some time looking.

Obviously, some people like to search out neighborhoods that
are full of English-speaking Americans and that offer all the ameni-

ties. Others opt for quiet, Ecuadorean communities in the hopes of learning the language and fully experiencing a different culture. If you don't have a car, you must consider the distance to supermarkets, pharmacies, and other businesses so that you can take a bus or a taxi, or walk.

The best way to find out what's available and to gauge prices is to check the classified ads in the daily newspapers. Prices have risen in recent years owing to increased demand for houses in Ecuador's major cities. Still, housing costs are cheaper than in most U.S. and European cities.

HOUSES, APARTMENTS, AND CONDOS

Quito has houses and apartments ranging from colonial stucco and tiled-roof mansions to ultramodern town houses with large windows and simple features. Most of the newer homes are split-level or multilevel. Many houses have three to five bedrooms, two or more baths, and servants' quarters. Most houses have walls or fences around the grounds and very small yards. Lower-floor windows will likely have protective grillwork. Apartment buildings usually have guards or doormen.

Some houses come with no fixtures, stoves, or refrigerators, so you should check with agents or owners before signing a contract. Also, make certain that a special water supply, required in Quito housing, is provided for in your lease.

THE PLACES WHERE RETIREES LIVE

Well-known residential neighborhoods in Quito that are popular with Americans—and therefore are more expensive—include one along González Suárez Avenue, near the Hotel Quito. Others are called El Batán, La Carolíña, Quito Tenis, Bellavista, and El Bosque. Less expensive and exclusive neighborhoods that can be quite nice include El Inca, Jipijapa, Granda Centeno, La Granja, and La Floresta. Obviously, you'll want to drive or walk around these neighborhoods both during the day and at night. Talk to other Americans and find out what they recommend. Ask neighbors about crime problems.

If you're looking for a more peaceful atmosphere—the traffic in Quito can be a nightmare—the Valley of Los Chillos, about twenty minutes outside Quito, is a pleasant place to live. The valley has general stores, banks, grocery stores, and the like, but it's calmer, and also a bit warmer, than Quito.

Quito

Quito is considered one of the most beautiful cities in the Western Hemisphere and is known for its astonishing location—more than a mile above sea level, nestled high in the Andes Mountains beneath the sparkling snow-cone of the Pichincha mountain and almost directly on the equator.

Quito is a small city, easy to navigate, but not so small that it does not boast a healthy nightlife of salsa clubs, all-night discos, and quiet, elegant drinking establishments. Popular residential areas include Gonzáles Suárez, about three miles from the city center and close to Quito's largest park; Bellavista, a hilly suburban neighborhood where many Ecuadorean diplomats live; and El Valle, a flat suburban community about ten miles from the city center. El Valle is well liked because it is less congested than other areas and less expensive, although it boasts commercial centers just like Quito.

Other districts favored by expatriates include La Mariscal for apartments, El Condado and La Caroliña for houses, and El Batán for both. Moderate-rent areas in Quito include Kennedy, El Inca, and Chaupicruz. Higher rents are charged in Pinar Alto and Montserrin.

Other Areas

After you've spent some time getting to know Quito, rent a car and take the Pan American Highway north to the province of Imbabura, fifty-five miles north of Quito. You can visit the town of Otavalo, situated in the rugged lake district about 8,530 feet above sea level. Locals say that about forty "gringo," or American, families live in Otavalo, taking advantage of houses that rent for less than $250 a month. Other attractions in the area include the town of Cotacachi, the Cuicocha Lake, the city of Ibarra, and the San Pablo Lake.

To ask questions about the area or to sign up for a tour, stop by the ever-informative Inti-Express in Otavalo at Sucre 11-06 y Colón. The phone number is 2-92-14-36. (You can also change money there.) An employee reports that apartments in Otavalo rent for $50 to $75 a month, and houses go for $150 to $250 a month.

A short (thirty- to forty-minute) flight from Quito is Cuenca, another spot you may want to consider for long-term residency. Ecuadorans consider Cuenca their most beautiful city, and most Americans would agree. Cuenca is the country's third-largest city—the population tops 300,000—but since paved roads were not laid between Cuenca and the cities of Quito and Guayaquil until the 1960s, Cuenca has managed to maintain its colonial architecture despite an influx of tourists. The city's skyline is marked by shining church domes. Cobblestone streets, winding rivers, graceful iron-work balconies, and beautiful gardens add to the atmosphere of this historic city.

You'll get a taste of shopping in this city by visiting the weekly fair on Thursdays and the weekly market on Saturdays, popular for crafts as well as fresh produce. Both are located at the squares titled 9 de Octubre and 10 de Agosto. I loved the daily flower market just off the central square. You'll see some Americans in this town, studying Spanish and sipping cappuccino at Café Austria, or eating a candlelight dinner for two of lobster and other delicacies, plus wine, for $35 at El Jardin restaurant. Believe it or not, Cuenca reminded me of a New York City neighborhood sometimes, especially at about 6:00 or 6:30 p.m. Everyone hustles and bustles about, picking up flowers at corner stands or smelling fruits and vegetables at streetside groceries. The sidewalks are narrow, and people walk fast. There are lots of antique shops, and bread shops, and wrought-iron balconies. Many art galleries and places featuring live music and Spanish schools are here, too. And there are plenty of police-men, so there's very little crime. As in Antigua, Guatemala, you'll find people in the churches day and night, and you might come upon a religious procession any day of the week. The mild climate, pre-colonial ruins, lake-studded national park, and Indian markets make Cuenca worthy of consideration.

Guayaquil, Ecuador's largest city, with more than 1.8 million people, might also be worth a visit, although you might not bump into any retirees who have made this busy seaport their home. The tropical city has an exciting nightlife, full of casinos, discos, night-clubs, and outdoor cafés. The seafood is tasty, and it's an easy drive to the beaches. Guayaquil is also popular with fishing and boating buffs. Still, this business-oriented city has never been known to draw large crowds of tourists, and most people stop here only en route to the Galápagos. Another problem is that Guayaquil can become sti-flingly hot from December to April, with temperatures hovering near 90 degrees.

RENTING: WHAT IT WILL COST

As with houses, some apartments in Ecuador are rented without appliances or fixtures, so you must check with the owner before signing a lease. Newer apartments can be hard to find, and so can furnished units. Check in the English-language *Q* magazine for apartments, as well as in the classified sections of local newspapers. Usually, one month's rent must be paid in advance, with an additional month's rent (or a bank guarantee) required as a security deposit.

An extremely nice one-bedroom unfurnished apartment in Quito will likely rent for $300 to $425; a two-bedroom unfurnished apartment will rent for $475 to $525; and a three-bedroom, or bigger, unfurnished apartment will rent for $900 to $1,250. Furnished apartments go for $450 to $550 for a one-bedroom; $750 to $800 for a two-bedroom; and $1,200 to $1,550 for anything three bedrooms or larger.

Two-, three-, and four-bedroom unfurnished homes may rent for $650 to $750; $1,000 to $1,125; and $1,300 to $1,600, respectively. For furnished homes, the prices may run $900 to $925; $1,200 to $1,450; and $1,500 to $1,800.

In Quito, condominium prices can range from $500 to more than $1,000. An American doctor named Cary Frouman says he pays $240 a month for a furnished, two-bedroom apartment with color television, washing machine, and all appliances, located in the Quito neighborhood of Las Casas. "Most Americans, like myself, live on the north side of town," he said. "You have to be careful because sometimes people charge foreigners more than locals."

Obviously, rentals are cheaper outside Quito. A long-time resident of Otavalo told me that apartments rent for $50 to $75 a month, and that houses rent for $150 to $250. In Cuenca, you'll pay $100 on up for a nice apartment, $400 to $500 for a condominium. When I was there, one apartment complex called Apartamentos Atorongo was renting one-bedroom furnished apartments for $225 a month, which included a refrigerator, stove, daily maid service, electricity, and water. The price also included a daily change of sheets and towels!

BUYING PROPERTY AND FINANCING THE DEAL

Officials at the U.S. Embassy say that most Americans pay cash when they buy property. However, with a special certification letter from the U.S. Embassy, some Americans have been able to get loans from banks in Ecuador. But, in general, payment terms are not very favorable and interest terms are so high that it is more attractive to pay cash if you can afford to. And, at best, many banks will provide mortgages of up to only 50 percent.

Quito has many real estate brokers. Most advertise in local newspapers and in the phone book. You should deal only with agencies that have a recognized reputation and experience. Agencies usually charge the owner of the house or apartment a commission to find either a tenant or a buyer. In the case of sales, the commission that the owner must pay ranges from 3 to 6 percent of the sales price.

A necessity for anyone buying a home abroad is reliable legal assistance from someone who speaks English. You can obtain a list of English-speaking attorneys from the U.S. Embassy.

UTILITIES: WHAT YOU'LL PAY

Utilities in Ecuador are not always reliable, but at least they are cheap. The cost of electricity, gas, and water is not usually included in rental costs. But, for two people, you're likely to pay just $10 to $30 a month for electricity, $2 to $3 a month for gas, and $10 to $20 a month for water. Costs are kept to a minimum because most homes and apartments in Ecuador, where the temperature is generally pleasant year-round, lack central air conditioning and heat, although many have fireplaces or electric baseboard heat.

Bills are delivered to each house each month. Take the bill to the nearest collection office (the addresses are printed on the back of the bill). Services can be debited from your bank account for your convenience as well, if you authorize it.

Electric current in Ecuador is 120V; 220V is also available and should be reserved for electric ranges and dryers. Square, two-pronged plugs are used most of the time. This means that you'll be able to use your appliances in Ecuador without using converters.

It's not easy to get a new phone line, as it is in the United States. I strongly recommend that if a telephone is important to you, and it probably should be, you need to rent or purchase a home or apartment that comes with this service because it takes a long time—sometimes years—for the phone company to process requests for new phones. Installation fees are also quite high, running $300 and up in some cases.

You are responsible for keeping up with your monthly telephone bill, even if you fail to receive a bill in the mail one month. You can either pay at the nearest Ecuadorean Telecommunications Institute (IETEL) office or authorize your bank to pay the bill.

There are many problems with telephone service, something you'll just have to learn to accept if you want to live in Latin America. However, it's not nearly as bad in Ecuador as it can be in places like, say, Guatemala. Still, there are reports of crossed calls, wrong numbers, dead telephones, and difficulties in making a connection. There are recordings to inform you when an exchange is congested or if a number dialed does not exist. The government is trying to privatize IETEL, and service is expected to get better in the next few years. If your telephone is out of order, call 132 (from a different phone, obviously) and they will take your repair order.

Setting Up, Settling In

Finding an apartment or house is only the first step in establishing a retirement residence. You'll want to know how to stay informed, receive mail, and telephone home, as well as furnish your home and obtain household help. These are all easily arranged.

NEWSPAPERS, MAGAZINES, TELEVISION, MOVIES

Quito has two independent morning newspapers, *El Comercio* and *Hoy*, and two afternoon papers, *Ultimas Notícias* and *La Hora*. Newspapers are sold on the streets and in neighborhood stores, and can also be delivered to the home. The *Ecuadorean Times* is available in English.

If you want to keep up with news from home, the international edition of the *Miami Herald* is usually flown to Quito daily and is available by subscription for $32 a month. The international editions of *Time* and *Newsweek* magazines are available weekly at about $2.25 and $75 a year by subscription. Also, *USA Today* has an international edition that is usually sold at major newsstands.

English-language books can be found at Los Libros del Mundo, which has locations all over Quito. The Binational Centers in Quito and Guayaquil subscribe to dozens of English-language periodicals. And the British-American Women's Club runs a small library of English-language books.

You can also keep up with the help of cable TV beamed from the United States. Cable is available by subscription, and costs vary from $15 to $35 a month, depending on the number of stations you choose. U.S. network TV is available, as are movie channels and CNN. Shortwave reception is very good. Both Voice of America and BBC can be heard clearly.

To make you feel more at home than you might want to feel, there are plenty of radio stations playing American pop music from the 1970s and 1980s.

MAIL SERVICE

Keeping in touch via mail does pose a minor problem, as it does in all Third World countries. However, in Ecuador, the postal system is at least adequate and better than in most Central American countries. The average time for a letter to reach the United States is seven to ten days.

Postage depends on the distance and weight. Airmail letters to New York cost about 20 cents. It is quite common not to mail packages abroad, but to send them with someone you trust who is traveling and can mail them in the country of destination. If a letter is important, it might be a good idea to certify it. When you buy stamps, request certificado so that the letter will be stamped separately.

The main post office in Quito is at Eloy Alfaro between 9 de Octubre and 10 de Agosto. There are branches around the city.

If you're worried about getting your mail from back home, there is a new mail service designed to assist you by picking it up and having it forwarded to you on a weekly basis. For more information, contact:

Personal Mail International (PMI)   Phone: 201-543-6001
P.O. Box 311
Mendham, New Jersey 07945- 0311

TELEPHONE SERVICE

The best way to contact friends and family back home by phone is through the use of credit cards or calling cards. This allows you to reach an English-speaking operator, then reverse charges or charge the call to any place you like.

To use an AT&T card, dial 119 to be connected with an AT&T operator. For further information within the United States, call 1-

800-874-4000, Ext. 359. For MCI customers, dial 170 to be connected with an MCI operator. For further information within the United States, call 1-800-444-2222. For Sprint customers, dial 171 to be connected with a Sprint operator. For further information within the United States, call 1-800-877-4646.

To dial direct to the United States from Ecuador without using a credit card, you must dial 00-1-area code-local number. Calls to the United States and Canada generally run about $2.50 for the first minute and about $1.50 for each subsequent minute. Calls are cheaper on Sunday and at night.

To call Ecuador from the United States, you must dial 593-2 plus the number for numbers in Quito; 593-4 plus the number for numbers in Guayaquil; and 593-7 plus the number for numbers in Cuenca. Remember that you must dial 011 before calling any number in Ecuador from the United States.

FURNISHING A HOME, FROM SILVERWARE TO APPLIANCES

It's not as easy to bring U.S. belongings into Ecuador as it once was. The government now imposes an import duty on personal belongings brought into the country by foreign retirees. Therefore it's not really a good idea to import appliances, although they are expensive in Ecuador. You should try to find apartments and houses that come equipped with what you need.

A few items you might consider bringing with you from the States, if you are serious about living in Ecuador, are small appliances because they can cost a bundle if you purchase them there. Because of the lack of central heat, it's also a good idea to bring electric blankets and space heaters if the cold bothers you. You might also want to bring a small television set. (Keep in mind though that there will be import duties charged on all these items.) A color TV in Quito can cost you $575 to $750. Because Quito experiences occasional blackouts—usually lasting only a very short time—all sensitive electronic equipment such as microwaves, stereos, and computers should be connected to surge protectors, and you should bring these from home.

There are companies that will supply you with a wide range of appliances for use around the world. Costs are lower than they would be overseas, and many provide dual-voltage appliances that may be used in the United States as well as in Latin countries. Be sure to provide the company with the proper voltage, cycles, and broadcast frequency for your new home. The companies normally handle all shipping details. For more information, contact the following companies:

Appliances Overseas   Phone: 212-545-8001
276 Fifth Avenue, Suite 407   Fax: 212-545-8005
New York, NY 10001-4509

East West International   Phone: 713-789-6611
6300 Westpark, Suite 600   Fax: 713-789-6662
Houston, TX 77057

L.A.W. International   Phone: 713-558-5600
13711 Westheimer, Suite L
Houston, TX 77077

Ecuador's craftspeople can make fine furniture, provided that the correct, well-seasoned woods are used. Good upholstery, coverings, and fabrics are expensive and hard to find. However, furniture repairs are good and easy to arrange.

CLOTHES YOU'LL WANT

Whatever you do, bring some warm clothes because it can get chilly at night in Quito, and downright cold in some other parts of Ecuador. Bring sweaters, jackets, and a raincoat. You'll be surprised in the countryside by how bundled up people stay, wrapped with layers of clothing. (Yet they go barefoot. Don't take this idea to heart.)

Of course, there are plenty of beautiful handmade sweaters and blankets that can be purchased throughout Ecuador. Sunglasses and a sun hat are also recommended. Informal or casual clothing is worn most of the time. For Guayaquil, only summer clothing is needed. Lots of stylish clothing can be purchased in Ecuador; however, women's shoes in sizes about $8^1/_2$ or larger are difficult to find.

BRINGING BOWSER AND BUTTONS WITH YOU

The one "comfort" you can bring from home is your pet, although it requires some advance footwork. Although prior authorization for entry is required, Ecuador has no quarantine for pets.

To import your pet, you must get a notarized Good Health Certificate from a veterinarian and a paper from the Ecuadorean consulate that says the animal was examined and is free of contagious disease. The certificate must include the animal's pedigree, species, sex, age, and license number. In addition, dogs require a rabies inoculation certificate issued within three months of arrival in Ecuador. (Rabies is a problem in Ecuador.) Besides all that, the airport of origin must send a telex or fax to the Ecuadorean airport at least twelve hours in advance of your trip so that a veterinarian can be present to inspect the pet upon its arrival. Pets also require an export permit when leaving Ecuador, which can be obtained from the head office of Agriculture and Livestock Ministry. While this procedure may seem like a real headache, at least Ecuador doesn't require your pet to be quarantined for six months, as do some countries.

THE QUEST FOR PEANUT BUTTER
AND OTHER NECESSITIES

One of the advantages of life in Ecuador is the vast supply of tropical fruits and vegetables all year long, with varieties not seen in the United States. You can buy avocados, artichokes, raspberries, strawberries, pineapples, papaya, and bananas every day of the year, and peaches, apples, pears, and other fruits in season. Several markets in Quito sell fresh produce, seafood, chicken, meat, cut flowers, and potted plants.

Beef, pork, lamb, and veal are plentiful in supermarkets and butcher shops. You'll pay about half as much for filet mignon as you would in the United States, but about twice as much for turkey. Chicken, too, is slightly more expensive. You might want to use meat tenderizers or marinades on your beef here, since it tends not to be aged and is a little tough.

Pasteurized milk is available in disposable paper cartons or plastic bags. Heavy cream can be found in supermarkets, along with sour cream. A wide selection of cheeses is available, along with several brands of ice cream and yogurt. Breads and pastries are especially tasty and inexpensive all over Ecuador.

Quito has large supermarket chains, the most popular of which are probably Supermaxi and Mi Comisariato, where you can find U.S. imported products, but at high prices. In Quito, there is a Supermaxi store at the Multicentro shopping center on the Avenida 6 de Diciembre, a complex that includes all kinds of stores.

The Centro Comercial Iñaquito, at the corner of Avenidas Naciones Unidas and Amazonas, is the city's largest shopping center, with stores selling books, toys, records, clothes, and kitchen supplies. You can even find a Supermaxi in the city of Cuenca, along with another good well-stocked supermarket called Supermercados Unidos.

Otavalo has one supermercado on the Parque Central. Most people shop in the open-air local markets.

Many Americans frequent smaller stores and delicatessens, which offer items like pastas, cold cuts, and pickles. In Quito, one of my favorite places to go is the Delicatessen El Español, with three locations, one at Avenidas Amazonas and G. de Villarreal. These delis sell brie, huge well-stuffed hero sandwiches, fancy olive oils, salmon, cakes, pâté, olives, and American imports like Tabasco. They also have a good selection of wines—you can buy a decent bottle of Chilean wine for $3.50.

In Cuenca, there are cafés like Café Austria, which serves desserts, Earl Grey tea, cappuccino, ice cream, and sandwiches for 50 cents. There are also a few expensive, upper-crust restaurants that will make you feel as if you're dining in the heart of Manhattan, instead of a tiny city in a Third World country.

METRIC MEASURES

Ecuador operates on the metric system of weights and measurements. Here are some conversions to help you adjust.

1 gallon	equals	3.8 liters
1 quart	equals	.95 liter
1 pound	equals	.37 kilogram
1 ounce	equals	31.1 grams
1 mile	equals	1.61 kilometers
1 yard	equals	.91 meter
1 inch	equals	2.54 centimeters
1 kilogram	equals	2.2 pounds
1 liter	equals	1.06 quarts
1 gram	equals	.035 ounce
1 kilometer	equals	.62 mile
1 meter	equals	39.37 inches
1 centimeter	equals	.39 inch

HOUSEHOLD HELP

Maids, gardeners, drivers, and even good caterers are available at very reasonable rates—more reasonable than in most Latin American countries. Domestic employees earn about $60 a month. Day workers earn about $5 a day or less. Laundresses and gardeners earn about $1 an hour.

Under Ecuadorean law, domestic employees must be covered by Ecuadorean social security, just as they're supposed to be in the United States. The laws that govern employment and termination are very strict. In addition to a salary, household help receive three months' salary as a yearly bonus. Some employees are also eligible for cost-of-living compensation, supplementary bonus, and/or a transportation bonus. Although the employer is required to pay only a portion of the monthly Ecuadorean social security payments, or about 9 percent, most people pay the entire amount for their domestic employees, which is about 17 percent.

By law, employees are entitled to one day off every two weeks, but in practice they receive a day off every week. They are given fifteen days paid vacation annually, more than most U.S. workers receive. Employers provide uniforms.

Getting Around

The most economical, and the most common, way to get around Ecuador is via one of the country's many bus companies or in a private car. As is always the case, buses are for spirited, adventurous people who don't mind some inconvenience.

PUBLIC TRANSPORTATION

Regular intercity buses are available, and major cities have lots of city buses. They are inexpensive, costing about 5 cents or so. You pay when you get in (except for some smaller and inter-city buses, which may charge you when you want to get off).

Buses have a sign above the windshield showing what route they run (by starting and ending points, usually). But be warned. They are crowded and often in need of repair. Sometimes, three people are squeezed into seats made for two. I don't know which is worse: being in the middle, which means you usually have two strangers

TRAVEL TIMES BY BUS

The travel times in hours from Quito to the main cities in Ecuador by bus are as follows (times will obviously be shorter for car travel):

Ambato	3 hours
Bahía de Caráquez	6 hours
Cuenca	10 hours
Esmeraldas	6 hours, 30 minutes
Guayaquil	8 hours
Ibarra	3 hours
Manta	6 hours
Otavalo	2 hours
Riobamba	4 hours, 30 minutes

pushing against you, or being on the aisle, where one of your legs is likely to be hanging over the side.

The Quito Municipal Transport Company has newer, both double-decker and double-length jointed buses. Also comfortable are the air-conditioned Viatur buses used for inter-city travel, complete with snacks and special attendants, that cost about $5 from Guayaquil to Quito.

Taxis are everywhere, and the fares are very reasonable. You can easily hail one on the street or telephone the neighborhood "cooperativa" to request one. However, taxis may be in short supply during rush-hour periods. If the taxi does not have a meter—almost all do—negotiate the fare before beginning the trip. Taxis are yellow and those that are members of a cooperative are marked. A five-mile ride across town should cost no more than $3. Taxis from Quito's Mariscal Sucre Airport downtown should cost about $5. Unlike in Quito, taxis in Guayaquil usually do not have meters, but the driver will usually have a schedule of rates for various locations.

Train service to Guayaquil was suspended in early 1983 because of damage to the roadbed caused by catastrophic rains. The service is being revamped across the country, and you can already travel by train from Quito to Riobamba, with many stops along the way, and from

Ibarra to San Lorenzo, a tiny port north of Esmeraldas. Autoferros, which are Pullman-style buses on rails, are comfortable and faster than regular trains. For more information on rail service contact the Railways Office at Bolívar 441 in Quito; phone 2-21-45-45.

DRIVING IN ECUADOR

Ecuador has a good road system, with the Pan American Highway stretching from the Colombian border to Peru, passing through Quito, and branching into Guayaquil and other coastal cities such as Esmeraldas, Bahía, Manta, and Machala. Branches also lead to Amazon basin cities such as Lago Agrio, Coca, Tena, Puyo, and Macas, as well as Cuenca in the southern highlands. In all, Ecuador has about 11,000 miles of road, about half of which are open year-round and 4,000 miles of which are paved.

Most cars can be serviced in the major cities, but replacement parts may be hard to come by, and repairs often take a long time while mechanics wait for these parts to be delivered.

Premium gas (92 octane) sold in Ecuador is similar to regular gasoline sold in the United States. A low-octane regular gas is also available. A gallon of super unleaded gas sells for $1.40 to $1.50 a gallon.

While international or foreign licenses are valid in Ecuador, long-term residents eventually must obtain an Ecuadorean license. You won't have to take a driving test, but you will have to present four 1-inch photos, and a statement of blood type. Contact local automobile clubs for help and further information (see below).

AUTOMOBILE CLUBS IN ECUADOR

In addition to providing maps and other information regarding driving routes, the following clubs should be able to help you obtain an Ecuadorean driver's license.

Automóvil Club de Ecuador	**Club Automobilismo y**
Avenida Eloy Alfaro 218 and	**Turismo**
Berlin, Casilla 2830	Avenida Almedo 212
Quito	Guayaquil
Phone: 2-23-77-79	Phone: 4-30-65-27

Car Rentals

You'll find many car rental agencies in Quito and Guayaquil, and a few in Cuenca. Some agencies require you to rent for a minimum of three days. Agencies charge a 10 percent tax on rentals. They will accept a U.S. driver's license.

Most rental car companies have offices at or near the airport, as well as in downtown Quito. Here are phone numbers of the top offices:

Avis:	airport 2-28-79-06; downtown 2-56-28-15
Budget:	airport 2-28-85-10; downtown 2-28-45-59
Hertz:	airport 2-29-30-11; downtown 2-32-78-95

As an alternative to renting a car, you might consider hiring a chauffeured taxi, since they are so inexpensive. This is especially recommended if you are concerned about driving in a foreign country, or are worried about leaving personal belongings in a parked car.

Importing Your Car

I would think twice—and then a third time—before bringing a car into Ecuador. It's not that Ecuador doesn't have good roads; it's that driving in Quito's downtown is quite hectic, and there's always a danger that your car could be stolen or that you'd have an accident and have to deal with insurance hassles.

Most important, while new cars can be imported, they are subject to size and price limitations. Permission was granted only in the last few years, so you should check with your embassy or consulate for the latest regulations before deciding anything.

Used cars cannot be imported into Ecuador. However, tourists may temporarily bring vehicles into the country, for a period of no longer than ninety days. But bringing a vehicle into Ecuador either permanently or temporarily involves driving to Panama, then shipping the vehicle to Guayaquil. Most people ship their vehicles from Panama to South America by sea, but some find air-freighting more convenient. It's usually faster and avoids many of the unpleasant customs hassles, but it is more expensive.

Prices for shipping vary considerably. According to the *South*

American Handbook, major carriers may charge about $1,500 for a four-wheel drive Subaru station wagon, although cargo lines and independents can offer more reasonable prices. You are generally not allowed to accompany the vehicle.

You might find it a better idea to purchase a used car in Ecuador if you do decide to stay permanently. Prices vary, but the cost of a new compact car can top $20,000 or $25,000. You can get an idea of how much used and new cars are selling for upon arrival by glancing through the classifieds of an Ecuadorean newspaper like *El Universo.*

Before buying a used car, take it to a garage for a complete checkup. When you purchase a car, the dealer must give you the guarantee, the title of ownership, and a free transit certificate, which allows you to use the car until you register it and get license plates. Keep in mind that if you choose to live in Cuenca or Otavalo, you can walk to many places.

SECURITY CONCERNS

Many expatriates prefer living in apartment buildings because they feel safer, since many such buildings have doormen, guards, and automatic security devices for access doors to apartments and garages. Although there is little danger of violent crime, burglary is not uncommon, and it is a good idea to take precautions.

People who wish to live in houses should make certain that they have some kind of protection, such as iron gates over the doors, bars over the windows, high walls, lights in the garden, alarms, and other measures. There are companies in Ecuador that will install electrical alarms on the doors and windows, and others that will provide guard service. When you leave town, it's important to keep some lights on. Better yet, if you hire a live-in maid, she will provide protection during your absence.

One issue that is of increasing concern is that of pickpockets, especially on public transportation. You should always secure your valuables by carrying your wallet in an inside pocket or body belt. Women should cling tight to handbags. While pickpocketing is a growing problem in Quito and Guayaquil, these cities are still among the safest in Latin America.

Car Insurance

A third-party insurance policy of about $800 minimum is required under Ecuadorean law, but full coverage is highly recommended. Rates average $178 a year. The general requirements of most insurers in Ecuador are as follows: that the vehicle be no more than six years old, that it be inspected by the insurer, that it have a current registration, and that the owner have complete documents available for review.

If you are unfortunate enough to have an accident while driving in Ecuador, don't move your car for any reason because regulations require that the car remain in the same position until a policeman arrives. The insurance company will not reimburse or cover the cost of damage caused if there is no police report. Immediately call the police. Write down the license plate numbers of all vehicles involved in the accident and get the names of witnesses. Get the name of the insurance company of the other party.

Accept no blame or responsibility. Make no statements about the accident, and don't sign anything that's not from the insurance company. Make certain the police report is correct, and make note of the policeman's name and identification number. Report the accident to the insurance company as soon as possible, and make no repairs without its authorization.

Staying Healthy

Quito stands at an altitude of 9,350 feet, or 2,850 meters. This is no myth. Therefore, don't be surprised if you feel slightly out of breath the first few days you're there. To alleviate any discomfort, you should avoid alcohol, and you should avoid doing too much too soon. Take it easy until you become acclimated to the higher elevation. But aside from the problems that stem from being at a high altitude, it's easy to stay healthy in Ecuador.

DON'T DRINK THE WATER AND OTHER SAFEGUARDS

The high altitude of Ecuador makes sunburn a prevalent hazard. I didn't find this a concern when I was there, but you should use a sunscreen if you plan to be outdoors a lot. A hat is advisable on particularly warm days or when on the beach.

In Ecuador, it is important to drink only bottled water, or to boil the water, as this will prevent you from getting amoebas. These microscopic parasites—which live in the water—attack one's intestines and liver. However, they are rarely a problem if you take simple precautions.

Because of Quito's high altitude, when boiling tap water for safety, the water should be kept at the boil for at least twenty minutes. (Higher altitudes cause water to boil at a lower temperature, making it necessary to heat it for a longer period of time to kill any parasites.) Although altitude is not a concern in Guayaquil, you should boil water there for ten minutes. Ice should be made only from boiled or bottled water. Good bottled waters available in Ecuador include Manantial and Gütig brands.

Because of improper fertilization, amoebas can also be found in fruit and vegetables. And they may be found on any uncovered food where flies have put their dirty feet. Therefore, it's a good idea to carefully wash whatever you're going to eat. If you feel tired or nauseated, have headaches, or suffer from diarrhea, you might want to ask a doctor to send a stool sample to the laboratory for analysis.

You should also avoid raw or uncooked seafood and cold seafood salads, which have been known to be important in the transmission of cholera. Avoid foods and beverages sold by street vendors, no matter how tasty they look. Milk is often pasteurized, but because some random sampling has discovered high bacteria counts, you may be wise to slow-boil, cool, and place milk in other containers before use.

Another health concern is due to the ups and downs of the temperature, which can lead to colds and flu. In Quito, it's said that if you don't like the climate, you should wait a few hours for it to change. Just bring your favorite cold medicine with you and get plenty of rest, and you should be fine.

Fortunately, you don't have to undergo a series of painful shots to enter Ecuador, although some inoculations, like those against hepatitis, typhus, tetanus, and typhoid, are recommended. You should call the Federal Centers for Disease Control in Atlanta, Georgia at 404-332-4555 or 404-332-4559 for more information about vaccinations.

DOCTORS AND HOSPITALS: WHAT IF YOU GET SICK?

You'll find excellent, inexpensive doctors in Ecuador. Many doctors and dentists speak English and have studied abroad. One that I know of is a doctor/chiropractor in Quito. He charges $12 for a visit—indeed, most doctors charge $12 to $50 for a checkup.

In general, clinics are privately owned, as are many hospitals. Public hospitals are funded by the government, and provide free care to the poor and to anyone else in an emergency. Patients entering a clinic or hospital may be required to pay a guarantee; in any event, they usually are asked to pay the bill when leaving the facility. It is possible to pay in many places with credit cards, and checks drawn on local banks are usually accepted.

Daily clinic or hospital rates vary according to the institution and the care provided: medicine, food, and extra expenses. An estimate of these rates, in private hospitals and clinics, is as follows, according to the type of room:

Private	$50/day
Semi-private	$40/day
Suite A	$70/day
Suite B	$65/day

There are lots of hospitals and clinics to choose from in Quito, and you can get a list of English-speaking physicians from the U.S. Embassy. You can also contact the International Association for Medical Assistance to Travelers (IAMAT) before leaving the states. It publishes a list of participating doctors, as well as clinics and participating hospitals, around the world. The phone number is 716-754-4883.

One American-run hospital is the Hospital Voz Andes at Villalengua 263; phone 2-24-15-40. The Clínica Americana Adventista is often used by foreigners. It's located at 10 de Agosto 3366.

If you choose to settle in Otavalo, there's one hospital there as well as many clinics. There's also a small hospital in Atantaqui, a town just north of Otavalo near the city of Ibarra. There are plenty of clinics in Cuenca, as well. If you should have an emergency, you can get from Otavalo to Quito by car in an hour and a half, and from Cuenca to Quito by plane in thirty minutes.

DEALING WITH EMERGENCIES

Heaven forbid you have to deal with a medical emergency while in Ecuador, but at least you can rest assured that there are places to turn for help if something unexpected does occur. To get more information about possible help in the case of an emergency, before leaving the States, contact the International SOS Assistance (address below). This organization provides subscribers with professional help around the world in any medical or personal emergency. Services range from telephone advice and referrals to full-scale international medical evacuations. SOS operates via a network of multilingual critical care and aeromedical specialists at SOS centers in many countries.

International SOS Assistance   Phone: 215-244-1500
P.O. Box 11568
Philadelphia, PA 19116

The Medex Assistance Corporation offers services similar to those offered by SOS, with a network of multilingual assistance specialists answering calls directly; an international communications network available twenty-four hours a day; and more than 10,000 providers worldwide. It is located at:

Medex Assistance Corporation   Phone: 410-296-2530.
P.O. Box 10623
Baltimore, MD 21285-0623

INSURANCE FOR OVERSEAS HEALTH CARE

Guidebooks and government officials will tell you that insurance for hospitalization, as well as accident insurance, is a must for someone who plans to retire in Ecuador. Still, many foreigners get by without it, choosing instead to pay all bills with cash or credit cards. Insurance companies in Ecuador offer various types of medical and life insurance, usually covering one-year periods. Most insurance firms do not offer individual insurance, but provide it only for groups of at least fifteen people. However, there are individual systems, such as Metromedical and Ecuasanitas, that cover all sorts of illnesses contracted after the policy went into effect. There are certain exclusions, such as illnesses caused by radiation, pollution, or nervous disorders, or those deriving from drug addiction or alcoholism, dental or eye treatment (not related to an accident), and plastic surgery. Rates are generally based on a variety of factors, including the average age of the group and the proportion of men and women (since women's life expectancy is longer).

According to employees at the U.S. Embassy, most older Americans living in Ecuador have Medicare and return to the United States when they need treatment. You should talk to your insurance company, your travel agent, and the nearest consulate's office regarding insurance coverage in Ecuador—what's available and what's recommended.

Since most U.S. medical insurance policies do not cover you once you have left the United States, you might decide to purchase some kind of traveler's medical insurance before leaving home. Below are some contacts to help you with the purchase of travel insurance.

Amex Travel Protection Plan Phone: 800-234-0375
P.O. Box 919010 or 619-622-3300
San Diego, CA 92191-9970

*Amex doesn't require that you be
an American Express cardholder in
order to obtain a policy.*

Travel Assure, Teletrip Company Inc. Phone: 800-228-9792
3201 Farnarm Street or 402-342-7600
Omaha, NE 68131

Travel Insurance Services Phone: 800-937-1387
2930 Camino Diablo or 510-932-1387
Suite 200, Box 200
Walnut Creek, CA 94596

MEDICINES, PHARMACIES, AND PRESCRIPTIONS

Foreigners are always amazed at the wide range of medicines and products available in pharmacies across Latin America, including Ecuador. You can find everything from sleeping pills to Ponds cold cream.

Drugstores take turns staying open twenty-four hours a day. Each day, the newspapers publish a list of pharmacies that are *de turno*, and the information operator (dial 104) also has this information. There is a sign in front of each drugstore, which will be lit if it is on night duty.

Americans are often shocked to see that medicine they considered prescription drugs in the United States is sold over the counter in Ecuador. Since one can buy so many different types of medicines, there's often an urge to prescribe for oneself and avoid seeing a doctor. And some druggists are very good at suggesting medicines for certain symptoms. However, if your symptoms persist or if you're seriously sick, you should also see a doctor. Understand that Ecuadorean physicians sometimes have a tendency to prescribe heavy doses of strong antibiotics, even for minor infections.

Reputable optometrists in Ecuador will fill eye-related prescriptions, but it's always a good idea to bring extra eyeglasses or contact lenses from the States. You can purchase contact lenses in Quito, although some people find it difficult to wear contacts, in general, because of the city's dry climate. (I wear soft contact lenses and never found this to be a problem.)

DENTAL CARE

There are many dental clinics in Quito, as well as in other cities, with competent professionals and modern equipment. They usually work only on weekdays, except for emergencies. You should try to arrange for appointments by telephone to avoid a long wait.

Several Quito-area dentists are listed as certified by the American Dental Association. Check with the U.S. Embassy for a current list of English-speaking dentists. In general, prices for dental care are going to be very cheap compared with those charged in the United States. Most retirees consider cheap medical and dental care the best perk when it comes to living in Latin America. Most visits will cost $20 to $40, or even less!

Staying Busy and Happy

Moving to the Third World doesn't necessarily mean you'll have to give up movies, or the theater, or libraries, or even Japanese food. And unlike the centers of many major U.S. cities, downtown Quito comes alive at night. Yes, Ecuador's big cities even have many things you might have wanted to escape from in the United States, like Happy Hours and the Golden Arches and disco music.

LEISURE ACTIVITIES

There are dozens of movie theaters, many showing English-language films, in Ecuador's big cities. Major U.S. releases usually arrive in Ecuador within a year of their release in the United States. And for theatre buffs, there's the Pichincha Playhouse at 758 Avenida Colón, where an amateur English-language group puts on several productions a year. Excellent Spanish-language plays are performed at the Teatro Nacional Sucre, also the site of concerts by the National Symphony Orchestra, and Teatro Prometeo. By the way, watching Spanish-language plays and films is an excellent way to learn the language.

Also, there are plenty of bookstores and libraries where you can find both Spanish and English-language books. There's a little-known place to buy English-language books for next to nothing called Café Cultura, which is also a good hotel, located at Robles 513 y Reina Victoria; phone 2-22-42-71.

A sports club can offer recreational opportunities as well as a chance to meet people. In addition to private clubs, there are very spacious public places where people can enjoy any sport free of charge, such as the La Caroliña Park, which has fields and courts for soccer, basketball, tennis, volleyball, roller-skating, and rowing.

Private clubs offer their members the opportunity to practice sports or participate in social activities, bridge tournaments, squash, soccer, luncheons, dinners, cocktail parties, and other gatherings. Club membership is usually limited, and those who wish to join must sometimes buy shares, which are sold openly and sometimes advertised in the newspaper. The price depends on the supply and demand and the services and equipment offered by the particular club. Private clubs include El Condado, Buena Vista, and Los Chillos. Call each to learn the rules, prices (sure to be high), and what they have to offer.

If the cost of joining a private club is too steep, check out one of the many gymnasiums that have cropped up all over Ecuador in recent years. These offer aerobics classes, weight rooms, sauna baths, and snack bars, and usually aren't that expensive.

One facility I recommend visiting is the Quito Tennis and Golf Club on Avenida Occidental. It has an eighteen-hole course as well as nine clay tennis courts and a pool. The club will usually sell temporary memberships to travelers. Its phone number is 2-53-81-20.

If you're just looking for a little exercise from time to time, there are plenty of free public tennis courts. Other sports that are quite popular in Ecuador include mountain climbing, spelunking, and various water sports. Quito and surrounding areas have several spots for swimming. Swimming memberships are available at the Hotels Colon and Quito. The Los Chillos Valley, south of Quito, has many pools and country clubs.

Fishing enthusiasts (licenses are a must) can enjoy excellent freshwater and deep-sea fishing in Ecuador. Off the coast, deep-sea tackle is needed for the abundant marlin, tuna, dorado, and other species. Areas close to Quito have good stream and lake fishing for bass and trout.

The three major parks in Quito are La Caroliña, bounded by Amazonas, Naciones Unidas, Shyris, and Republica avenues; El Ejido, bounded by 12 de Octubre, Patria, 10 de Agosto, and Tarqui avenues; and La Alameda, bounded by Gran Colombia, Sodiro, and Luis Felipe Borja avenues. El Ejido is across from the U.S. Embassy and there's an open-air art exposition in the park every Saturday and Sunday. It's a great spot for people-watching, as families come here in droves on the weekends to play volleyball, enjoy carnival rides, and eat cotton candy. Ecuador also has a vast national park system, and geographically offers everything from snowcapped mountains to crystal-clear lakes.

If you're a beach person, Ecuador is the place for you. It has many miles of lovely beaches, surrounded by totally untouched natural environments. Although the resort towns tend to be crowded and dirty, you can find clean, quiet beaches by traveling a bit farther. The most frequented beaches include Salinas, a two-hour drive from Guayaquil (there are apartments for rent, restaurants, hotels, and the Salinas Yacht Club), and Atacames, a four- or five-hour drive from Quito (with endless beaches bordered by palm trees).

Guayaquil also boasts a healthy recreational and social life. Swimming, tennis, basketball, volleyball, bowling, jogging, and golf are all part of life in the Guayaquil area. The Tennis Club and the Country Club have swimming pools, although membership is expensive. The clubs Nacional and Garibaldo are lower-priced alternatives with tennis and swimming facilities.

You can find out about social and cultural events in Guayaquil and Quito, as well as in Cuenca and Otavalo, by purchasing *Q,* Ecuador's English-language magazine. It's available at most hotels, newsstands, and bookstores.

HOW TO MAKE FRIENDS

Ecuador is a friendly, welcoming country and its cities are easy to maneuver. You should have little trouble assimilating into the local network. U.S. citizens tend to live in their own neighborhoods, so meeting other English speakers shouldn't be a problem. I've always found North Americans much more willing to strike up a conversation when they're in a foreign country than they'd ever be at home.

I've met people sitting on park benches, in breakfast cafés, in museums, and on buses.

One good way to meet people is by attending church, if that's something you'd like to do. St. Nicholas Anglican Church, located at Gustavo Darquea y Carrión in Quito, has Sunday services in English. So does the Advent Lutheran Church on Isabel la Católica. Another way is by visiting nightspots popular with travelers and English-speaking residents. These include El Pub Inglés, across the street from the Hotel Quito; La Licorne, located in the Hotel Colon; and Bar Reina Victoria, a U.S.-run establishment in the Mariscál district.

If drinking is not your idea of a good time, there are lots of cafés frequented by North Americans. In Cuenca, Café Austria serves desserts, cappuccino, ice creams, and Earl Grey tea. When I was there, couples sat at tables studying Spanish and discussing politics. Speaking of Cuenca, there are lots of galleries and live-music establishments here, as well as Spanish-language schools. All would be good places to meet people. If you have any questions, there's a CETUR, or Corporación Ecuatoriana de Turismo (government tourist office) in town. When I stopped by there recently, a group of older Americans just happened to be there asking for directions to Las Cajas, a group of lakes great for fishing, and the hot springs at the secluded town of Baños.

There aren't many formal organizations for Americans in Quito. In Guayaquil, however, the International Society has monthly dinners and dances throughout the year, providing a good opportunity for socializing.

LANGUAGE SCHOOLS:
HOW MUCH SHOULD YOU KNOW?

Spanish schools are prevalent all across Ecuador. Needless to say, prices and quality vary. Ecuador is a much better country for learning Spanish than, say, Costa Rica because fewer people in Ecuador speak English, thereby forcing you to speak Spanish.

You'll have to know at least a few words of Spanish before visiting Ecuador for a long period of time, and you should carry a Spanish dictionary with you at all times. If you just want to spend a few weeks here, then you'll probably be fine just speaking English if you never stray too far from Quito and stay in a tourist hotel. But if you really want to experience the culture, and feel a part of a new place, you'll have to hunker down and learn some Spanish.

To be honest, I've never attended a Spanish school in Ecuador. However, it works like this. You usually pay by the week, or by the month, and cost depends on how many hours per day you study. Some people prefer four hours a day; others, eight. My personal preference, formed by studying at schools in Guatemala, is that somewhere in between is probably best, maybe five or six hours. You want to absorb all you can, but you don't want to wear yourself out in the process.

Most schools offer one-on-one tutoring for beginning, intermediate, and advanced students. Many give you the option of staying with an Ecuadorean family, which will only make the learning process easier. It's also cheaper to do it this way, as meals are usually included in the price.

Whatever you decide to do, I'd avoid signing up for a long-term program in the beginning, if possible. Attend a school for a week or two to get a feel for whether it's the right one for you. Don't get locked in to anything if you can help it. Prices usually range from about $40 to $100 a week depending on how many hours a day you study. To live with a family may cost $30 to $60 more a week.

Below is a list of some Spanish schools in Ecuador that should at least give you a place to start. Spanish schools are located in all major cities, although the list below includes only those schools found in the city of Quito. I can't recommend any particular one, but you might visit each to see what you think. You might also check with Quito's Information Center (the address is listed on page 232) for recommendations.

Academia de Español Equinoccial
Roca #533 and Juan Leon Mera
Quito

Phone: 2-52-94-60

Academia Latinoamericana de Español
Catalina Aldaz 115 y Eloy Alfaro
Quito

Phone: 2-24-56-58

Amazonas Spanish School
718 Jorge Washington Street
and Amazonas Avenida
Building Rocafuerte
Washington block, 3rd floor
Quito

Phone: 2-50-46-54, 2-67-35-53

America Spanish School
768 Carrión and 9 de Octubre
Streets
Quito

Phone: 2-23-73-59, 2-51-25-65

Instituto Superior de Español   Phone: 2-52-38-13, 2-56-86-64,
Ulloa 220 y Jerónimo Carrión   2-23-07-01
Quito

VOLUNTEER OPPORTUNITIES

Volunteer opportunities are harder to come by in Ecuador than in countries like Guatemala, Mexico, and Costa Rica, perhaps because the U.S. community is not as well organized here. However, if you're adamant about wanting to donate a few hours of time each week to a good cause, you might try checking in *Q,* Ecuador's English-language magazine, which contains all sorts of classified advertising where volunteer opportunities might be presented. Churches and the staff at the U.S. Embassy also might be able to offer some ideas.

Your Exploratory Trip

Anyone considering retiring to Ecuador should first visit the country. Most Americans start a tour of Ecuador in Quito. If making your first tour of Ecuador, you should also definitely spend a few days checking out Cuenca, and plan to visit Otavalo, both popular spots for retirees.

ADVANCE PREPARATION

Obviously, you'll want to stop your mail if you're going to Ecuador for only a short time, or find someone who can pick it up and sort through it for you if you're going to be gone a few months. Bills must be paid up while you're away. Newspaper subscriptions stopped. Utilities turned off.

You won't need to get any vaccinations to enter Ecuador, although inoculations against typhoid, typhus, tetanus, and hepatitis are sometimes recommended. For people planning to live or travel in areas of Ecuador below 5,000 feet, malaria prophylaxis is essential. Call the Federal Centers for Disease Control in Atlanta at 404-332-4555, or 404-332-4559 for more information about vaccinations and health concerns.

If you don't have a passport, you'll have to get one. To apply for a passport, you must submit, in person, a completed passport appli-

EXPATRIATE ORGANIZATIONS: A USER'S GUIDE

Ecuador offers a range of expatriate organizations—organizations that assist U.S. citizens living or traveling in Ecuador. These groups can help make your adjustment smoother and happier.

BUSINESS SOURCES

Ecuadorian-American Chamber of Commerce
Multicentro Bldg.
Fourth Floor
La Niña & 6 de Diciembre
Quito

Phone: 2-54-35-12

GENERAL INFORMATION

Quito's Information Center
International Contact Office
1242 Guayaquil and Olmedo Streets
or 768 Carrión and
9 de Octubre Streets
Quito

Phone: 2-51-25-65, 2-23-73-59

U.S. Embassy in Quito
Avenida Patria y 12 de Octubre
Quito

Phone: 2-56-28-90

For information about Spanish schools and tourist information.

PARKS AND WILDLIFE INFORMATION

Fundación Natura
Casilla 243
Avenida America 5653 y Vozandes
Quito

Phone: 2-44-73-41, 2-44-73-42

SAILING INFORMATION

Federación Ecuatoriana de Yachting
Circunvalacion Norte 301 y La Primera
Guayaquil

Phone: 4-38-36-95, 4-38-19-04

TOURIST OFFICES

Corporación Ecuatoriana de Turismo/CETUR
Reina Victoria 514 y Vicenta Ramon Roca
Casilla 2454
Quito

Phone: 2-52-70-02

Also CETUR/Branch Office
Avenida Venezuela y Chile
Quito

Phone: 2-51-40-44

cation at a U.S. State Department Passport Agency or at one of the several thousand federal or state courts of U.S. Post Offices authorized to accept passport applications.

Along with your application, you'll have to have proof of U.S. citizenship (such as a certified copy of your birth certificate), an ID that includes your signature and photo, and two identical 2-inch photos. The fee is $65, and the passport is valid for ten years. If you need to renew your passport, you can renew by mail by picking up an application at U.S. Post Offices or at a Passport Agency. The mail-in procedure costs $55 and can take up to four weeks during busy periods.

Before you go, you might also consider contacting the Ecuadorean Embassy with questions or for more information. Or contact the Ecuadorean Consulate General in New York. (See below for addresses.) Consulates are also located in Boston, Chicago, Los Angeles, San Francisco, Baltimore, Houston, and San Diego.

Ecuadorean Embassy   Phone: 202-234-7200
2535 15 Street N.W.
Washington, D.C. 20009

Ecuadorean Consulate General   Phone: 212-808-0170
18 East 41st Street, 18th Floor
New York, New York 10017

Because Ecuador doesn't claim the expatriate population that other Latin countries do, not a lot has been written about life in Ecuador. However, there are several good tourist guides to choose from. For example, the *South American Handbook* has an excellent chapter on Ecuador. Also, once you get to Ecuador, you might stop by the Ecuadorean-American Chamber of Commerce, which publishes a book called *Living in Ecuador* that will be helpful. Ecuador's English-language magazine is called *Q,* which you will find sold in Ecuador at most newsstands and hotels.

FLYING TO ECUADOR

Ecuador's two main airports are Mariscal Sucre Airport in Quito and Simón Bolívar Airport in Guayaquil. These two are the only airports handling international flights. From the United States, Ecuador's Saeta flies direct to Quito and Guayaquil from Miami, as do American Airlines and Ladeco, the latter strictly to Guayaquil.

Whatever you do, don't worry about mass confusion setting in the moment you step on Ecuadorean soil. The Mariscal Sucre Airport in Quito is a breeze to maneuver your way through. Money-changing booths, including one that will change traveler's checks, stay open in the airport until the last flight comes in.

Taxis are just outside the airport's doors and they're cheap—it costs just $5 from the airport to most hotels. Speaking of hotels, you should probably make a reservation before you go, at least for the first night you're there. There are plenty of travel guides to help you decide where to stay. For more information, you might consider writing the Ecuadorean tourism agency, which used to have offices in Miami and New York, before both were closed. Now you must write to:

Corporación Ecuatoriana   Phone: 2-52-70-02
de Turismo/CETUR
Reina Victoria 514 y Vicenta Ramon Roca
Casilla 2454 Quito

Will You Be Retiring in Ecuador?

If you've discovered the secret of Ecuador, you'll find a retirement destination that's not only very inexpensive but also welcoming. The people are friendly and the climate is pleasant year-round. Though the economy is a little weak right now, as a retiree you won't be affected. You can spend all your time getting to know the people of the high Andes and learning to love the relaxed pace of life there.

Index

The Night Before
Summer Camp

Grosset & Dunlap

To Gillen Martin and Tess Arntson for sharing their camp experiences—N.W.
For Rachel, a brave camper!—M.P.

GROSSET & DUNLAP
Published by the Penguin Group
Penguin Group (USA) Inc., 375 Hudson Street, New York, New York 10014, U.S.A.
Penguin Group (Canada), 90 Eglinton Avenue East, Suite 700, Toronto, Ontario, Canada M4P 2Y3
(a division of Pearson Penguin Canada Inc.)
Penguin Books Ltd, 80 Strand, London WC2R 0RL, England
Penguin Ireland, 25 St Stephen's Green, Dublin 2, Ireland
(a division of Penguin Books Ltd)
Penguin Group (Australia), 250 Camberwell Road, Camberwell, Victoria 3124, Australia
(a division of Pearson Australia Group Pty Ltd)
Penguin Books India Pvt Ltd, 11 Community Centre, Panchsheel Park, New Delhi - 110 017, India
Penguin Group (NZ), 67 Apollo Drive, Mairangi Bay, Auckland 1311, New Zealand
(a division of Pearson New Zealand Ltd)
Penguin Books (South Africa) (Pty) Ltd,
24 Sturdee Avenue, Rosebank, Johannesburg 2196, South Africa

Penguin Books Ltd, Registered Offices: 80 Strand, London WC2R 0RL, England

Library of Congress Control Number: 2006100692

ISBN 978-0-448-44639-4   10 9 8 7 6 5 4 3 2

The Night Before
Summer Camp

By Natasha Wing • Illustrated by Mindy Pierce

Grosset & Dunlap

'Twas the night before day camp
when at the town park
the counselors were working
till well after dark.

The canoes were moored
by the boat dock with care,
in hopes that young paddlers
soon would be there.

The children were nestled
all snug in their beds
while visions of butterflies
danced in their heads.

But not everyone was happy
about going to camp . . .
especially Rick,
who was the worry-bird champ.

In the morning Mom woke him.
"Rise and shine, kiddo!"
But he pulled up the covers.
"I don't want to go.

"I don't know anyone there.
I'll be gone all day.
Can't I just go over
to Tommy's and play?"

"Camp is one giant playtime,"
Mom said, "so don't you stress.
And it's not an overnighter."

"Okay. I'll try it, I guess."

The bus picked him up
at the end of the street

**and dropped off the kids
where the sign said to meet.**

**There was a whole bunch of children—
none that Rick knew.
He felt lost and lonely.
"What do I do?"**

"Come join the Lion's Cubs!"
said his counselor Kim,
who today was teaching
the kids how to swim.

"Kick your feet! Move your arms!
Place your face in the water!
Excellent, Rick!
You swim like an otter!"

For the rest of the morning,
the Cubs explored nature trails.

They saw butterflies, birds,
crawly bugs, snakes, and snails.

They gathered up sticks
and found bark to make boats.
Then set them a'sail—

"Hey, look! Mine really floats!"

When what at the edge of the lake should appear,
but a beautiful doe and two baby brown deer.

Their eyes—how they twinkled! Their bobtails so twitchy!
Their legs were so slender, while Rick's were so itchy!

"Anybody starving?" asked Kim.
"It's time to eat lunch!"

But Rick wasn't hungry.
He missed his mom a whole bunch.

Counselor Kim sat beside him
and asked, "Are you okay?"
"I want to go home," Rick told her.
"I'm kind of nervous today."

Kim smiled and said, "Hey, little Cub.
I'm nervous, just like you.
This is my very first job.
I'm away from home, too.

"Last night I tossed
and turned in my bed.
I couldn't get the
jitters out of my head!"

"Same here!" replied Rick.
"I really understand!
So whenever you're nervous,
just hold onto my hand."

"It's a deal!" said Kim.
"And thanks for the talk.
Could you help me carry
the jump rope and chalk?"

For the rest of the week,
Rick had oodles of fun!

There were three-legged races,
which he and Kim won!

He made a scrapbook and drum
at the arts and crafts table,

starred in a play
from an old Aesop's fable.

**Day camp ended on Friday—
oh what a bummer!**

"I want to go back
for *two* weeks next summer!"